Illu.

Three Rousing (

AN AUTOBIOGRAPHY

By ELIZABETH JORDAN

Three rousing cheers for Elizabeth Jordan who writes this absorbing chronicle of a busy life—a life enriched by intellectual and social activities, by good fun and not a little reflection. At once a "personal history" and a fascinating sheaf of literary reminiscences, this autobiography is notable for the freshness of its material and for the delightful flavor of its writing.

Elizabeth Jordan made her intrepid entrance into the newspaper world of New York as a very young woman fresh from a Milwaukee Convent school. She handled almost every type of story. Her career on the New York *World* lead from the start to splendid friendships and professional success. While still a young woman she became editor-in-chief of *Harper's Bazar*. Her enthusiasm for her job, her pleasure in her friends (such as Arthur Brisbane, George Harvey, Frances Hodgson Burnett, Mark Twain, William Dean Howells, Henry James, to name but a few) are communicated in intensely interesting pages crowded with brand-new literary anecdotes. Like many a good editor, Miss Jordan had an influential connection with the course of literature in this country, playing her part in the discovery of such authors as Sinclair Lewis, Zona Gale, and Dorothy Canfield. In addition, she has written successful novels herself; has had her fling in motion pictures, and has had a play produced on Broadway. The zest, the vigor, the sense of humor, the love of life which are Elizabeth Jordan's communicate themselves to the reader in the pages of this book, a life story of remarkable vitality and interest.

D. APPLETON-CENTURY COMPANY

New York   *London*

THREE ROUSING CHEERS

By ELIZABETH JORDAN

Elizabeth Jordan
From a portrait by A. Garfield Learned, 1929

THREE ROUSING CHEERS

by

ELIZABETH JORDAN

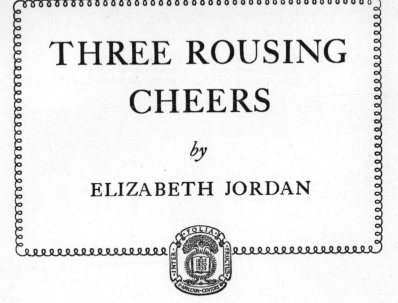

D. APPLETON-CENTURY COMPANY

INCORPORATED

NEW YORK   LONDON

1938

TO THE MEMORY OF MY
FATHER AND MOTHER

Let me explain with my first drops of ink that these reminiscences are not the offspring of any delusion as to my individual importance. I am merely the chain on which they are strung. Neither does their ringing title acclaim my own activities. It expresses in some degree my mental attitude toward life; and, in a much greater degree, my devotion to the memory of the friends who, for a quarter of a century, used the refrain so constantly and so gaily that it became the rallying call of our clan.

It is those friends, among others, whose lives and achievements justify these pages; and it was perhaps the cheerful philosophy underlying our clan cry that best held us together. By many of us it was used on any and every occasion. It was greeting, it was farewell, it was comment. It covered our grouches, pointed our successes, and underlined our disappointments. Looking back now, I can see that we over-used it; but none of us realized this at the time. It had become a basic feature of our daily speech.

In the beginning it was Frances Hodgson Burnett and the Otis Skinners and I who sent the old adjuration on its new rounds. Eventually it became so much a part of our vocabularies that we often brought it out unconsciously, as in this instance:

"Hello, Otis. Three rousing cheers!"

"Three rousing cheers, Elizabeth! I hear you're just back from the war zone. Are things going as badly over there as we're told they are?"

Habits like that are contagious. The first group of us who tossed the phrase about soon included Colonel and Mrs. George Harvey, Arthur Brisbane, Frederick Duneka, and Mark Twain. After that it spread rapidly among the literary guests Colonel and Mrs. George Harvey were constantly entertaining in their country home, Jorjalma, at Deal, New Jersey. Colonel Harvey was then President of Harper and Brothers, and during the ten years I edited *Harper's Bazar* I passed more week-ends at Jorjalma than at home. Many authors and editors had the same happy experience, and dozens of life-long friendships began there. We injected our slogan into the speech of most of our fellow-guests—even into those of William Dean Howells, Henry Mills Alden, and Henry James. Those three looked rather startled when they caught themselves bringing it out. They were not natural cheerers, as the rest of us were.

Possibly I exaggerate the importance of the bond created by such frequent use of a rallying cry; but there *was* a bond. The habit of using it was picked up by group after group, many of whom had no close affiliation with the other groups. It became a recognizable clue that identified and widened circles. When any of us entered a room full of strangers, and overheard it uttered in the airy and off-hand fashion in which most of us used it, we knew that we were at least among the friends of friends.

It is now many years since I have used or heard it frequently, for most of the members of that great company are dead. But the old refrain, heard from any lips, still brings them back for a wonderful moment.

As further illustration of the moods in which we brought it forth, and to prove that we were not always beating drums and tinkling cymbals when we did so, I quote a letter from Frances Hodgson Burnett, written from the unconquerable spirit of the woman and from the heart of the child she was:

PLANDOME, LONG ISLAND.
December 21st, 1916.

DEAREST ELIZABETH,

I am preparing for my Christmas with the kind of a cold I had last year. Three rousing cheers! This time its richness is added to by an intensifying of the pain in my eyes, caused by the oculist's giving me overpowering glasses. Nevertheless, three rousing cheers! I cannot write and I cannot read. I can only lie in bed feeling mizzable. However, three rousing cheers! Edith is as badly off as I am. The chauffeur has left, the waitress is leaving, and we are expecting guests. All this being so, I still *insist* on three rousing cheers!

And well or ill, I shall arrive for your luncheon a week from Tuesday, either triumphantly erect upon my feet, or crawling on my hands and knees.

F. H. B.

Few members of that gallant clan ever uttered much criticism of the world, or of the experience we call living. I myself can truly say, as old Lord Lackington said in his last moments, "Life has been very pleasant." Like Margaret Fuller I can cry, though without her ecstasy, "I accept the universe." And like Carlyle, when this gracious concession was quoted to him, I can comment, "Gad, she'd *better!*"

Yes, we were a buoyant lot, carrying our various responsibilities without too many words but with high hearts and banners flying. Looking back over the road on which we traveled so long together I see the milestones where one friend after another dropped—Colonel and Mrs. Harvey, Frances Hodgson Burnett, Kate Douglas Wiggin, Maud Skinner, Mary Harrison McKee, Mrs. Herbert Houston, Mark Twain, Mr. and Mrs. Henry Mills Alden, Mrs. Arthur Dodge and Mrs. Spencer Trask, Frederick Duneka, Charles

A. Conant, John à Becket, Arthur Brisbane . . . and so many others! I am appalled to discover how few are left. . . .

Often I seem to hear Frances Hodgson Burnett's laughter bubbling down the years, or Mark Twain's dry chuckle, or Colonel Harvey's quiet speech, or Colonel Cockerill's unique monologues, or Henry James's considered phrases, as clearly as I hear the voices that are still around me. But this is an emptying world—well worth living in, however, if one has continued interests, memories, and the Great Hope.

CONTENTS

xi

ILLUSTRATIONS

CHAPTER I

Two Talks and a Bargain

THE day of my graduation from the Convent of Notre
Dame in Milwaukee was the turning point of my life.
To the observer it would not have seemed so. My age was
tender—only seventeen; not the point at which one normally
sets one's compass for the trek through the years. Nevertheless, two conversations that day shaped the course I have
followed ever since. The first began and ended with one
sentence. The second was an hour's talk.

The sentence was pronounced by Reverend Mother Mary
Caroline, Mother General of the great Order of the Sisters
of Notre Dame. The Convent of Notre Dame in Milwaukee
is the Mother House of the Order. It was also Mother
Caroline's headquarters, when she was not on the wing
visiting the hundreds of institutions under her direction. We
students saw very little of her, but we adored her from a
distance and we chattered about her unwearyingly. All sorts
of stories were told of her, most of them, no doubt, pure
romance. "In the world," as the phrase went in the convent,
she was supposed to have been an Austrian Archduchess
before she joined the Order, and to have lived a glamorous
life in Vienna. She was certainly well-born; and she had the
beauty and graciousness and charm an Archduchess should
possess, as well as a personal magnetism that drew even
the unwilling into her orbit.

The only "unwilling" I knew of were a few girls who
passionately announced before they met her that they would
never be her "satellites." After they met her—if they did—

I

they lurked at points she was apt to pass, and their critical voices were silent. Mother Caroline knew little of all this adulation, and would not have liked it. But she had a vast amount of worldly knowledge, whether it had been acquired in Vienna or elsewhere; and she must have been touched by the awe and admiration in the eyes of her students.

We all saw her, of course, on Commencement Days, and in the Chapel, or occasionally walking in the garden. That beautiful old convent garden, the size of a squared city block inside its high brick walls, was a favorite haunt of my own. The etiquette of the occasion, when one encountered Mother Caroline there, was to bow and pass on. But one May evening, when she and I happened to be the only human figures against that enchanting background, she shook my young heart by stopping to speak to me. After we had chatted a few minutes she drew me to a bench beside the big fountain, and we sat there together while she asked me about my routine studies and my music.

I was only fourteen, and in addition to the academic course I was giving two hours a day to piano practice, as I had done since I was eight. It appeared that Sister Cecilia, head of the music department and a musician whose fame extended far beyond convent walls, had told Mother Caroline of my mother's plan that I should be a concert pianiste. Mother Caroline was herself a good pianiste and a music lover. She seemed interested in knowing the details of my practice, and my musical likes and dislikes. I was already valiantly assaulting the works of Beethoven, Bach, Chopin, Mozart, and other masters, and I had my opinions of them all. Words have always gushed from me far too freely. That evening they flowed like streams from a fountain in full action, and Mother Caroline listened with an amused smile.

I had the thrills of later chats with her. When I was fifteen the four performances of the Nibelungen Ring were given in Milwaukee, on four successive nights, with the three greatest Wagnerian singers of their day in the leading rôles—Lilli Lehmann, Max Alvary and Emil Fischer. They had been giving the cycle in Chicago for weeks, and had come to the German and music-loving city of Milwaukee in response to a popular clamor. Mother Caroline arranged that four of the convent's music students, including myself, should be allowed to attend every performance—properly chaperoned, of course.

It was a great adventure. We rode somberly to and from the Opera House in the convent's curtained bus, but the hours between were pure rapture. The operas began at seven and were given almost uncut. This meant that we were not back in the convent till midnight, and naturally we were expected to go to bed at once. Instead, too excited by the music to sleep, we stole to one of the great convent's innumerable music-rooms, remote from the cells of the nuns. There, till the startled dawn peered in at us, we went over the piano score of the opera we had just heard, as well as that of the opera we were to hear the next night. We were not discovered; but Sister Cecilia reported a gratifying progress in our piano work that year.

A year later one of my special friends among the veiled novices—Sister Mary Clare—was to take the black veil of the Order, with fifty other Sisters. The ceremony is a very beautiful and poignant one and at that time was witnessed only by the nuns and the immediate families of the novices. More than I had ever wanted anything else, it seemed to me, I wanted to see that function, but it never occurred to me to ask permission. However, on the morning of the investiture Mother Caroline's secretary told me I might attend it. It was an experience I did not confide to any one. Many years later, in 1935, a really beautiful moving picture was exhibited in New York showing the same ritual taking place in a European convent. The fact that it was given with the approval of the Catholic Church was an interesting illustration of the changes of viewpoint time brings about.

I did not realize till the day I graduated why I had been allowed to see the ceremony. The knowledge came during the Commencement exercises, through Mother Caroline's pregnant remark. Notre Dame was a cloistered Order. We always had a final rehearsal of the entire Commencement program for the nuns, as they never appeared in public except in times of war or pestilence. Then they went forth as a gallant young army, to risk their lives in serving the world they had left. The only nun who appeared before our Commencement audiences was Sister Cecilia, and this was because she was in charge of the musical program and directed the orchestra. Mother Caroline and our favorite class teacher, Sister Ethelbert, were always there; but they remained in the wings, seeing everything on the stage and invisible from the auditorium.

Toward the close of this Commencement program I, too, was in the wings, waiting to go on for my valedictory. Unexpectedly, I found myself standing beside Mother Caroline. She put her hands on my shoulders and turned me to face her.

"Your graduation gown is very becoming, my dear," she said smilingly, "but"—her face grew very serious and she gave me a deep look, "I think the Habit of Notre Dame would suit you even better," she ended slowly.

I had no time to answer. I don't think I could have answered if I had. From the opposite wings I had received my signal to go out on the stage, and even the Mother General of a great Order does not keep an audience waiting. Mother Caroline bent and kissed me on each cheek, and I went.

When I came off the stage my attention was taken up by my family and friends from the audience. But I went home with Mother Caroline's words burning in my mind and heart. I knew exactly what they meant, and how almost unprecedented they were. One of the unwritten but fixed laws of the Notre Dame Order, and indeed of all other teaching Orders, is that no proselyting is done to encourage students to become Sisters. This, the Communities rightly feel, would be disloyalty to the parents of their students, who entrust the children to them. The Sisters lean backward in their determination to avoid such a danger. Both Sister Ethelbert and Sister Clare were close friends of mine, and remained so up till the time of their deaths many years later; but during my student days neither would ever discuss with me the ambition I had held from my childhood to be a nun myself. Gently, perhaps regretfully, but very firmly, they changed the subject whenever I brought it up.

Mother Caroline herself had never touched on it even obliquely, in those talks of ours so memorable to me. She appeared to have accepted my mother's ambition to have me develop into a concert pianist. Milwaukee was saturated with music, and its pet method of raising money for its charities was by concert. The soloists were usually local amateurs, turned loose on friendly audiences to gain experience. I played at many such concerts, and my mother had arranged with the convent authorities that I should always be available for them. Mother Caroline was interested in these public appearances, and naturally anxious to have me do credit to my training. She must also have known of my convent aspiration. Certainly I had made no secret of it, though I was growing sensitive about it. I could always lighten the atmosphere of any gathering by a mere mention of that ambition—and my classmates laughed the loudest. They said I was not the material nuns are made of, and they were right. I was a high-spirited and irrepressible young person, and usually in trouble. Only a vivid imagination could picture me in a religious Habit.

Nevertheless, Mother Caroline's imagination had taken that leap, and in doing so it had healed a sore spot in my pride. Also—and this was as vital—it linked up with and soothed another hurt that had ached since I was fourteen. I had gone through an experience then that was very funny to every one except the victim. For years afterwards I could not think of it without a sinking stomach and a rush of blood to the head. Now, on my graduation day, I could remember it without these distressing accompaniments. My heart rose, singing.

In memory I went over that old tragedy as I rode home after Commencement. It had begun so nicely. I had a secret. I had begun to write. I had actually sold my first story to the *Evening Wisconsin,* of Milwaukee, when I was just fourteen. Misled by the maturity of my style, the editor had addressed me as "Dear Madam." He had also sent me a real check—for two dollars. All these phenomena I had concealed from my family. I had a Plan. I had decided to hold the great news till the story was published. Then I would read it aloud to our domestic circle with no hint of the authorship. I would bask in the family's absorption in the tale, and in the adulation that followed the announcement of the author's name. That is a dangerous experiment for any author to make at any age. The results of it in my case were shattering.

The plan meant that I had to keep careful watch every afternoon for the arrival of the *Evening Wisconsin,* which the newsboy delivered daily at our house at about five o'clock. It would never do to have the family see the newspaper first. But it was summer time and I had leisure for sentinel duty, though it cramped my social activities. I kept guard for a month. When the copy containing the story was finally delivered I scurried up to my own room with it, and hid it there till evening.

That night, after the family had been soothed by dinner and was assembled in the library, I brought forth my surprise. My grandmother and two of my mother's younger sisters were with us. With my father, mother, and little sister, there would be an audience of six.

When I announced that I wanted them to listen to a story I had just found in the *Evening Wisconsin,* a depressed silence settled over the gathering. My young aunts could think of many things they would rather do than listen to a tale of my selection. My mother and father had plans of their own for the evening. My small sister, Alice, alone was interested. She liked stories, and she hoped the reading would give her an extra half hour before bed-time. It did. After the first shock of the suggestion they all settled down to listen philosophically, and I began the story.

I read it with love and fire. To me it seemed a remarkable tale. But it could not stand that acid test. My young aunts yawned. My grandmother's beautiful old head nodded. "Allie" fell asleep on a rug before the fire, like a young puppy. When I finished the tale and waited for applause, still desperately clutching the newspaper, my aunts started a ruthless dissection of the story.

"What's the use of giving space to a yarn like that?" one of them began. She proceeded, with the other's help, to pick out the story's flaws. There were plenty of them, and she was witty. Enchanted by the interest of her listeners, which was far beyond any aroused by the reading, she developed the theme. The others laughed and agreed with her. They called attention to the faults she had overlooked. A perfect picture of a happy family, united in its interests, was before me. I sat silent and crushed. Then my father spoke.

"What was there about the story that you liked so much, my dear?" he asked. "Why did you want to read it to us?"

The question was the turn of the screw.

"Because I wrote it," I wailed, and burst into loud sobs. Life was over. I wanted to die, or at least to go into the convent, without an hour's delay.

There was a moment of stunned silence. After it the excitement was as intense as any author could wish it to be. My aunts explained that they were joking. They assured me they were simply crazy about that story. My grandmother said the incidents in it could happen anywhere. Allie promptly awoke and climbed into my lap to tell me she thought it was "perfeckly be-au-ti-ful." My mother and father were sick at heart over their understanding of what the episode meant to me. No praise or assurance could comfort me now. Niobe weeping for her children would have seemed debonair in contrast to me, as I sorrowed over my literary first-born.

My father crossed the room, sat down beside me, and began to talk—very gently and sympathetically. He explained that they had all assumed the story to be written by an established "grown-up" author. They had judged it solely from that viewpoint. Looked at thus, it wasn't very striking. As the first effort of a little girl only fourteen it was good. Surely I saw the difference, didn't I? I did. I stopped crying. But I had been hurt to the soul, and the wound bled for years. In fact, it never wholly healed till twenty years later, when I published the experience in *Harper's Magazine* as fiction.

A little of my confidence returned while I was a girl, but very slowly. I had another story accepted a year later, and my price leaped to the sun-tipped peak of five dollars, paid by *Texas Siftings*. However, there were plenty of returned manuscripts to chasten me, and I kept my ambitions and activities to myself. My mind was occupied with a grave problem. If neither literature nor the convent would have me, what would I do? Perhaps, after all, I might have to be a great pianiste like Teresa Carreno, and put my broken heart into my music. That thought cheered me a little. I put the broken heart into my music at once, and my practice hours sent the members of the family into outer space for long walks.

The severe mental problem of those days came back to me many years later when our young French ward, then an infant of five, approached me with a momentous decision of her own. A member of our family had just died and Clothilde, who had loved her deeply, was taking the blow hard.

"Aunt Sarah's gone to heaven," she announced, "so I'm going to heaven, too. Where's my best hat?"

I had to explain to Clo, at some length before she understood, that one does not project one's self into heaven in that abrupt fashion, even in one's best hat. One has to wait for an invitation. My own problem had been similar to Clo's, and its solution was about the same. I must wait for my invitation. It was not for me to thrust myself into Orders or literature if they didn't want me. I must have at least some intimation that I would be welcome if I knocked. In Mother Caroline's words on my graduation day the intimation had come.

I took it up with my father that night. It was not an opportune time. As usual, the house was full of guests. My mother's young sisters were again with us, and some of their friends, and a girl chum of my own who had come from Illinois to see me graduate. However, the general excitement occupied my mother's mind and made it possible for me to lure my father into his study and have an uninterrupted interview. It was on him I was counting for support from the family. My mother, I knew, would oppose my dream to her last breath. She was not a Catholic, and she did not approve of cloistered life. Moreover, she was a woman of great strength of character and her plans for me were made.

I was not sure that I could count on my father. The happiness of our home—and it was an unusually happy home—was based on the success of an agreement between my parents. It had been made very early in their married life, and was faithfully lived up to by both. By this, Mother was in control of the house and the two children, with Father as a Court of Appeal, while he ran his business and his personal life without interference or unasked-for advice. It was an excellent arrangement and we all benefited by it. But my mother and I were very close. I dared not hope that in a matter so vital to her happiness Father would side with me against her. Still, there had been one or two show-downs during the years, when he had quietly but firmly taken command. That night I put the whole situation before him, after making him promise not to comment on it until I had finished all I had to say.

When he realized what I was telling him he got up from his desk, walked over to a window, and stood looking out with his back to me till I stopped talking. When he turned I was struck by the change in his face. He actually seemed older. I had some of my mother's will-power, and he knew exactly what all this might lead to. However, I had also inherited his undying sense of humor. It has been my most precious possession, and up till the time of his death it held us together like a steel cable. We could conduct any and every discussion with the utmost good feeling. We could always make each other understand. Mother was usually serious, but she liked our laughter and our high spirits.

Father dropped into his desk chair and swung it around to face me. He had himself in hand now and he began to talk in his usual easy fashion. From our earliest childhood he had always talked to my sister and to me, and to other children as well, as if he were speaking to his equals. It was one of the characteristics that had won our devotion.

"It's your turn now to listen without interrupting, isn't it?" he asked. I agreed that it was.

"Then I'm going right into a long monologue," he said.

He began with a little flattery. I was only seventeen, he reminded me, but I had acquired the habit of thinking quite early in life, and he had considerable respect for my judgment. He hoped my judgment was too sound to let me make a decision which would shape my whole future, without taking time to consider the effects of the decision. It was very unwise, he suggested, to give up life without knowing something of what life was, and what one was giving up. Moreover, the sacrifice of a thing one had hardly possessed was not much of a sacrifice. The thing to do, he thought, was to give life a tryout. As it happened, I already had two other irons in the fire. I was interested in music and in writing.

At last he had firmly put his finger on my weak spot, and I knew it. I had always kept too many irons in the fire, and the habit has followed me through life. I have been pianiste, reporter, newspaper editor, magazine editor, public speaker, playwright, dramatic critic, and novelist, which helps to explain why I have never done any one thing superlatively well. I even took a hand in the moving-picture game. But these different activities have given me an interesting life and a lot of those "vital human experiences" clubwomen love to discuss.

My father went on talking. I had tried out my music to some degree, he reminded me, and had not been disappointed in the results. Why didn't I try out my writing—go at it more thoroughly and make a real job of it? He and my mother had hoped I would remain at home for a time. Why

didn't I go into newspaper work, which was so interesting
and exciting? I could begin in a small way in Milwaukee—
getting familiar with the newspaper atmosphere, learning the
A.B.C. of reporting and editorial work. He was quite sure
our friend, George W. Peck (then world-famous as a humorist and editor) would take me on the staff of *Peck's Sun.*
Or perhaps Mr. Cramer would give me a chance on the
Evening Wisconsin. After six months or a year of such
experience I could go to Chicago and win my spurs there.
He would pull some wires for me. And then—this last with
a returning buoyancy in his voice—if I had made good, New
York stretched before me, a new world to conquer!

He was an exciting talker and, as always, I was fascinated by him; but I expressed the fear that haunted me
from the first.

"How about the music—and Mother?"

"You have given the music a good tryout here in Milwaukee, and you can keep it up as a side interest if you have
time. As to your mother—well, that problem is up to me and
I'll handle it. I'll make a bargain with you. If you will promise to drop for the next four years all thoughts of entering
the convent, I'll promise to advance your interests in music
and writing in every way I can, and I'll stake you to a tryout
in Chicago and New York if you make good here. Wait
a minute, before you interrupt. I'll make another promise.
If after four years of outside work and experience, you
still want to enter the convent, your mother and I will let
you do it without any more argument. Think it over for a
few days. In the meantime, don't mention the matter to your
mother."

My father's promises were the unbreakable kind. I thought
it over for a week. The world or the convent? At the end
of the week I accepted Father's plan, and after that he confided in Mother. I think his mental attitude during the inter-

Elizabeth Jordan at Seventeen
Photographed in her graduation dress

view was that of Whistler toward William Chase, when
Whistler remarked, "I'm not arguing with you, Chase, I'm
telling you!" But Father was as tactful and beguiling with
Mother as he had been with me. He convinced her that his
plan would save the whole situation. As to taking me away
from home, it could not do that more effectively than a concert career would have done it. He reminded Mother that her
program had included at least two years of study in Germany. By his plan the ocean would not lie between us. He
talked her over. Neither she nor I, nor both together, could
match him when he took a stand.

My sole confidant, outside of the family, was Mother
Caroline.

"Your father is quite right," was all she said. "But—keep
up your music!"

Long afterwards I learned that from the first she had had
me in mind as an eventual successor to Sister Cecilia, who
was growing old.

Father was not a man to map out a course and then forget
it. He vigorously followed up this one. So did I. I went to the
Spencerian Business College in Milwaukee and studied shorthand, on the general assumption that it would be useful
in my newspaper work in Chicago and New York. No one
outside the family quite understood why I wanted to work.
Careers were not inevitable in those days, as they are now.
My father had not as much money as most people thought
he had, but the interest on his capital would have supported
us all very comfortably, and every one knew it. However,
R. C. Spencer took my efforts as seriously as if my daily
bread depended on them. He personally saw to it that I had a
thorough training, and I found my shorthand helpful for
many years. I could probably earn my living as a court reporter to-day—always assuming that I could get a job.

My father found my first job for me. In a few weeks

I was editing the new woman's page of *Peck's Sun,* in Milwaukee. Our friend George W. Peck was wonderfully kind but, of course, this was not the newspaper work of my dreams. "Sunshine," Mr. Peck insisted on calling the department; and he wrote a flowery introduction for it which conveyed the impression that I would personally supply light and warmth to the universe. I myself was not a sentimentalist. It is a miracle that the stuff I had to carry in "Sunshine" did not permanently destroy my interest in newspaper work. "Sunshine" succeeded, however, because Mr. Peck was quite right about what his readers wanted. We were giving them the sort of thing they loved. There was no growth in such effort, however, and at the end of a year I dropped it with vast relief.

Undaunted by this calamity to his newspaper, Mr. Peck went into politics and became Governor of Wisconsin. In later years, when I was on the New York *World,* he always came to see me when he visited the big city, and I saw to it that he met the newspaper men he most admired. He had given me letters of introduction to them all when I came to New York, but he had never met them. This had not disturbed either of us. We both assumed that though they were strangers they would have honored introductions from the leading humorist of his day. No doubt we were right; but I was always too busy in New York to present letters of introduction.

I had my eyes on Chicago. My father, ostensibly an innocent bystander but really manipulating the chessmen in the game we were playing, and convinced that it was too soon for my move to Chicago, found another job for me before I could get one there. He was a member of the Milwaukee School Board. William E. Anderson, Superintendent of Milwaukee schools, needed a private secretary, and asked Father if he knew of the right person for the job. Father thought he did. His daughter called on the Superintendent the next morning, and had the situation ten minutes later.

I was disgruntled. It was too easy. I had done nothing toward getting it except to earnestly assure Mr. Anderson that I had no experience as a secretary and would undoubtedly make a very bad one. The work wasn't at all the kind I wanted. However, the position was really excellent for me. I was a city employee, with a salary generous for the period, a pleasant office, and a very considerate chief. Moreover, as my father pointed out, it was "something different." I was in an atmosphere where I could study human nature and other subjects interesting to embryo authors. Also, I had Saturdays, Sundays, and my evenings free, and this gave me time to keep up my music and writing.

CHAPTER II

First Stop—New York

I HAD plenty of opportunities to study human nature in the school board offices, and I found it as interesting as my father had predicted. To a youngster who had just passed eighteen, it was rather fascinating to know all the secrets of a big school system and most of the professional secrets of the teachers. There were some exciting episodes in which efforts were made to depose certain teachers. Battles were fought out in the school board offices.

Also, in that year, I had my first encounter with tragedy. The school board's treasurer, Henry Schattenberg, a man we all liked and trusted, was discovered to have been embezzling from the city for years. Before the police came for him he shot himself, to avoid a long prison term. I remember every detail of the story of his death: his keeping his four-year-old son with him while he wrote his farewell letters: the child's interest in what his father was doing; "Daddy, how fast you write": his kissing the boy and locking him in a distant room in the house, where the youngster could not hear the shot that sent Henry Schattenberg out of the world. The dignity and reserve with which the *Milwaukee Sentinel* and the *Evening Wisconsin* presented the story the next morning gave me a first and lasting lesson in good newspaper writing.

The following summer I left home for what was on the surface a holiday jaunt through Canada and the East. I had plans. I was growing restless and uneasy. Two years of those promised four years were gone and it seemed to me that I had made no progress. In reality I was working very hard—putting in eight hours a day at my office, reading a great deal, writing short magazine stories which went forth and came back with considerable regularity, and writing for the Chicago newspapers with better results. William Van Benthuysen, managing editor of the Chicago *Tribune,* was especially kind and hospitable. I kept a firm young eye on him. Chicago loomed before me. . . .

I was also keeping up my music, playing at occasional concerts, and very frequently going to Chicago with my mother for Saturday afternoon piano recitals, or for operas that did not come to Milwaukee. The distance between the two cities was only eighty-five miles. We went down on a morning train, lunched in Chicago, heard Teresa Carreno, or D'Albert, or young Hoffman, or some opera, dined on the train coming home, and reached Milwaukee about ten at night. But all this was not progress. Progress, to me, meant one thing only—New York and a place on the New York *World's* staff. I was not yet sure the world in general was a better place than the convent. A New York experience would give me the right answer.

The next move on life's chess-board, I decided, was to be made by me, not by Father. My real destination in that holiday jaunt was New York, and my intention was to get a situation on the *World* before I left the city. However, on my way, I took a look at Canada—Montreal, Quebec, the St. Lawrence—and I also passed a week in Boston. I had never been East before. Then I was ready for New York. But I wasted no time on sight-seeing when I got there. I went straight from the train to the *World* building, and asked for the editor. I didn't even know his name.

Colonel George Harvey once told me, in my later Harper days, that he had done the same thing on his arrival in New York. Having no faith in the elevated trains, he had walked

all the way downtown from the Grand Central Station to
Park Row—a little stroll of three miles. I did not do that.
I took a horse cab—and I was so stunned by the cost of the
ride when I reached the end of it that I was glad to have
time to catch my breath in the waiting-room before I saw
the editor. I was not kept waiting very long. Without realizing it I had come at the ideal time, immediately after luncheon and thus before the real rush of a newspaper day. The
September heat was intense. Colonel John A. Cockerill, then
editor-in-chief of the *World,* was leaning back in his chair
smoking a cigar when I entered his office.

It is on such small details as this that vital turns in fortune often rest. There was no reason at all why Colonel
Cockerill should see me. I had not brought Mr. Peck's letter. I was determined to put this episode through without
help from any one. The Colonel did not know my name or
anything about me. He was idle for a moment or two, while
he finished that cigar—and I had my chance!

I did know enough not to waste time. I made my applica-
tion with my first breath. Colonel Cockerill looked amused,
and leaned back to study me. He decided that I would kill
time as well as anything else till he had finished his cigar.
He asked questions and I answered them. He was amazed
to learn that I had come all the way from Milwaukee to find
a place among the *World's* workers. He said something
about the big responsibility an editor assumed in taking on
an untried candidate so far from home. Did I know the city?
I did not. I had never been in it before that day—but I would
know it in a week. Had I any experience at all in practical
reporting? None whatever—but it was the work I wanted.
Had I done any interviewing? Never, but I hoped he would
give me a lot of it. My contributions to the Chicago *Tribune*
and other newspapers—those clippings he had just glanced
over—were all special features.

But by this time we were past such trivial considerations as experience. We were having a heart-talk, and the entente between us was perfect. Several times I rose to go, but the Colonel waved me back into my chair. Never before, I am sure, had he come into contact with such a combination of ignorance and ambition, frankness and reserve, self-confidence and childish modesty, as I was revealing. Looking back I see that I had them all and that I must have been extremely amusing. I admitted that I didn't know a thing. I was quite sure I could learn, but just then a violet would have seemed an arrogant object beside me.

"One has to start somewhere," I blithely pointed out.

The Colonel knew the answer to that, but he did not make it. He asked if I had any social experience—had I "mingled" as it were. Well, I had spent my school life in a great convent, among a thousand nuns and several hundred students. There had been quite a lot of mingling. The Colonel lit another cigar and said he didn't doubt it.

His office boy left a growing collection of cards on the desk between us. The Colonel's secretary thrust his head around the door once or twice and reverently withdrew it. It was all very much like a fairy-tale to me—a fairy-tale with a wonderful ending. For toward the end of our talk Colonel Cockerill promised me a tryout.

After that understanding the Colonel and I took up the little matter of details. This was September. I explained that I must give Superintendent Anderson and the city of Milwaukee six months' warning before I separated myself from them. It was settled that I was to come to New York and begin my work on the *World* about the middle of April. I felt a natural reluctance to begin the first of April, and when I said so the Colonel grinned understandingly.

Up till the moment he promised me a tryout he had been merely a beneficent god in my machine, more than human, less than personal. That vital point decided, I had time to observe that he was a big man, six feet tall, and that he must weigh about two hundred pounds. He had a massive head with graying hair, an expression suggesting power combined with a valiant kindliness, and strained, tired eyes that usually held a friendly twinkle. He was coatless, and cigar ashes flowed in and out among the crumpled folds of his waistcoat like tiny streams of lava.

The office boy came again with some message that annoyed the Colonel. The twinkle in the tired eyes disappeared and the editor sent up a fountain of profanity that made me stare. It was the first time I heard him exercise this gift, for which, I discovered later, he was famous. He swore as naturally and as easily as he breathed, and it was held by his admirers that he could swear ten minutes at a time without repeating a phrase. He had the unique habit of inserting oaths between the syllables of his words, as if he were in too much of a hurry to swear again to wait till the entire word was pronounced. One of the things he said in the outburst I had just listened to was that the man who had sent in the message was "too—inde—God-damned—pendent."

The office boy grinned and scuttered out. Nobody was afraid of Colonel Cockerill. His staff, from the smallest office boy to the most impressive of his editors—always excepting Ballard Smith—really loved him. This, of course, I also learned later. He was frequently disgusted and often annoyed, but rarely angry. His swearing was a turgid stream that flowed from his lips as freely as water from a faucet, and as unconsciously.

Many months later, at two o'clock one morning, I was privileged to listen to one of his prolonged addresses to his night office boy—an utterly useless but fat and lovable infant of nine or ten who looked seven or eight. No one else would have dreamed of giving such a job to such a baby; but Colonel Cockerill had taken a fancy to the infant, so there he was.

On this night the child was peacefully sleeping at his desk, his head on his folded arms, when the Colonel awoke him with a slap on the shoulder and gave him an order. The youngster was too dazed and sleepy to understand what was said to him. He stood blinking and wobbling on his legs, while the Colonel swore for five minutes. The climax of the monologue was the boy's discharge. He was to go home on the instant and never come back. The baby—he was really no more than that for the moment—stumbled out of the office.

"He doesn't even know what's happened to him," the Colonel grumbled; and went on with the instructions he was giving me.

In less than five minutes the office door reopened. The infant stood on the threshold. His face was wet with tears and white with fury. He was gasping for breath, because he had run back upstairs.

"Say," he howled at the top of his voice, "did you fire me?"

"I did," said the Colonel.

"Well, what I want to know is why the —— —— —— —— —— —— —— —— —— —— —— you did it!" the infant roared.

The Colonel looked at him and then at me. We were in the Cockerill office high in the gold dome of the new *World* building. On the same impulse we turned our backs to the boy and stared hard at the boats bellowing up at us from the river.

"Is it possible this kid got that from me?" the Colonel asked in an awed tone.

"It seems to be. It all sounds very familiar."

"Well, he's got to stop it. See here!" Colonel Cockerill rearranged his features and turned sternly to the boy.

"Stop that swearing and get back to your work."

The child gulped.

"Ain't I fired?"

"No, but you're going to be the next time I hear an oath out of you—and that time you'll *stay* fired. Nobody under twenty-one swears around these offices. That's an order. Now, hustle."

This was Colonel Cockerill as I learned to know him— the kindest, biggest-hearted man in the newspaper world, and with abilities and idiosyncrasies that made him one of the most discussed editors of his day. But on the day of our agreement he was shaking hands in farewell and advising me what to read and learn in preparation for the new job in the spring.

In later years I might well have been a bit skeptical about that casual contract between an applicant and an editor. There was no shadow on my faith then, and that faith was justified. The Colonel and I seemed to have read each other very accurately. I knew he would give me a tryout and he knew I would return and do the best I could with it. I wrote him a brief letter of appreciation as soon as I reached home, and received a short but pleasant reply confirming our agreement.

I did not write him again until I was about to start for New York. I was too busy. I had to announce the new plans to my family and reconcile my mother to them. Father took them like the good sport he was. He knew I had not been contented, and he reminded Mother that my next sortie might be into the convent if they did not give me my head. I resigned my position, and with equal surprise and appreciation refused an offer to remain at an increased salary. It was my lucky year and everything was going my way. Mother was very difficult, but finally came 'round. It was no doubt of my ability to take care of myself in New York that disturbed her. She was the most independent woman I have ever known. She had been one of the few college girls of her day—an honor student at Mendota Female College, with her cousin Mary Breckinridge, and she had expected to be a physician. Her marriage upset all that, but she had assumed that I would "carry on" with the music which was her greatest passion. I loved music, too, but literature came first—and I saw in newspaper work the best training for it. Human interest in plenty, human contacts, increasing knowledge of life. Five years of these, say; then magazine work, and after that an open door to the world of literature. This was my program, and to me it was as definite as a blueprint.

Nellie Bly was making a triumphant tour through the West that winter, after her big feat of going around the world in seventy-two days. When she came to Milwaukee Charles Ledlie, city editor of the *Sentinel,* and I were appointed a committee of two to meet her at the train and arrange a reception for her. We did it, and I was thrilled. But Miss Bly was not at all interested in the news that I was to join the *World's* staff in the spring. I failed to make matters any better when I explained that I was not to attempt the wonderful things she and Nell Nelson were doing, but was to confine myself to news reporting. I hoped this was true. I had warned Colonel Cockerill that I was not up to "stunt" reporting and that I did not like it. Miss Bly remarked briefly that she had just resigned from the *World* and that she was sorry for any one who was going to work on that sheet. The entente between us took on a delicate layer of frost.

As the day of my departure for New York drew near Superintendent Anderson gave a farewell dinner for me and flowery speeches were made by him and others. I have forgotten most of them but I recall a really charming little talk, simple and sincere, contributed by Paul Binner, then the distinguished head of Milwaukee's well-known School for the Deaf and Dumb.

Every one I knew, it seemed to me, was giving me letters of introduction to friends in New York. I brought a trunkful of letters with me when I came East, but I never used more than two or three of them. For the next ten years I had little time for anything but work. I did, however, present one of the letters to A. M. Palmer, then manager of Wallack's Theatre, because I was immensely interested in plays and players. He immediately put me on his free list and sent me tickets for first-night performances of all the plays presented at Wallack's. I distinctly remember the opening night of *Beau Brummel,* among others, and Clyde Fitch's panic-stricken eyes and shaking legs, as he stood before us trying to make a speech.

It was well that so many pleasant things happened just before I left Milwaukee. During my first months in New York I needed the memory of them to sustain me through the successive jolts and disappointments life handed me. On the other hand, I also needed those jolts and disappointments. Things had been going far too smoothly. It was high time I learned that I was not really the darling of fortune I had begun to fancy myself.

CHAPTER III

BETWEEN TWO MILL-STONES

THE twinkle had left Colonel Cockerill's eyes when I reported to him in New York. He looked many years older and very tired. He received me with what a more suspicious nature would have diagnosed as weary resignation. Even I could not believe it was enthusiasm.

I knew nothing of office politics, nor of the fierce internal warfare that went on in many newspaper offices. In those of the New York *World* and the New York *Herald* this warfare was then particularly hectic. In both offices the continued absence of their owners, Joseph Pulitzer of the *World* and James Gordon Bennett of the *Herald,* was the basic cause of the conditions. Mr. Bennett chose to live abroad. The tragic condition of Joseph Pulitzer's eyes kept him away from his desk and in the care of European oculists.

Given a choice Mr. Pulitzer would never have absented himself voluntarily, as Mr. Bennett did. The *World* was his life and he would have asked nothing better than to devote all his time to it. But he was slowly going blind. Nevertheless, with the aid of a large staff of readers and secretaries he kept in amazingly close touch with his newspaper.

He usually lived on his yacht, which dropped anchor in American waters several times a year. The sound of that dropping anchor seemed to be heard in the *World* offices, which Mr. Pulitzer's unseen presence was always sweeping through like a high wind. From the hour of his arrival in New York that effect deepened. The nerve tension of the editorial staff, always at the breaking point, tightened. Mr.

25

Pulitzer was a mighty leader, and a very generous one; but his editors lived in extreme awe of him.

Moreover, the inevitable result of his absence was that an incessant life-and-death struggle for supremacy went on among them. It was said at the time that Mr. Pulitzer rather fostered this. He was the author of the often-quoted remark, "The indispensable man has not yet been born." He seemed determined that no editor should have the impression that he was necessary to the progress of the *World*. The respective authority of his editor-in-chief and his managing editor was never clearly defined for them. Certainly each man, throughout my subsequent ten years on the *World,* usually considered himself the head. The results were combats that rose between them like pillars of fire; and both men wasted a vast amount of nerve power in keeping that flame alive. After a year or two of this struggle one of the combatants conquered, had his little day of power, and soon went down before a new-comer.

At the time of my arrival the final stage of one of these struggles was in progress between Colonel Cockerill and Ballard Smith. It was probably the biggest and the most fiercely fought in the *World's* history. Colonel Cockerill was editor-in-chief. He had held the position for years and had been very close to "J P," as Mr. Pulitzer was always called in his offices. Colonel Cockerill was a born newspaper man, a great worker, a great leader, but of the old school. Ballard Smith, the managing editor, was young and dynamic. He was a really brilliant newspaper man, and he carried his ambition like a flaunting flag. He had locked horns with the Colonel almost as soon as he was appointed, and the long contest was on. By the time I appeared the old leader was almost down. Mr. Smith had reached the point of feeling that no person should be added to the staff except by himself. Any one brought in by Cockerill was anathema to Smith, and was marked for immediate slaughter.

I knew nothing of all this at the time, and Mr. Smith was afterwards so kind to me that I hesitate to mention it. But it explained Colonel Cockerill's new manner, his weariness, and his distressing uncertainty as to what he could do with me now that I was there to be reckoned with. Much can happen on any newspaper in six months, and Colonel Cockerill's power had waned steadily since the day I first met him. He should have written and put me off, but his natural kindliness and a lingering optimism forbade this. He had received me at once, and shaken hands. Now he was looking at me worriedly. I felt his vagueness, his uncertainty, and a chill ran down my spine. I had come to him with such utter confidence, such overwhelming enthusiasm! The situation was not one he could explain to me. He uttered a few generalities, turned me over to a sub-editor, and my troubles began.

There is no doubt whatever that I needed them. It had all been too easy, and the farewell celebration in my home city had been too heady. I was dizzy with self-confidence, and I needed an immediate and a very thorough lesson. I received it. The assignments I was given were trivial. I worked from fourteen to eighteen hours a day, running all over town on leads that rarely developed and would hardly have been worth while if they had. When I crossed Ballard Smith's line of vision he simply did not see me. When Colonel Cockerill gave me an assignment, Mr. Smith struck it from the schedule.

No one else was deliberately unkind, but every one had his own troubles. The city editor was a young man as ambitious as Smith himself and as determined to succeed. He was a protégé of Ballard Smith and could not afford to get caught in the machine in which I was whirling so helplessly.

I was a stranger in New York. I had no time to present my letters of introduction. As yet I had not a friend in whom I could confide. I remembered and tried to follow my father's parting advice when I left home.

"Don't lean on *any one*. Stand on your own feet."

I had to stand on my own feet. I was young and as strong as a pony, and my optimism was indestructible. I set my jaw and took what came, though my pride was a tattered flag. I had given some time during my last months in Milwaukee to a careful study of New York city maps. Now I extended this study in my rushes about town. I watched the star reporters in the City Room and studied their style and methods. I read every line in the *World* every morning, and as many of the big stories in the rival newspapers as I had time for. I made suggestions for specials which were always turned down.

The thing that most impressed Colonel Cockerill, he told me later, was that I never made a complaint to him or to any one else. This was mere common sense, but he considered it unusual. I saw him rarely, but gave him the best impersonation I could offer of a cub reporter in a condition of beatific well-being. Very soon I understood the whole situation, and my heart ached over him. He was my hero and I let him see that, at least. I was on salary, and the salary was large enough to pay my expenses. Smith could not change this. He could only try to force me off the newspaper.

This went on for two months. Then Colonel Cockerill saw an opening for me and grasped it. When I learned the nature of the opening I nearly collapsed and fell into it from shock and humiliation. Nevertheless, I realized there was nothing to do but take the new assignment and try to make good. It was on the Brooklyn edition of the *World*. It would take me out of New York and leave me planted there. Worse

still, it was almost commercial. It had to do with a series of
special articles to be written about Long Island summer resorts—articles frankly designed to please hotel proprietors
and stimulate advertising, local pride, and *World* circulation.
I think Colonel Cockerill was sure he had me off his hands
for good. His parting grin was almost a benediction. I believe, too, that my own steadfast smile must have slipped
off for a few seconds. If it had, it was securely back in place
when I reached the Brooklyn office an hour later and reported to Vincent Cook, managing editor of the Brooklyn
edition.

That was many, many years ago, but I can see Mr. Cook
as I write, and my heart warms at the memory of him. He
gave me a wonderful welcome. Later he told me he had heard
all about my experience between the Smith-Cockerill mill-
stones; but this day there was no hint in words or manner
that I was a novice, and that I had my spurs to win. He
assured me I was to be his right hand man in a big scheme
that had all sorts of possibilities in the way of public attention and circulation increase.

I was to begin at Sea Cliff the next morning, which was
Friday morning, by going there for the week-end, taking up
quarters at the best hotel, and writing an illustrated story
of the place and its charms, to which Mr. Cook would give
half a page in the Sunday edition. I had the rest of the day
to get ready for the expedition, and I used it in studying
maps of Brooklyn and Long Island, and getting all the information I could about Sea Cliff. Despite Mr. Cook's brave
words I had no illusions about the situation. Anything I
wrote would be read in Brooklyn and Long Island and nowhere else. I was out of New York almost as definitely as if
I were working in China.

I arrived at the Sea Cliff Inn Friday, presented Mr. Cook's
letter, and was received with considerable empressement.

The prospect of getting half a page of free advertising of
Sea Cliff at the beginning of its social season struck the
proprietor of the Sea Cliff Inn very favorably. He gave me
a beautiful room and bath overlooking the Sound, and assured me that the hotel was mine.

It was now about the middle of June. During the following month I visited and wrote up every important summer
resort on Long Island, and Mr. Cook's fairest dreams came
true. Hotel managers and town authorities were equally delighted by this free publicity. Hotel proprietors bought thousands of extra copies of the Brooklyn editions and sent them
all over the country with their circulars and announcements.
They all wanted their towns written up at once. The circulation went up and advertising came in. Mr. Cook boasted to
Colonel Cockerill, and the Colonel saw to it that the boasts
and the figures reached Ballard Smith. Mr. Smith had copies
of the Brooklyn edition brought to his desk and looked over
the specials. He made no comment on them, but from that
time it seems that he regularly skimmed them as part of his
routine morning work.

I was more cheerful. My mother had come to New York
to make the first of those visits which, according to my
father, she subsequently made four times a year, remaining
three months each time. I had been away from home two
months and she felt that a reunion was indicated, as well as
a personal investigation into my goings on. I took her with
me on the Long Island assignments and the jaunts were
healing and soothing to us both. Mother carried back to
Milwaukee an undying conviction that newspaper work was
just one pleasant experience after another. Compared to the
black period which had preceded it those weeks seemed a
time of dalliance, even to me. We passed the week-ends at
the bigger resorts, a day and a night at the smaller ones. All
I had to do was to take Mother sight-seeing, absorb my

own impressions, select good photographs of the town, and write my special in the evening—a column, or two columns, or more.

I put in from one to three hours on the actual writing. The remainder of every day was given to what seemed mere holiday enjoyment. I felt guilty about it. Was I earning my salary? As a matter of record, I was very definitely doing so. I was writing on an average ten columns a week, which at the space rates then paid would have cost the *World* seventy-five dollars. I was getting thirty dollars a week, and all my expenses. The *World's* circulation and advertising were increasing in the most gratifying manner. Vincent Cook was jubilant. He raised my salary, brooded over coming triumphs, and assumed that together we would carry the Brooklyn edition to new heights. This was not my dream, but I was acquiescent for the time.

In July the situation changed with amazing suddenness. Things had been happening in the New York offices. Ballard Smith's star reporters had failed on a story on which Mr. Smith had set his restless heart. The fact that most of the other star reporters in town had failed on the same story held no comfort for him. General Benjamin Harrison, then President of the United States, had moved with his family from the White House in Washington to a seashore cottage at Cape May, New Jersey, lent him for the season, it was said, by that eminent philanthropist, George W. Childs of Philadelphia. There had been considerable newspaper criticism of the President's acceptance of this hospitality. There were, as of course there would be on the slightest provocation, hints of high finance making its ignoble uses of our statesmen. Ballard Smith wanted a description of that cottage and a story of the life the presidential family was living there. But the Harrisons had entrenched themselves in their seaside refuge and would not be seen. Their feelings had been hurt by press criticisms. Newspaper men from all over the country battered at the cottage doors in vain.

The family at that time consisted of President and Mrs. Harrison, their daughter, Mrs. James Robert McKee (afterwards a life-long friend of mine) and Mrs. McKee's infant son, Benjamin Harrison McKee, then about five years old. Mr. McKee was there for week-ends only. "Baby McKee," as the child was affectionately called by the American press, was supposed to be the vulnerable spot in Benjamin Harrison's cold make-up. The President was devoted to the youngster and liked to have him around, playing at his feet, even in the presidential offices.

Inevitably, the newspapers of the country had become almost hysterical over that baby. They printed innumerable columns about him. His small interests and activities were described as if they were world news. His photographs smiled from the pages of all the leading journals. There had been nothing quite like it before. There have been few things like it since. Ballard Smith wanted a story about the Cape May life of the whole Harrison family, with special attention to Baby McKee. Smith was a hot-tempered man, and now he was infuriated by the repeated failures of his staff to get that story.

"Do you think that girl over in Brooklyn could get it— the one that's doing this Long Island series?" he yelped at his secretary one morning, while he was glancing over the Brooklyn edition.

"I do not," the secretary snapped. "We've had half a dozen of our best men on that Cape May door-step for two weeks. What chance would she have where they've failed?"

"Get her over here, anyway," Smith ordered. "I want to talk to her."

The secretary, who afterwards repeated the little conversation to me, hastened to recall me to the *World's* hearthstone. Its temperature was still tepid. The talk with Mr. Smith was brief and on his side, at least, without much optimism. I was to go to Cape May and get that story. Mr. Smith would give me as much space as I could fill. He wanted the daily life of the Harrison family—their diversions and relaxations. I was to draw on the cashier for my expenses and start at once. I started that night. At a few minutes after nine o'clock the next morning I, too, was on that Cape May door-step.

Right here I must turn aside to correct one of the few inaccuracies I found in Ishbel Ross's recent and excellent book, *Ladies of the Press*. In writing of the Harrison Cape May "beat"—the biggest of its day in New York—Miss Ross says: "Elizabeth Jordan so overawed Benjamin Harrison's butler with her elegant costume and ostrich feathers that she got an interview at Cape May when the door was closed to all other reporters."

I was at that time and for many years afterwards one of the most severely tailor-made young persons in New York. It would no more have occurred to me to do my newspaper work in "elegant costumes and ostrich feathers" than it would have occurred to me to do it in no clothing at all. I had hanging in my closets one or two afternoon and evening gowns, kept there in the artless hope that some day or evening I might have time to wear them. I never had. In my working hours I dressed with the utmost simplicity. It was a very hot July morning when I rang the door-bell of that Cape May cottage, and what I wore was a fresh white linen tailor-made suit, white canvas shoes, a white sport hat, and white wash gloves. I suppose I looked clean and informal and very much alive when I asked the butler if Mrs. Harrison was at home, but I certainly did not impress him by my elegance. He said she was, and stepped aside to let me pass him. As I entered the hall Mrs. Harrison walked out of an inner room, wearing a beach hat and leading Baby McKee by the hand.

Again I am impelled to remark that on such slight chances as this do vital changes in fortune rest! If I had been formally announced, if Mrs. Harrison had been upstairs, it is almost certain that I would not have seen her. As it was, I went forward at once, told her exactly where I came from and what I wanted, and gave my attention to Baby McKee during the moment in which she took me in and decided that it was safe to accept me. The next moment we were shaking hands, while she explained that she and "Ben" were just leaving for the beach for his first sea bath. It was an occasion. Did I care to come? I did!

The Harrisons had a private stretch of seashore, and it was too early for bathers using the rest of the beach. There were only a few men sprawled on the distant sands or floating out in the water. Mrs. Harrison and I seemed alone in the universe as we sat down together and talked for more than an hour, while Baby McKee "did his stuff" as if his little hour had struck. He intrepidly tackled the ocean. He dropped on the sand and let the waves roll over him. He made short sorties into the water, tentatively at first, then more boldly. He came back at intervals, incoherent with rapture, and dripped on us. We watched him as we talked.

Mrs. Harrison was a simple, maternal type of woman, but her face was touched with tragedy. She was already, and consciously, in the grip of the disease which caused her death a few years later. She talked of the baby, of the routine of these seashore days, of the welcome change from the strain of official life in Washington, of what she was reading. She answered fully and frankly every question I asked her. She had no knowledge that she was starting me out on a new life, but she would have been interested if she had known it. Under her simple morning blouse beat the heart of a gentlewoman. I built a shrine for her in that hour, and I have kept a little candle burning there throughout my life.

Long before the hour was over I had the story which in the next morning's *World* was the newspaper "beat" of the period, and which set me on the straight road I had elected to travel. I wanted both Ballard Smith and Mrs. Harrison to like that story, and they did. I had a nice letter from Mrs. Harrison two days later. Ballard Smith reacted to the episode with characteristic enthusiasm. I was ordered back to New York at once, my salary was again raised, and I was put on Mr. Smith's personal staff of reporters. Mr. Cook and I parted almost with tears. My real working life had begun. But what I recall most vividly, next to Mrs. Harrison's kindness, was the grip of John A. Cockerill's hand the next day.

CHAPTER IV

TRUE STORIES OF THE NEWS

WHAT I wanted to do was straight reporting. That, fortunately, was what Mr. Smith usually wanted me to do, so we were in happy accord. I need hardly explain, however, that I was not entering upon a career of uninterrupted triumphs. I had some good assignments, enough successes to keep me cheerful, and enough failures to keep me chastened.

In September I had my first "model story" posted on the wall of the *World's* City Room. Morrell Goddard (still happily alive as I write, and one of the last of the old *World* group) was by that time the city editor.* He was an up-and-coming young man, already showing the forceful qualities that won his later success. He was outwardly cold, inwardly kind, and always absolutely just. He introduced various innovations into the *World* City Room. One of these was to cut out of the morning *World* what he considered an especially good story,† and paste it on the wall as a model for the members of the staff to study and imitate. A few of them studied and imitated. I was one of these. The model stories were rather rare, and notwithstanding our assumed indifference the reporters kept an eye out for them. We were all more or less impressed when one appeared.

There was sentiment in Mr. Goddard's nature, but there was absolutely no sentimentality. It must have been the bare

---

* Mr. Goddard died in 1937.
† The word "story," as used in newspaper circles, covers almost any article that appears in a newspaper, except an editorial.

facts of the episode that hit him so hard in "The Death of Number Nine." This was the simple tale of a sick baby, carried three miles through New York streets one night in its mother's arms, only to have her discover at Bellevue Hospital that the child was dead. She had had no money for car fare. She had no money to bury the baby. She was forced to leave him in the city morgue, as Number Nine, to be buried in Potter's Field. One of the Bellevue nurses I knew telephoned me about the case. I went to the morgue and found the tiny pine box in which Number Nine, who had never known comfort or proper care in his little life, lay in peace at last, waiting to be carted away in the morning. I was determined that he should have proper burial. On the cover of that box I wrote in chalk:

Hold this baby till instructions are received from The New York World.

I went back to the office and wrote the story, finishing it with a plea for contributions to bury the baby. I wrote very simply, remembering a bit of advice Sister Ethelbert had given me during my senior year at Notre Dame.

"Let your readers shed their own tears," she penciled at the end of one of my vaulting efforts. It is the best literary criticism I have ever received, and I have preached and tried to practise it ever since.

The Death of Number Nine was published the next morning. Possibly what most impressed Mr. Goddard was the fact that by the time he reached his desk at ten o'clock enough contributions had been received to bury almost every dead child in New York that day. He was a young man of brisk action. In the next half hour he had read the story, posted it on the City Room wall, telephoned to Bellevue Hospital, and started me off on a "follow-up" special for the next day. Number Nine was laid away with the dignified simplicity with which a child should be buried. The remainder of the money that poured into the *World* offices rescued his mother and his brothers and sisters from starvation. Permanent work was found for the mother and her two oldest boys, and the tragic family faced a happier life.

The story created a little newspaper stir out of all proportion to its importance as a bit of writing, and I suppose my *World* associates felt that I needed deflating. From the first they had all been extremely considerate and friendly. Now they proceeded to have some fun with me.

What was represented as a delegation from the entire *World* staff impressively came to me in the City Room the evening after the funeral. There were eight on the Committee, as I remember it. One of them, I think, was Bayard Veiller, then a cub reporter like myself, later one of New York's leading playwrights. They were provided with notebooks, pencils and other paraphernalia. They were unsmiling and extremely dignified, and they had an eloquent spokesman. He called the meeting to order, ushered me to a chair in the center of the circle, and embarked on a burlesque tribute which included a brief but hectic story of my life. As he went on I became a composite character made up of Nellie Bly, Maud Ballington Booth, Lydia E. Pinkham, and Mary Ellen Lease. He solemnly presented me with a wreath of immortelles contributed by my associates.

Next, assuming a different tone and manner, he declared that my fellow workers had found in me a Flaw, and they were pointing it out that I might drop it and become Perfect. The Flaw was my convent manner. I did things that were contrary to all newspaper traditions. He enumerated some of them. I stood up when my elders and superiors came to my desk. I did not interrupt when others were speaking, as others always were. Later, he promised, he would go into the problem of how I retained the power of speech under these conditions. I said "Please" and "Thank you" and "I beg your pardon." When I fed with the bunch I kept my elbows off the table and my face out of my plate. For four months, off and on, they had tried to live up to all this, but the strain was too great. The strongest among them were weakening under it. The desperate expression in the eyes around me in the City Room was due to it. Would I, for God's sake and for the love of Mike, drop the damned formality and the convent polish and be a regular fellow like the rest of them?

Dazed by the yells of rapture that greeted the speaker's strong points, I said I would. We all went to Mouquin's for supper, where I sat at the right of the chairman and, by special request, wore the wreath of immortelles. Three months later, as Christmas approached, I was initiated into the *World's* secret holiday club—the T.H.W.T.M.Y.T.— formed to relieve the feelings of those who had to work on Christmas Day and on all other days except Sunday. I have no intention of interpreting the initials, but any one who cares to may do so.

Other experiences came fast. Mr. Smith had a special flair for "human interest stories." He could detect one in a two-line bit of local news telegraphed from remote hamlets throughout the country. It developed that in October I must go down to the mountains of Virginia and Tennessee for a series of special articles he had been brooding over for months. He had read some item about an old preacher loved and revered by all the southern mountaineers. My first duty when I reached the mountains would be to find this man and write a story about his life and work.

Mr. Smith was vague about details. Could I ride a horse? I could. Good! Most of my journeying in those remote fast-nesses would have to be done on horseback. "Possibly" I'd need a guide. There were no hotels, of course, in the region, but there was plenty of "hospitality." "Probably" I could find food and shelter when I needed them. I must "decide"

such things for myself. "Perhaps" I'd better go from New
York to Bristol, Tennessee, and from Bristol by wagon to
Big Stone Gap, Virginia. There I would drop my last connection with civilization and plunge into the wilderness for
a fortnight or more. When I had obtained the preacher's
story I was to follow up the little matter of mountain feuds,
and also cover anything else that might seem dramatic and
heart-pulling to *World* readers.

I was enchanted. This was real adventure. It was a dream
come true. I was as airy about details as Ballard Smith. I left
for Bristol the next morning and reached there late at night.

I don't know what the hotels in Bristol have developed
into during the years, but the one I went to—recommended
as the best—lacked everything a hotel should have. It was
dirty and down-at-the-heel, and the meals had been prepared
with a can opener. The sagging door of my bedroom had
no lock. Compared to that hotel the makeshift boarding-
house at Big Stone Gap, when I reached it, seemed almost
luxurious. Ore had been discovered in the mountains and a
developing company was beginning work there. The board-
ing-shack was reasonably clean, and there was one woman
in the settlement. She was the young bride of an engineer,
and so pathetically glad to see another woman that I have
never forgotten her. Both she and her husband were appalled
by my project of pushing on into the mountains, but the
husband recommended a guide to me and helped me to select
two horses. The guide he chose was a Negro, one of his
own helpers. He had known the Negro for years and considered him more trustworthy than any of the white "riff-
raff" of the camp.

I myself had not the slightest conception of the risks I
was taking. I had passed most of my life, except my vacations, in a convent. Everybody had always been kind to me.
A small amount of theoretical knowledge lay lightly on the

surface of my mind. If I had been put through a primer in-
terrogation as to what might happen I could have answered
questions glibly. I was already sure I knew life to its core.
Was I not a newspaper reporter in New York? But my
ignorance was incredible, and most of what my associates
were kind enough to call my courage was due to that ignorance. To me the southern mountain assignment was merely
a high adventure; and a high adventure it remained from
start to finish.

The engineer's faith in the Negro guide was justified, so
far as the man's character was concerned. He was gentle-
natured, docile, reasonably intelligent, and he took good care
of the horses. On the first day of our journey, however, I discovered that he had no more knowledge of those mountains
than I had. He was forced to ask our way at every cabin.
After a week of this I paid him off and sent him back to Big
Stone Gap. By that time I was taking care of him. Also, he
was a nuisance when I had to take baths in running streams,
which was my only way of keeping clean. At such times I
had to send him off for an hour and take chances that he
would be able to find me again. He rarely could. I usually
had to pursue and rescue him. But all that came later. The
month was October. The weather was perfect.

I reached the cabin of the mountain preacher the evening
of the first day of the journey, just at sunset. We had
traveled since sunrise, stopping only once—to eat the luncheon we brought from Big Stone Gap. The preacher's name
was Joseph Wells, and that visit to his home gave me my
first experience of mountain hospitality and family habits
and customs. The news of my coming had already spread
through the hills. Every member of the family came out into
the clearing to meet me—the old man, his wife, his three
grown sons, his married daughter, her boy, fourteen, and
her baby, six months old.

I passed two nights in that mountain hut, and became all too well acquainted with the family; for I slept with the married daughter, her baby, and her fourteen-year-old boy, and assisted at the morning and evening toilets of the others. The lad reposed on the outside of the bed, and across its foot. Incidentally, he reposed on our feet. On the opposite side of the room was another bed, in which the old minister and his wife slept. Leading from that one room to a small loft was a home-made ladder up which the three sons climbed to their blankets on the attic floor.

Before this experience, I had been greeted by the family, had explained my errand and accepted an invitation to remain, had heard the despairing squawk of a young hen as her neck was wrung, and had helped to eat her an hour later, as we all sat at our supper of chicken and corn-bread.

"Sometimes we got butter an' sometimes we haint," my hostess explained. "Jest now," she added peacefully, "we haint."

She was a dear creature and I have never forgotten her. In her God had given the fiery-souled old minister the companion he needed—a woman quietly cheerful and steady of heart.

"I cain't read an' I cain't write," she confided to me. "But I c'n listen when Joe reads an' I c'n un'stan' whut he says. I wisht ou' Bible wuzn't so wored out."

The old Bible was indeed in tatters, and I remember with pleasure that I sent "Joe" a new one as soon as I got back to New York. That in itself was an enterprise. The Bible had to be expressed to Bristol, taken on by wagon to Big Stone Gap, and then on horseback to the Wells cabin.

My first evening with the family brought out all I needed to know about J. B. Wells. We talked for hours, seated around his field-stone fireplace. I had also learned much about him at Big Stone Gap. He lived fifty miles from a railroad, and he had never seen either railroad tracks or trains. He had no more conception of the outer world than his baby grandson had. He had never seen nor heard any musical instrument except a jews'-harp, played on by a local youth who had made a sortie into Big Stone Gap. But Joseph Wells, while he knew nothing of this world, held mighty convictions about the next one. He meant to see to it that his congregation would have a better time there than it had here. In some way he had got possession of the battered Bible and had taught himself to read. With the help of his mountain neighbors he had built a church—a crude thing of logs and unpainted pine boards. There—and this was the Big Stone Gap end of the biography—he preached every Sunday, with homely eloquence that out in the world would have carried him far. Even in the mountains his fame grew. Mountaineers throughout the region came on horseback to hear him, riding fifty miles and more. He had to build an annex to the log church.

Uninterested though he was in the outside world, he was passionately interested in the physical health and progress as well as in the spiritual development of his neighbors. He had a little knowledge of the medical value of roots and herbs, and of first aid in accidents. He would not travel six feet to attend a dance, or a party of any kind. He would and constantly did ride over the mountains at all hours of the day and night and in all sorts of weather, summer and winter alike, to help other human beings. He had plenty of opportunities. Around him the mountain feuds were raging, and the cemeteries were being filled with young men in their prime, whose fathers or grandfathers had been shot by some member of a neighboring family, and who had grown up with the cancer of revenge in their brains and hearts.

I did not, of course, get this sort of information from J. B. Wells or his family. I did not, at any time, hear any-

thing like self-praise from the old man. He was the nobly
primitive type one so often reads about and so rarely meets
—simple, kind to the depths of his nature, obsessed by a
burning zeal for the welfare of souls and bodies, and utterly
sincere. He was modest because he had no realization that
he was in any way unusual. He was not surprised because I
had come from New York to write about him. He had no
real idea of what New York was, or where it was. He asked
me some amazing questions and the boys asked more. The
boys could not read or write, and they hadn't let "pap"
teach them to. They had been all the way to Big Stone Gap,
a metropolis in which several hundred men and one woman
were living. New York, they had heard, was a big town.
How big was it? How many folks lived in it? What kind of
houses did they have?

I answered in the simplest way I could. Almost immediately I made the humiliating discovery that they did not
believe me. The boys obviously thought I was "pulling their
legs." They exchanged glances, then listened with chuckles
and dancing eyes, delighted with the wild yarns they were
sure I was spinning. That they could consider me capable of
this conduct, even though they were so willing to forgive it,
hurt me. I did my best to convince them that I was talking
seriously and giving them facts about their country's greatest city. I might better have saved my breath.

The boys, all in their early twenties, guffawed and slapped
their knees. Their mother was dozing in her chair. The
married daughter was pouring her baby into its night garment—a little brown meal sack with a homemade string
around the neck. I don't know what the old preacher thought,
but I can imagine. A city with more than two million human
beings in it; cars that ran through its streets or on trestles
in the air; a *World* building twenty-two stories high—New
York's architectural triumph at that time—all this was too

much for J. B. Wells, as it was for his sons and his grandson.

In desperation I turned to the West—to its wheat-fields, corn-fields, and orchards. They understood those things, but not for long. When I answered their questions about the acreage of those fields and the size of those crops the boys again roared and the old man ceased to listen. He sat with us quietly, his eyes on the fire and his thoughts, I am sure, with his people.

I turned to the topic of the mountain feuds. That woke him up. He had set his strong old will against those killings. He was determined to end them—and he had no illusions as to the difficulty of the task. The things he told me were as strange to my ears as my talk had seemed to him. I remember a fifty-year-old feud and nine deaths, all the result of the theft of one rooster. The cause of another feud, almost equally long and bloody, was the accidental discovery by one man of a neighbor's mountain still. The owner was ill in bed, and the neighbor had mounted guard over the still for a night and day—only to be shot at sight, before he could explain his friendly purpose, when the owner returned. That had led to six deaths during the following thirty years.

We all went to bed at ten o'clock. I had unconsciously delayed the ceremony two hours past the usual time. I lay awake most of the night, listening to the cries of wildcats in the woods that closed around us, while my hair fluttered in the breeze that blew through the wide chinks between the logs forming the cabin walls. I fell asleep toward dawn. When I awoke at five in the morning the oldest son, "Shep," about twenty-four, was standing beside the bed looking down at me with deep interest. As our eyes met he smiled without embarrassment.

"Don't you-uns git up yit," he kindly advised. "Fire ain't burnin' right sma't."

I remained over Sunday to hear the old man preach. The sermon was all I had expected.

After two weeks of days in the saddle and nights in mountain cabins, after fording countless mountain streams and getting wet and letting my clothes dry on me, after experiences in the feud regions that in themselves would fill a book—in short, after getting my mountain stories—I developed an ailment I never had before or since. It was rheumatism. When my right arm and shoulder became so helpless that I could neither dress nor undress without help I returned to Big Stone Gap, and from there drove to Bristol.

The weather had changed. The day was cold and rainy. The driver and wagon I had hired for the latter pilgrimage deposited me at the door of the so-called hotel, and departed. I made my explanations to the proprietor. I wanted a doctor and a nurse, to get me into condition for the railroad journey to New York.

The man reflected, staring out at the rain with vague eyes. Following his glance I saw a woman gallantly striding along the muddy pathway across the road from the hotel. The proprietor shot out into the street with unexpected energy, waving his arms and shouting.

"Mrs. Carrington!"

The woman stopped and waited, evidently expecting him to cross the road to her. But his flicker of energy had died down. When he did not move she came over to him through the mud. I inferred that he was about to ask advice concerning me, and I strolled out into the rain to hear the result. My arm was in a sling. "Mrs. Carrington" looked at it and at me and smiled sympathetically. I was in pain, and no doubt my expression showed it.

Before I could speak the proprietor, vastly relieved by her appearance, told her who I was and put my case before her.

"You can't possibly stay here," she decided at once. "You must come right home with me. Send her luggage to my house," she told the hotel proprietor.

This did not suit either the hotel man or me. We both protested passionately. He was unwilling to lose a boarder, and I had no intention of being a burden to strangers. The whole matter was taken out of our hands. In twenty minutes I was a guest in the home of Mrs. Wirt Cabell Carrington, in a charming room whose three windows offered a fine view of the deluge and the countryside. My hostess's Negro mammy, the best amateur nurse in the region, was looking after me. It was the finest example of southern hospitality I have ever known, and I enjoyed it for three nights and two days, until I was able to travel. Mrs. Carrington's father, General Imboden, had recently married a second time—a young and charming woman. I saw much of them all, and I recall them with deep gratitude.

As a young officer, General Imboden had been on General Lee's staff and he was one of the historical group present at Lee's surrender. He described the scene—very much as I have often heard it, but added a new touch that impressed me.

"Every Confederate officer there was in tears," he said, "and when Grant returned Lee's sword to him some of us younger chaps almost blubbered. But both General Grant and General Lee were as stiff and remote as manikins. Neither man seemed to feel *anything!* We talked a lot about that afterwards. We decided they were both so worn out that they hardly knew what they were doing. They moved and spoke as if they were in a dream!"

When I left Mrs. Wirt Cabell Carrington's home on a midnight train for the North, not only she and her entire family came to the station with me but—as it seemed— most of the other citizens of the town as well. Life was uneventful in Bristol,* Tennessee and Virginia. The arrival of a New York reporter had furnished a break in the routine.

When I got back to New York and turned in my mountain material the other specials went into the *Sunday World* as Mr. Smith had planned. But he put the story of the old preacher on the front page of a regular morning edition, a space which from the beginning of time has been and still is the exclusive home of news. The excitement this unique position aroused was much greater, I am sure, than any interest in the tale itself. The story was nothing to write a song about. But Mr. Smith was now in a mood to approve anything I did. He had discovered that I was willing to work twenty-four hours a day—in his opinion one of a reporter's most necessary qualifications—and to take any assignment except society news. I drew the line at that.

When the proofs came to him Mr. Smith brought them to my desk. In one corner they bore the eloquent direction *Must. B.S.*

"We're going to use this in the morning," he said. "Build a news head on it and put in subheads."

"But I don't know how to build a news head or put in subheads," I explained anxiously. "I've never done it."

"Then you sit right down and learn," Mr. Smith directed in high humor. "Perhaps you'll have my job in six months and be firing Cockerill. You might as well know some of the practical details of bringing out a newspaper."

He grinned expansively and Colonel Cockerill, who happened to be in the office at the moment, favored me with a large wink. We had traveled a bit since those spring days when Mr. Smith looked past my profile every time he met me.

Mr. Smith had found at last some one who was really

* The state line ran through the center of the town.

interested in writing the human-interest stories his nature seemed calling for. From the first, of course, the dream of writing fiction had been with me. Now Mr. Smith gave me an assignment that was directly in line with my plans. It had begun to dawn on me that after all there might be a few things about life I had not yet learned. The new assignment held vast opportunities for study of different types and phases.

I was to write a series of half-page daily specials under the standing caption, True Stories of the News, such as the *Petit Journal* was publishing in Paris. They were to be taken from the daily happenings in New York—those bits of drama which are often covered by a few lines in a newspaper. The finding of an unknown body in the river; the suicide of an unknown girl; some pregnant incident in the prisons or courtrooms or hospitals of the big city. All I had to do, Mr. Smith smilingly assured me, was to dig up all the facts back of the news leads and write each story as fiction, hung on its news hook.

I became a daily frequenter of the Tombs, of Bellevue Hospital and the Charity Hospital on Blackwells Island,* of the Police Courts and the city prisons. Friendly men and women in these institutions telephoned me "tips."

"I think we have a true story of the news here for you," was the sentence that usually started my working day.

Very often they had. More often, of course, they had not. I followed up every tip, and the series took me into all sorts of places and among all types of human beings. My mother, fortunately for her, was filled with happy memories of our Long Island jaunts, and still pictured me as passing lightly from one pleasant excursion to another. If she had known what I was really doing peace would have fled from our Milwaukee home. She did not know it. My letters were

* Now Welfare Island.

numerous but short, and very vague as to the details of my work.

Sometimes I found my story in the underworld; sometimes in the Chinese quarter; sometimes among the tenements; occasionally on Fifth Avenue. Once I found a really charming old lady, well-born, well-bred, over eighty, and looking very much like my own grandmother, who was about to be evicted from a tenement because her rich son-in-law would not pay rent for her, or allow his spineless wife to do it. One of her neighbors telephoned me late that evening. The gas in the old lady's tenement rooms had been turned off.

After an interview with her, as she sat in darkness with her few possessions piled around her, ready to be put out on the streets in the morning, I went to her son-in-law and put the fear of God and the newspaper world into him. He was a well-known man. He had no wish to figure in a newspaper story as leaving his mother-in-law to starve on city streets. He was a miserable creature, lying and whining—as contemptible as his wretched wife. I kept a close watch over him and saw to it that he supported his mother-in-law in comfort until she died several years later. That story, of course, was never written. Its withholding was the price of an aged gentlewoman's safety and comfort. I kept in touch with her, as well as with him, to be sure that she had both.

The writing of those "stories of the news" represented one of my most strenuous periods. It was no simple task to find from the news climax of some dramatic episode all the facts preceding it, to write two or three columns about them, and to do this six days a week. If I had not been in perfect health I might have worked myself to death. Mr. Smith took it all as no more than his due and the *World's*. It never occurred to him, as it did to Colonel Cockerill—who actually spoke of it several times—that I was missing sleep, missing meals, and taking all sorts of chances in covering that series —which ran for many months. Inexperienced as I was I marveled sometimes over the callousness of editors. Eventually, when I became assistant editor of the *Sunday World,* I may have been as callous—though I tried not to be.

I recall two cheery episodes with maniacs who figured in these stories of the news. I had gone to one well-known woman who had escaped from an insane asylum and who was suing her family for illegal incarceration there. She was in bed when I saw her, and as I bent to shake hands in farewell she suddenly caught me by the throat. She had an unpleasant face with huge black eyes and a wide red mouth that leered up at me.

"Aren't you glad I'm sane *now?*" she whispered, and tightened the grip of those clutching hands. The nurse rushed forward from the shadows of the room. Her patient was having a lively struggle with her when I departed, pausing only to send in help. For years afterwards that episode was a feature of my most unpleasant dreams.

Another, of whose peril I was happily unconscious at the time, was the case of a charming looking patient who suddenly showed a desire to kiss me good-by. I had no wish for the caress and was tactfully avoiding it when the nurse interfered and dragged the woman away with what seemed to me unnecessary violence. After she had quieted her patient, who seemed strangely upset by the slight disappointment, I learned that the woman was a "biter," whose unpleasant impulse was to take an occasional mouthful from the faces of those around her.

But the most thrilling episode of that period was the night in the haunted house, which deserves a chapter to itself.

CHAPTER V

GHOSTS AND THE WITCH OF ENDOR

THE haunted house was news, of the sort that even the least enthusiastic editors accepted as big news. It stood remotely in its ample grounds outside of Sea Cliff, Long Island, and it had just been sensationally vacated by Mrs. Paran Stevens, of New York and Newport. Mrs. Stevens was at that time New York's social leader, with some slight assistance from Ward McAllister, who had recently tabulated his famous list of four hundred citizens he thought worthy of forming the city's most exclusive circle. He and Mrs. Stevens ruled society with an impressive effect of harmony. Anything that happened to either of them was sure of a first-page position in the newspapers.

Many of the outpourings printed about them were excellent conductors of nausea, but the episode of the haunted house was really dramatic. Mrs. Stevens had left that house, she repeatedly and hotly asserted, because it *was* haunted and because neither she nor her family nor servants dared to remain in it with the ghosts there. She had taken the house for the summer season. Although she had occupied it only a few weeks she was being sued by its agents for the entire season's rent, which she refused to pay. The house, she claimed, had been rented to her on the false assurance that it was safe and habitable. It was neither. There was something indescribably horrible about it. The horror, she mentioned, was so universally admitted by the residents of Sea Cliff that few of them would even pass the house at night.

No one seemed to know why Mrs. Stevens had abandoned her beautiful home at Newport to rent a furnished house at Sea Cliff that season. Possibly she had acted on a whim. She was a woman of quick impulses and sudden actions. Possibly some member of her family was ill, and needed to remain in touch with New York physicians. Whatever the explanation, Sea Cliff had felt that her presence would add a new luster to the town. To have that luminous presence removed so abruptly, and with such distressing publicity, had been a bitter blow to Sea Cliff. The social season of the little resort threatened to go down under it. The village seethed with excitement, with anger, and with fear. Inevitably, among citizens with nothing to lose by the publicity, wild tales were first whispered and then shouted.

The situation of the house, aloof from neighbors, set in large grounds that sloped down to the shore of Long Island Sound, guarded by sentinel trees that were dark and gloomy, lent itself nicely to sinister gossip. Blood-curdling manifestations were said to be occurring there. Footsteps with no flesh and blood feet to explain them; cold unseen fingers touching the faces of the family, and not even sparing Mrs. Paran Stevens' resentful countenance; the sounds of groans, falls, and clanking chains; the incessant sense of unseen figures in bedrooms at night; terror, and finally panic in the heart of every member of the Stevens household.

The servants departed first. Some of them, they said, had been with Mrs. Stevens for years; but they were not loyal enough to wrestle nightly with the terrors of that house. Its new human inmates, Mrs. Stevens claimed in her defense, were themselves objects of suspicion and fear. There must be something wrong with them, the eyes of Long Islanders hinted, or they would not be willing to live there. The agent of the house scoffed at the stories, and suggested that they were due to another of Mrs. Paran Stevens' sudden impulses—in this instance an impulse to go back to Newport.

To all this and much more the New York newspapers rapturously gave full cry. The public was fascinated. New York had not had a haunted house for a long time. Anything about Mrs. Paran Stevens was interesting—but this!

Mr. Smith turned his mind on the subject and inspiration burst in his brain like a star shell. He would send me to that haunted house. I would pass the night there, and write the story of my experiences, whatever they were. After that, he gaily pointed out, we would know what all the fuss was about.

It did not occur to me to protest. Neither did I think there was anything supernatural to face. I have been afraid of many things during my life, but never of ghosts. My only fear was that there would be no story.

I went to Sea Cliff in the late afternoon, and had myself driven directly to the haunted house. The driver of the station cab gave me a quick and startled glance as I mentioned the address. But he was young and carefree and he put me down as one of those tourists who are urged to such pilgrimages by newspaper reports. It appeared that there had been others. He told me of them, and threw in a few hair-raising tales as his horse clumped along the country roads to the house. When we reached it I had him drive through the grounds, that I might study them and the building from every angle. He showed a coy unwillingness to do this, but finally spurred himself and his steed to the task.

The house was a big, comfortable, mid-Victorian structure, set in many acres of land, with well-kept lawns and trees on all sides of it, and a broad veranda extending across its front. I had intended to stroll around the grounds on foot and learn every turn of them; but a heavy rain was falling and it was growing dark. In the wide carriage-drive before the front door I got out of the cab, opened the house door with the key the agent had trustfully given me, and walked in leaving the driver gaping in his cab. He could not understand my possession of that key. I had no intention of inspecting the whole house then. That would come later. I merely looked into the rooms on the ground floor, made a mental map of their respective positions, and left candles and candle-holders I had brought with me at points where I could reach and light them easily when I returned to the house that night. I had been warned that the gas and even the water were turned off. I set two candles in the front hall, two in the room at the left of the entrance, and three more in a connecting room in the rear.

The place was depressing and I was as glad as the driver to leave it and get on to the Sea Cliff Inn. The weather was steadily growing worse. A big storm was coming up and high winds drove the heavy rain against the windows. I grew more cheerful. This storm would certainly lend "atmosphere" to my story. Also the lighted rooms of the Inn were bright and colorful, and I had an extremely good dinner at seven o'clock.

I had brought a traveling bag containing books, candles, matches, and other needs for the night. All my plans were made. I was not going to bed in that haunted house. Instead I would sit up all night and read, fully dressed and ready for any developments.

When at nine o'clock I was ready to start, the hotel proprietor and his wife looked at me with eyes that held tragic farewell. They were old friends. This was the Inn I had visited when I gave Sea Cliff its place on Long Island's social map. Now its host and hostess were appalled. No young girl, they protested, should be asked to do this sort of thing. They were sure they ought to take some action about it. At last

Mrs. Blank—I have ungratefully forgotten her name—suggested that she might prepare a midnight lunch for me. This struck me as true first aid. She put up the luncheon, and a few tears may have fallen into it. Certainly there were tears in her kind eyes when she and her husband saw me off. I had engaged one of the Inn's carriages to take me back to the haunted house. The driver was not the one I had picked up at the station that afternoon, but I knew this man well. He had driven me around the countryside on many of my first Sea Cliff excursions. When I gave him the address he stopped his horse, turned in his seat, and stared at me in horror.

"But—that's the haunted house!" he stammered.

There was nothing to do but take him into the secret. I did so, and engaged him to return to the house for me at eight o'clock the next morning. I also impressed him with the importance and secrecy of the adventure and explained that his employers knew of it. He clucked, shook his head, and unwillingly drove on. The storm had now settled down to an impressive exhibition of its possibilities. I had rarely seen a heavier rainfall or heard a higher wind. There could not have been a more perfect night for such an undertaking as mine. The deluge might have almost washed the dead out of their graves in the village cemetery.

The old horse breasted the gale with his head down, plodding heavily through deep pools in the road, and the driver let him take his time. I suspected that the man did so deliberately. Certainly neither horse nor driver was in a hurry to reach that house. We got there finally and found it black and forbidding in its soaked setting of whooshing pines and cedars. When we reached the gates the driver turned a stricken face to me.

"Say, Miss, I don't like this," he quavered. "I guess—we better not go in."

"You don't mean that you're afraid to drive to the front door, do you?" I scoffed.

"No, Miss, I don't mean that. What I mean is, I don't like *you* doin' it. It ain't safe. There's queer things goin' on in there. Every one knows it."

"I'll tell you all about them when you come back for me at eight to-morrow morning," I promised.

He offered to see me safely inside the house, but he was greatly relieved when I refused the escort. However, he waited outside the front door while I fitted the agent's key into the lock and entered the hall. As I said good night and closed the front door I heard the old horse start off at a gait that was almost a gallop.

The sound gave me my first sensation of depression. I lit the two waiting candles on the hall table. Then I went into the room at the left of the hall, which happened to be a library, and lit the two candles there. The momentary sense of depression had gone, and my spirits were rising. Libraries were an accustomed background to me. I had spent my infancy and early childhood toddling around our library at home, or lying on my stomach before the fire reading first *Cock Robin,* then *Chatterbox* and *St. Nicholas,* before the family realized that I could read at all. I think it must have been the cook who taught me, when I was five. I remember pleasant hours with her in the kitchen, both of us absorbed in literature, before I startled my father by reading aloud to him *The Sweet Story of Old* while I was still having my intellect protected in the kindergarten. After that I put in my free hours in our library, gulping every book that came to my hand. I remember reading a translation of *Les Misérables* in four volumes when I was nine. At ten, Father decided I was reading too much fiction, so he started me on *Rollins' Ancient History.* That was hard going and he paid me twenty-five cents a page for giving him the gist of what

I got out of it. What I got always interested and amused him very much.

These memories have come to me ever since in private libraries, and they were with me the night I entered the library of the haunted house. It would not be as soul-satisfying as our library at home. No other private library ever has been, not even my own. But it would be fascinating to investigate this one, which looked as if it held some good books.

I had brought two books with me to lighten the heavy hours, and had selected them with special care. At the time they seemed appropriate. They were two very grisly ghost stories, Bulwer Lytton's *Strange Story,* and Marion Crawford's *The Upper Berth.* I had felt in selecting them that they would lend atmosphere—would help to put me in a mood suited to a night with spooks. Now, for the moment, I didn't know.... To steady a suddenly sinking heart I picked up two of the lighted candles, and with one in each hand went over to the shelves and looked at the titles of some of the books. They were familiar companions, old friends. Again I felt better.

The big rooms and the spectral, linen-covered furniture still looked grimly forbidding. The candles were only tiny flickering points of light in dark spaces. The agent had promised to have all the shutters on the house fastened tightly, and all the heavy inside curtains drawn together, and this had been done. It was a necessary precaution, of course. The discovery by passing citizens of lights in the house would have brought forth another crop of stories, and probably a police investigation at once. Also, the shuttered and curtained condition was reassuring. I should not have liked to feel that from the outer darkness unseen eyes were staring in.

I abandoned the book shelves with an inner promise to

return to them, and went over to the library's writing table. It, too, seemed a familiar friend. I placed my two candles on it, and lit two more for other parts of the room. I had made sure of having plenty of candles and candlesticks, but the effect was still sepulchral enough to satisfy any ghosts. I unpacked my case, put the two ghost stories within easy reach on the library table, and surrounded them with my matches. I was wearing a tailor-made suit, as I always did at work—Miss Ross to the contrary notwithstanding. Now I filled the side pockets of my coat with boxes of matches, and thrust a screwdriver and file into the skirt pocket. I was about to begin a careful and complete examination of the house; and that, I admitted to myself, was an enterprise I was not looking forward to with pleasure.

The only thing I was really afraid of—and from the first I had been afraid of it—was that in going through the old house some door might snap shut and lock behind me, leaving me trapped. This would not have been fatal. Some time the next afternoon or evening Mr. Smith or Mr. Goddard, annoyed by my failure to show up with my story, would probably look into the matter of my whereabouts. On the other hand, they might assume that I was writing the story in Sea Cliff. It was possible, though not probable, that I would be left there for thirty-six hours before any real investigation began. Then I gratefully remembered the cabman. He was to return for me at eight in the morning. I had not, of course, asked him to break into the house and rescue me if I did not answer the door-bell; but I thought he might do it, with reinforcements. Still . . .

My imagination, which had coldly refused to have anything to do with ghosts, played briskly around the possibility of being trapped. I had reached the point when workmen were finding my skeleton in the cellar years hence, when the absurdity of the picture made me laugh. However, the picture wasn't really funny! The proper course for me was to avoid being trapped. I picked up two of my candles, put more matches and candles in my pockets, and started my room-by-room inspection of the house.

It was a long task, and a trying one. It filled two hours, of which I gave the first thirty minutes to self-reproach as I poked and pried—being very careful not to close any door behind me. A word to the agent, if I had thought of it, would have meant that the gas could have been turned on for that one night. I would not have used it much, of course. It wouldn't have fitted into the general plan. I could and would have turned it on during those two hours of inspection.

I went through every room. I searched every corner of the attic and cellar. There were so many doors that in the end I grew careless about leaving them open. Toward midnight a door in the cellar suddenly closed behind me. I whirled and leaped for it even as I heard it snap. I am quite sure I have never moved so swiftly before or since. But it opened as easily as it had closed and I breathed again.

The result of my inspection was a deepening disappointment. Moving about had steadied my nerves. I had not expected ghosts; but I had expected unusual noises, at least. There should have been some of those groans and clankings and rattling of chains we had heard so much about, and which probably could be explained by a wind-mill or a rusty weather-vane somewhere near. But there was absolutely nothing disconcerting around the place except the wildness of the storm. The old house was on its dignity—outraged perhaps by the charges against it.

I had an odd feeling that it was watching me as I went about; watching and listening—and breathing! I did hear something like that from time to time—quiet breaths, deep sighs. But they were caused by the frantic wind, making its way through the unweather-stripped windows in little puffs of air against the curtains. Through the shadows I saw heavy draperies move around me, for the same reason, quite as if something or some one had stirred behind them. A closer view always showed them swaying gently in a draught. There were plenty of draughts.

At last I returned to the library and its books. The inspection had killed two hours, and all I had gained from it was a clear impression of the habits and cast-off clothing of former residents of the house. I had poked into every closet. I had opened medicine chests and looked back of bathtubs and toilet shelves. There was always a chance that some humorist had set up a concealed electrical contrivance which would stimulate the imaginations of the nervous and susceptible. If anything of the sort was there, I failed to find it.

I looked at my watch. Ten minutes to twelve. I looked at the box containing my supper. I was not yet hungry. I would examine the books again and then read for a time. My feet at least needed rest.

I began *The Strange Story*. It was creepy enough to chill any spine. The storm, too, was working harder than ever at its task of understudy to a night of horror. I increasingly realized that I was not getting a "break." That reflection is horror enough for any reporter, but it does not interest an editor. I should be forced to pass on the tales that were blowing through Sea Cliff like icy winds. I grew restless. I got up, browsed among the books, found another volume that interested me, and stood glancing through it by the light of the candle in my left hand. It was now midnight.

Suddenly I pushed the book back into its place on the shelf. I had heard a sound at last—a very definite and disturbing sound—the sound of footsteps on the front veranda. They were light footsteps and swift ones. They pattered along the veranda like the feet of some small wild thing, but they were human feet. They stopped and I heard a slight rattle of the bars of a shutter near me. Some one, something was at the shutter, trying to look in.

That was not strange. It was quite possible that a passing policeman or citizen had seen a thin line of light through the shuttered and curtained window, and had stopped to investigate it. But he wouldn't move like that or act like that! I stood still, waiting. The steps scampered to the front door. The bell rang furiously, sending strange echoes through the old house.

I walked into the hall very slowly. I was still almost convinced that this was somebody looking into the matter of light in a vacant building. Still—the thing outside was a *little* thing—seemingly as light and quick-moving as a child. What little thing would be visiting this somber house at that hour? The bell rang again. I did not answer it. Then a screech—no other word describes the sound—tore through the storm.

"Open this door! *Let me in!! Let me in!!!*"

Those wild piercing shrieks were not sent forth by any man. They did not sound human. They had to be very loud to be heard above the banshee lamentations of the wind. They *were* very loud. They conquered that outer turmoil of nature without effort. The bell rang repeatedly. There were sounds of beating hands and kicking feet against the door.

Something must be done. I had reached the point when it seemed easier to open the door and face the thing outside than to stand still and wonder what the thing was. My two hall candles were still burning, but there was little more than an inch of them left. I went close to the door and asked who was there. The answer was a renewed outburst of screeches and commands to be let in. I had left the key in the lock. I turned the key, braced myself, and opened the door an inch. I had never done anything more unwillingly. The one thing worse than opening that door was to leave it locked and listen to those frantic outcries on the other side of it.

I meant to parley through the narrow line of space. I thought I had a firm grip of the door. But it was struck open and against me as if by a battering ram outside, and with a force that sent me backward and almost over. The next instant something was in the hall that sent me still further against the wall. A small figure faced me, chattering with incoherent fury.

There could hardly have been a more perfect impersonation of the witch of tradition, fresh from a ride through the storm on a broomstick. It was feminine, very small, and very hunchbacked. Its clothing was soaked to its skin. Straight black hair hung dank and wet over its face, its eyes, and its shoulders. Worst of all, it was fighting, spitting mad, almost out of its head with rage, unable to articulate. I had never in my life seen such fury. I was paralyzed with fear. I was also convinced at last that this could be nothing human. There was something animal-like in its rage, and in the crouching attitude it held before me, as if ready to spring.

While it choked and sputtered, my classification of it changed slowly from witch to maniac. At last the creature brought out coherent speech.

"Why didn't you let me in?" it howled. "What did you mean by keeping me out in that storm?"

The words at least were normal words, and the voice began to seem human. I pulled myself together.

"I will ask the questions," I said. "Who are you and what do you want here?"

She, too, seemed to be getting herself in hand. She straightened as much as she could, which brought her a bit above the level of my waist. She stood quiet, dripping on the rug, breathing hard, and pushing the wet hair off her face with tiny clawlike hands. It seems to me that she could hardly have been four feet tall, but perhaps she was. Shoulders hunched and head thrust forward, she stared up at me with eyes that still blazed with anger. But she was now making a strong effort at self-control. At last she spoke again.

"I suppose I scared the life out of you," she muttered.

"You certainly did," I admitted.

I kept my eyes on hers; partly, I suppose, from fascination, partly with some idea of controlling her and preventing another outbreak. My heart was still thumping hard.

"Well," she said on a deep breath, her anger rising again, "you'd be red-hot, too, if some fool kept you out of your own house half an hour at midnight, and in a deluge like this, till you were like a drowned rat. That idiot of a driver wouldn't come into the grounds, so I had to walk up from the gate. I was soaked through before I got to the house, and the wind and rain have been blowing me around that veranda like a feather ever since. It was all I could do to keep my feet. If I don't have pneumonia after this, I'm a lucky woman."

I walked over to the hall door and locked it. Then I went back into the library. I was feeling better, but of course I had to be "shown."

"Come inside," I invited, "and prove that you're the owner. If you're the owner why haven't you a key to this house?"

That stirred her up again.

"Because that imbecile agent of mine gave it to you," she yelped, and set her jaws with a click. "If I live through this night I'll discharge him to-morrow morning if it's my last act."

She was scampering around the room now, very much as she had scampered around the veranda, evidently too overwrought to sit down. Her soaked shoes left wet tracks on the waxed floors and her skirt dripped like a small fountain.

"You must have cooked up this plan with that agent to-day," she went on. "The utter idiot! The twaddle you'll print in the *World* in the next day or two will put the last touch on the ruin of my property. My fool of an agent didn't realize that till ten o'clock to-night. Then he telephoned to my house in Brooklyn, and I've been on my way here ever since. He couldn't come himself because he's sick in bed with the grippe. He'll be sicker before I'm through with him. So will you, and a lot more scandal-mongers."

"You'd better stop talking now," I advised. "There's a limit to what I'll stand."

She was still hysterical. She was the most grotesque look-ing and the worst-tempered human being I had ever met. But she *was* human! I went to my lunch box and took out the pint of Sauterne Mrs. Blank had packed with my supper. I filled a glass and handed it to her.

"Drink this," I added. "Then go upstairs and get a rub-down and some dry clothes on, if you mean to stay here. Your agent had left some water in the second-floor bathroom. When you come back I'll share my supper with you, and we'll talk."

"That fool said you hypnotized him," she muttered. "You won't get around me—and you won't write any more news-paper drivel about my house."

She drank the wine and grew calmer.

"I suppose it would be a good idea to get off these soaked clothes," she ended.

"It would be a better plan if you gave yourself a rub-down and went to bed," I suggested.

"And let you cook up more lies about my house, and ruin me? No, young woman. You've done enough with your sen-sations. I'm here to-night at the risk of my life to stop all that —and I'm going to stop it!"

My temper was straining at its leash. In the old days

in Milwaukee—old days of less than a year ago!—I, too, had been "temperamental" and had put up some lively exhibitions for my awe-struck family. Very early in my *World* days I had found it necessary to check these outbursts. With almost every one around me oozing temperament from every pore it behooved some one to keep steady. My calmness seemed to impress my companion.

"My name is Emma Yost," she threw back at me as she started for the staircase.

"*Miss* Yost?" I called after her.

"Yes, *Miss* Yost," she snapped.

All this had taken time. It was now past one o'clock. I set out our banquet while Miss Yost was gone. There was enough food for half a dozen persons. Apparently Mrs. Blank had expected me to eat steadily all night.

Miss Yost was back again in half an hour, dry as to clothing and even drier in manner. She appeared to have strengthened her resolution not to be hypnotized.

"What I needed was a hot bath," she said, and looked at me as if I were a negligent lodging-house keeper who had failed to provide the comforts she expected.

I returned her inspection with interest. She had found some of her old clothes—outdated and faded, but clean and warm. She explained that she had taken a hard rub-down. Her black hair was smoothly arranged as she probably wore it normally—in two heavy braids wound around her head. She had begun to look something like the well-born and educated woman she really was. It seemed incredible that half an hour earlier I had thought of her in connection with witches and maniacs.

Although she was so much more reassuring in appearance her manner was still very cool and remote. She ate a good supper and enlarged on her wrongs. This property we were in, she said, was her most valuable real-estate holding.

The house and grounds had been worth fifty thousand dollars—in fact she had refused that amount for them. Now they were practically worthless. Even if she burned down the house, she added, the site would still be taboo. Mrs. Paran Stevens' idiocy and the newspaper sensations I had started ...

"Now stop right there," I interrupted. "We'll get that end of it straight, anyway."

I explained that this was my first assignment in the haunted house, and that I had had nothing whatever to do with the preliminary press excitement.

"What difference does that make?" Miss Yost asked bitterly. "The *World* is the worst sensation-monger of the lot. You'll write some wild yarn that will terrify every idiot within a hundred miles of here."

For the moment I had become the *World*.

I explained that I was there to get the truth. She ate sandwiches and sniffed. I added that I had been in the house since nine o'clock, that I had inspected every foot of it from top to bottom, and that thus far I had seen and heard nothing that could not be easily explained. Miss Yost seemed somewhat soothed by this. She finished her second glass of wine and stood up.

"Let's go through it again," she suggested.

She could not be said to be mellowing, but her manner was certainly milder. I, too, was feeling better. I had my story. If nothing else developed I could describe her arrival and our night in the house together. I had no wish for another two-hour expedition through that gloomy mansion but I fell in with her plan and we started for the cellar. We would begin there and work our way up through the house.

As we descended the cellar steps Miss Yost told me almost cheerfully it had been suggested that a band of counterfeiters or other under-worldlings might have taken refuge down there; might be using the cellar as a workshop or hide-out; might have staged the ghost scare to get rid of legitimate tenants. She seemed to like the theory.

"I can handle anything that's flesh and blood," she assured me, "except newspaper reporters that start lies about my property."

I had already heard the gangster theory and had reflected on it during my first visit to the cellar. Miss Yost was as free from forebodings about ghosts as I was. She stalked around the cellar in front of me, a gnomelike little figure that threw strange shadows on the whitewashed walls. She examined the floors, tapped the walls with a small hammer she had picked up, and continued to express her sense of outrage. I confessed my earlier nervousness about being trapped by spring locks or something of the sort and she sniffed again.

"It might be a good plan for me to lock you up here till the *World* comes to my terms," she said. "I owe you something for that terrific drenching. I'm not a young woman and I'm not a well woman," she went on. "This experience may easily be the death of me. How would you feel if you were kept out in that storm a full half hour, getting madder and wetter every second? And with a good prospect of having to walk back two miles to Sea Cliff Inn because you couldn't get into your own house?"

"I'd be very grateful to the kind reporter who finally took me in and fed me," I told her.

She grinned like an impish monkey.

"You took your time about it. But I must have scared the life out of you," she repeated coolly. "I must have looked exactly like the Witch of Endor."

"You did," I agreed. "For a few minutes I thought you were supernatural, or at least insane."

The second tour of the house was as fruitless as the first

had been. Back in the library we looked at each other doubtfully.

"Why don't you go to bed?" I asked again. "It's after
three o'clock in the morning."

"Why don't you go?"

"There's one thing I haven't done yet," I confessed. "I
haven't blown out all the candles and waited and listened in
the dark. Heaven knows these candles make the place spectral
enough—but perhaps ghosts don't like even that much light.
We might go to bed in the connecting rooms on the second
floor, blow out all the lights, and see what happens. The
objection is that if I get warm and comfortable in bed I'm
afraid I'll go to sleep."

"No, you won't," Miss Yost said grimly. "I won't let you.
I never sleep well, and I'm not apt to begin to-night. We'll
see this thing through."

We blew out all the candles but two, and each carried
one of these as we went upstairs. The rooms I had suggested ran from the front of the house to the back—the
first facing the writhing and protesting trees, the other overlooking the Sound. Both, like all the other rooms, were now
tightly shuttered and curtained and offered no views.

"Which will you have?" Miss Yost asked.

I took the rear one. She went away and came back in a
few minutes with some yellowed nightgowns smelling of
camphor.

"There are no sheets or pillow cases on the beds," she
told me, "and I can't find any. Do you mind?"

"Not a bit. It's wonderful to have a nightdress." I had
brought nothing with me but a few toilet articles.

Miss Yost opened the door between the two rooms and
we tossed friendly comments at each other as we undressed.
It was half past three when I got into bed. Miss Yost was
still moving about in her room.

"I'm going to blow out my candle," I called. "All right?"

"All right. So am I."

I heard her get into bed, muttering something about the comfortable bed in Brooklyn where she ought to be. The connecting door between our rooms was still open. I blew out my candle. I had left more candles and plenty of matches on the little table at the head of the bed. It had been impossible to open the locked and shuttered windows. Miss Yost's candle went out.

"Call me when the ghosts come," I said, and drew the blankets and quilt around me.

Miss Yost did not answer. Darkness and silence closed in—such darkness and silence as I had never experienced before. Even if there had been an opening in those barred shutters no light could have come in, that wild night. . . .

I heard sounds now, things scampering in the walls. Miss Yost called out.

"Those are mice and perhaps squirrels. They get into the attic sometimes."

"I know."

"There's a cheery little death tick, too. You'll hear that later."

"I heard it just before you came, in the walls downstairs."

"Good night."

"Good night."

It was pleasant to feel that she was in the next room.

I kept awake a long time—at least it seemed a long time. There was nothing but darkness, accentuated by the ordinary night sounds in an old house. Shutters rattled. The wind roared around the corners of the building. The wet branches of a tree lashed an outer wall of my room. At last I lit a match. Miss Yost spoke, in a very wideawake voice.

"What's the matter?"

"Nothing. I'm looking at my watch. It's half-past four."

Silence and darkness again. Then a figure stood by my bedside. Was it the murdered girl who had disturbed the repose of Mrs. Paran Stevens? It was not.

"It's half-past seven," Miss Yost was saying. "The rain is still coming down in sheets and there isn't even a cracker in this house. We'll have a bracing walk to the Sea Cliff Inn for breakfast."

"I'll let you ride in my cab," I said smugly.

The story of the haunted house brought me no laurels. I was handicapped by the lack of any dramatic happenings except Miss Yost's appearance, and by the obvious impossibility, at that time, of describing it with the abandon I have shown here. Now she is safely in her grave. If any of her descendants happen to see and resent this picture of Great-aunt Emma under stress I can only say that it is a correct one, and that the lady's hot temper and frail little body had been sorely tried that night. Years later, I worked the episode into one of my *May Iverson* stories, then appearing serially in *Good Housekeeping*. That was fiction. This is fact.

The acquaintance between Miss Yost and me never developed into friendship. I had felt from the first that it would not. We parted cordially and with respect. I am glad to add that the lawsuit was settled out of court, and in Miss Yost's favor.

CHAPTER VI

THE WORLD AND MR. PULITZER

TIME whizzed on and I settled more firmly into the hectic routine of a reporter's life. Little assignments and big ones. Promising leads that led to nothing, and unimportant leads that sometimes unearthed big stories. My father, reading between the lines of my letters something of the strain of all this, wrote me asking how I could endure such an irregular life. I replied that I could endure it because the irregular life was so regular.

It was the correct answer. In newspaper work as in warfare one adapts one's self to abnormal conditions. One eats when one can, sleeps when one can, strains one's nerves to the breaking point, draws constantly on one's reserve of vitality, and for a time actually seems to thrive on the excitement. Certainly that was the condition on Park Row forty years ago, and I have no reason to believe that it has greatly changed. One of our cub reporters, writing a story about a man's escape from a fire, and warmed by a still greater fire of ambition in his own soul, included in his report an inspired apostrophe: "Jump, James Johnson, as you never jumped before!" We were all James Johnsons. We jumped as we had never jumped before.

The swift and incalculable changes of newspaper work took place. My associates were a fascinating group—young and cheerful, high-spirited and ready to die at their posts if need be. Some of them did. Many of them risked doing it. The atmosphere demanded supermen and superwomen and it seemed to me that most of my fellow workers were just

72

that. I was still a novice. I could only leap from one to another of my assignments in the professional monkey-house, and try to keep pace with the more experienced workers around me.

In his Homeric conflict with Ballard Smith, Colonel Cockerill soon went down. He left the *World* and started a newspaper of his own. Ballard Smith had his day of complete control, but already the shadow of his successor was falling across his path. The successor was Colonel George Harvey, then in Washington and handling national news so brilliantly that Joseph Pulitzer was hot on his trail.

During my early years on the *World* my friend Christine Terhune Herrick came to me one June day and asked if I could secure a "tryout" for her brother, Albert Payson Terhune. She explained that "Bert" had recently graduated from Columbia University and that he would like a summer on a newspaper before he began his "real work" in the autumn. I persuaded Ernest Chamberlin, then managing editor of the *Evening World*, to take Bert on his staff. The young man was a success from his first hour there. He ended by remaining with the *Evening World* for more than twenty years. Then he inherited Sunnybank from his mother, "Marian Harland," and started his "real work"—his famous collie kennels. But I don't think he dreamed in those early days what that "real work" was to be.

I made some new friends and had some new experiences. Kate Field came swinging down the lane of life and we promptly foregathered. Like so many of my friends then and later she was much more than twice my age, but she was still a fine horsewoman and we sometimes rode together in Central Park, getting up at six o'clock in the morning to do it.

We had other interests in common, especially the theater. Kate was then the editor and owner of *Kate Field's Wash-*

ington, but she seemed to pass more time in New York than
in the Capital, and we saw many plays together. I had frequent pathetic telegrams from her business manager, Ella
Leonard: "Can you tell me where Kate is?" Sometimes I
could, but often I could not. Only Kate Field always knew
where Kate Field was. She was a fascinating, lovable, disappointed woman, who had some bitter moments. She had
not made the most of her brilliant gifts, and she could neither
understand nor forget this. She was an indefatigable trav-
eler and she died, as I think she would have wished to die,
at sea, and after only a few days of illness.

Another new-comer of that period was Annie Besant,
making her first visit to America. William Q. Judge, then
head of the American Theosophical Society, took me to see
her almost as soon as she landed, and left us together for
an entire evening. For several hours we talked before an
open fire in her hotel room, and I have rarely been more
interested.

Among other episodes she described to me that evening
her first meeting with her friend and associate, Helene
Blavatsky. She explained that at first she had not liked the
Russian. She was repelled by the woman's huge bulk, her
incessant smoking, and her nicotine-stained fingers. But
when, after several hours of talk, Blavatsky suddenly turned
to her and said impressively, "You and I have much work
to do together," Mrs. Besant immediately realized that this
was true. Everything in her responded to the call.

"Come to me to-morrow morning," Blavatsky ended; and
Annie Besant went, changing all her own plans to do it.
That was the simple beginning of their long years of close
association.

I asked her if she had ever seen Blavatsky do any of the
amazing things she was supposed to be able to do by occult
aid. I could no more have withheld that question ten minutes

longer than I could have held my breath during the same period. Mrs. Besant smiled.

"Of course I have, many, many times," she answered, but she looked patient. She admitted that the question affected her much as it did Blavatsky. It always annoyed the Russian, she added. Blavatsky considered exhibitions of occult power far beneath her dignity. "Why should I perform for fools?" she often asked. On special occasions, Mrs. Besant conceded, her friend sometimes consented to give a little exhibition.

Mrs. Besant described several of these episodes. One of them was for James Russell Lowell. He was brought to meet Blavatsky and Mrs. Besant, and he let them see at once that he was a courteous skeptic. Madame Blavatsky was urged to do something which would impress him. She hesitated and he waited, smiling but doubtful. It was a cold winter day, and snowing.

"What's your favorite flower?" the Russian asked, abruptly and even irritably.

"Roses," Mr. Lowell told her.

"What color?"

"Red."

"Look up!"

Mr. Lowell looked up. From the ceiling a rain of red roses was pouring down on him. They fell on and around him, covering the rug and almost burying the old man as he sat in a big chair facing his hostess.

"It was no niggardly showing," Mrs. Besant added calmly. "There were hundreds and hundreds of roses. There seemed no end to them. They fell and fell till Mr. Lowell cried out in amazement. I was there, and I saw it all."

"Did Madame Blavatsky ever do anything off her own bat?" I asked. "Anything spontaneous—to meet an emergency, say?"

"Yes," Mrs. Besant told me. "She had a way of working all night and expecting me to do it, too. She was never tired. Sometimes I was. Even when we were traveling and arrived at hotels at two or three in the morning Helene would open her portfolio and sit down to write. One night I rebelled. I was hungry, and it was too late to get food at the little Inn we had reached. I grumbled.

" 'What do you want?' Helene asked in surprise. 'You can have anything you want, of course.'

"Suddenly I remembered that without a doubt I could have anything I wanted.

" 'I will have some milk,' I said, 'and some sandwiches and fruit.'

"We were sitting at the small table where Helene had just set down her portfolio.

" 'Eat, then,' she said impatiently, and waved her hand. She was anxious, as usual, to get on with her work. I looked at the table. There before me was a basket of fruit, a plate of sandwiches, and a glass of milk. I ate and drank."

I watched Annie Besant closely while she told me this story. At first glance she had seemed to me a tired, middle-aged English woman of a rather commonplace type. When I met her eyes I changed that impression. They were unusual —very luminous and a bit hypnotic. As she talked of her friend and her work they glowed. It was easy to fancy them blazing if she became excited, but I never saw her excited. Then, and in our later encounters, she gave me the impression of a woman well poised, very much in earnest, and wholly sincere in her convictions. She said strange things and told strange stories; but no unprejudiced listener could doubt that she herself believed them.

She assured me that she and Madame Blavatsky were always in perfect mental communication, however great their physical separation was. She said nothing important could happen to either of them without the other's immediate knowledge.

Years later, when Annie Besant was lecturing in Boston, she suddenly stopped, hesitated, and then made an apology to her audience.

"I must ask your indulgence," she said with a break in her charming English voice. "I have just had a message from Helene Blavatsky. I—I must ask you to excuse me."

She left the stage. In England, at that very moment, so the story goes, Helene Blavatsky had died. There are doubters who believe she died before Mrs. Besant began that lecture. But we had no transatlantic telephones or radios then.

The best feature of newspaper life is its variety. It could not have been very long after this that I passed a day with Helen Keller and her teacher Miss Sullivan, later Mrs. Macy. They had decided that Miss Keller was to have a college education. Both were working toward it under full physical and mental steam. For hours I watched them work together. They sat side by side, with clasped hands. At that period Helen Keller's education and most of her association with the outside world came to her through those touching fingers.

In communication with others, unless they had learned Miss Sullivan's code, Helen put her right thumb under one's chin, her index finger between one's lips, and her second finger on the side of one's nose. In that way she commanded the entire range of the speaker's head, lip and throat response to verbal expression. I remember very distinctly the strange sensation I had when that exquisite little hand rested on my face—the awe I experienced in feeling it there. Miss Keller liked, before speaking, to pass her fingers over one's face and get from the contact her kind of mental picture of her visitor. After that, her fingers went about the task of getting the message this human bulk before her was sending to her brain. To a stranger the whole experience, and the touch of that delicate hand, was very stifling to eloquence. One sought wildly for words worthy of such an occasion; and unless one had prepared them in advance—or even then —one sought in vain.

Even now, when communication with others has become a commonplace experience to her, Miss Keller's face still holds more interest and expectancy than any other face I know. In those days it held an almost ecstatic eagerness, a kind of rapture. She had learned that wonderful things were going on outside that body in which she was imprisoned without light or sound or the power of speech. She longed to know about them all, for so far as she knew they were all thrilling. Certainly they were all wonderful and fascinating to her beyond the power of another imagination to conceive. It is not to be wondered at that those of us who, however briefly, sat in the presence of Helen Keller and Miss Sullivan in those days were too awed and too poignantly moved to contribute much of interest to either of them.

Mr. Pulitzer came to the office only a few times during my ten years on the *World,* but he knew all about every member of his editorial staff. He had a charming habit of sending extra checks to individual employees with his compliments, when they did something that especially pleased him. I received my share of these. He also celebrated his own birthdays by giving checks to the employees he approved of at the moment. Once he gave E. A. Grozier "a bag of gold" —a silk purse containing one thousand dollars in twenty-dollar gold pieces. On another birthday he failed to send a gift to Frederick A. Duneka, then city editor of the *Evening World,* who usually received one from him on these anniversaries. Mr. Duneka wrote him a heart-warming letter of thanks. He assured Mr. Pulitzer that he knew he had momentarily overlooked the little matter but that this was no reason why he, Duneka, should forget his manners. Mr. Pulitzer was delighted by this characteristic effusion, and sent the check by return mail. He hadn't much sense of humor; but he knew this was funny because Mr. Duneka did it.

Mentally and physically Mr. Pulitzer was an extraordinary man. He was more than six feet tall. He had heavy red hair, a red beard, a look of great power, and phenomenal vitality and magnetism. He had a unique gift for picking men, but his impulsiveness led to occasional mistakes. When the editorial department was tied into hard knots, as it sometimes was, he sent to St. Louis for Mr. Florence White, one of his St. Louis editors, in whom he had a justifiable faith. Mr. White always arrived smiling, got rid of the undesirable one, straightened out the office tangle the editor had left, and found his reward in his report to Mr. Pulitzer. He once told me he always reported in the same words: "The *World* is now ready for another genius!"

Mr. Pulitzer's blindness and general ill-health made him high-strung and hard to please. He loved good talk. He himself was a fascinating talker. He took fancies to certain members of his staff, whose talk he enjoyed, and frequently sent for them to join him at his home in Bar Harbor, or in Europe, or on his yacht. They all dreaded these visits, which were an intense nervous strain. I have seen strong souls like Colonel Harvey, Frederick Duneka, Arthur Brisbane, and Foster Coates wilt over such a summons. In certain moods J. P. himself would not talk at all. He sat grimly silent, putting the entire burden of his entertainment up to the companion of the moment. There were usually several of his editors visiting him, in addition to his large corps of secretaries and readers, and they had established a system of signals.

When one of them felt that he had reached the limit of

his power to interest Mr. Pulitzer, he raised his hand as an appeal for help. Mr. Pulitzer could not see these distress signs. His associates could, and one of them immediately came forward to interrupt the tête-à-tête and take on himself the burden of talking to the chief. Many of these incidents occurred on Mr. Pulitzer's yacht, and all the favorites were occasional victims of them.

On one occasion, Foster Coates told me, he and Mr. Pulitzer were sitting alone on the deck of the yacht, and the chief was out of sorts. Mr. Coates put forth his best efforts—which I can testify were always good. Mr. Pulitzer, his sightless eyes turned seaward, sat as unresponsive as if he were alone. After fifteen minutes of this Mr. Coates looked wildly around. No rescuer was in sight, but at the other end of the yacht he saw the slim young figure of Ralph Pulitzer, then a lad of eighteen or twenty, disappearing down a companionway. He said, "There's Ralph, just going below."

The silence thickened. Mr. Pulitzer saw nothing thrilling in this announcement.

"He's a good-looking chap," Coates added desperately. The sightless eyes turned from the water.

"Is he?" J. P. asked.

Mr. Coates grasped the verbal life line. He drew a picture of young Pulitzer from the top of his handsome head to the tips of his white canvas shoes. He described the color and cut of the boy's clothes, the pattern of his tie, his cuff links, each of his features and mannerisms, his changing expressions. When he finished tears were rolling down J. P.'s cheeks.

"Thank you, Coates," he said huskily. "Now, for the first time in many years, I know how my boy looks!"

Dr. W. S. Rainsford, then rector of St. George's Church in New York, also gave me a vivid picture of J. P.

Mr. Pulitzer's daughter Julia, a remarkably brilliant young girl, had just died. Her father adored her. He could not pull himself out from under the pall of her death. He fell into a melancholia that alarmed his family and friends. Then he learned that the year before her death Julia had thought of entering the Episcopalian fold. She had even visited Dr. Rainsford several times, to talk to him about doing so.

Mr. Pulitzer, whose life was spent summoning others into his presence and giving them their orders, humbly called on Dr. Rainsford. What he wanted was to talk about Julia. He wished to know how she had looked, what she had said, what Dr. Rainsford had thought of her during their interview. Dr. Rainsford, a sympathetic man, answered his questions fully and understandingly. At the end of the interview Mr. Pulitzer collapsed. Dr. Rainsford shook his head at the memory of the scene.

"I have never before seen a man in such utter despair," he ended. "He was almost beside himself."

As Mr. Pulitzer could not always call the world's leaders to him, he often sent his editors to them for private information he needed. It was understood that this information was given the editors in confidence; and theoretically, at least, the leaders talked to them as frankly as to Mr. Pulitzer himself. Mr. Pulitzer sent me on a number of such assignments, but the most important one was a call I made on John Hay and President McKinley.

J. P. had been reading up the case of Mrs. Maybrick, an American woman who had married an Englishman and who, according to the English courts, had subsequently poisoned him that she might marry another man. She was tried, convicted, and sentenced to life imprisonment. She had served many years of the sentence at the time Mr. Pulitzer's interest in her was aroused. He had looked up the records of the trial and discovered that it had been notoriously unfair. According to the testimony, the husband was an invalid who had announced several times that he would kill himself and leave suspicion of the killing on his wife. This testimony was ignored. The judge had been openly prejudiced against Mrs. Maybrick. His charge to the jury was said to be a blot on the history of British court procedure. Incidentally, that judge went insane within a few months of Mrs. Maybrick's conviction. The most strenuous efforts were made to obtain a pardon or at least a new trial for her.

For reasons no one seemed to understand all these efforts failed. Mrs. Maybrick's mother stormed all earthly gates in her daughter's behalf. According to rumor she also assailed those of heaven and hell; but without success. Mr. Pulitzer was inclined to throw the *World's* strength back of a new petition for a pardon, to be circulated throughout the United States. First, however, he wanted the inside history of the case. Even more he desired to find out whether our American Administration would back such an effort, and what was behind the British refusal to consider a petition for clemency. He sent me to President McKinley to get this information.

That mission worried me. I had grasped in some way, probably through one of the hidden wires that connect great newspaper offices with the White House, that the subject of Mrs. Maybrick did not interest Mr. McKinley, and that wise persons did not bring it up in his presence. I wrote to John Hay, then Secretary of State, asking if he would arrange for my appointment with the President. I explained that I represented Mr. Pulitzer himself, and I told Secretary Hay what my mission was.

He replied at once, enclosing a card for the appointment and adding that he would meet me at the White House and introduce me to the President. I was delighted but not surprised. I had met Mr. Hay half a dozen times, and he had

been amazingly kind. My unconscious "line" at that time
was starry-eyed admiration of the great. It must have been
effective, for it was absolutely sincere. It invariably gave me
a big thrill to meet a world-leader; and then, as always, Mr.
Hay was a glamorous figure. As I looked at him I saw him
not only as he was—wise, witty, sophisticated, and wholly
charming—but as the secretary and young friend of Abraham Lincoln. He had helped to make history!

My eager young face must have revealed my reverence as
well as my gratitude when we met that day, for Mr. Hay
was amused and perhaps rather touched. He had reserved
a White House office for us. He led me directly into it, sat
down opposite me, and talked to me like a friend and a
brother. I can see him now, exactly as he looked then, very
fresh and immaculate and handsome in a light gray suit
with a blue tie that had a star-sapphire pin in it. The sapphire held a moving twinkle that matched the twinkle in
his eyes. I must have gazed at him like a fascinated child,
for suddenly he laughed out.

"How old are you, really?" he asked. "Sixteen?"

I was hurt, and a bit deflated. I had been feeling so important. He saw this and sobered at once.

"I'm sorry," he apologized, "but I'll soon prove that I'm
taking you very seriously. I'm going to accept you as a
woman of the world in both senses, and talk to you very
confidentially. Here's the inside of the Maybrick situation."

He set it forth at some length, and I hardly breathed till
he had finished. To-day, after all these years, I could almost
repeat his monologue word for word.

He told me that from its beginning President McKinley
had been interested in the Maybrick case. When he became
President, McKinley's immediate impulse was to help the
woman, but he hesitated a long time. He had heard that
Queen Victoria was not welcoming petitions in Mrs. May-

brick's behalf. He hesitated to take any action that might imply a criticism of British justice. At last, however, he whipped himself up to the task and wrote Queen Victoria a personal letter.

"It was informal, and very tactfully expressed," Mr. Hay commented; and added that he himself had seen that letter.

Mr. Hay sent the letter to England with some other state papers and America's President waited for a reply. For many weeks none came. The President could not understand this. He was a modest man, but he had a strong sense of the dignity of his position. When he had begun to think the letter could not possibly have reached the Queen he received a reply, or rather an acknowledgment. It was not from Victoria herself. It was from an under-secretary who wrote with extreme formality. He assured the President of the United States that his letter had been received. He added that the question of Mrs. Maybrick's guilt had been settled by a British court, and that nothing more could be done about it.

"In short," Mr. Hay ended, with a wide and boyish grin, "the President of these United States was told by the Queen of England, firmly and none too courteously, to mind his own business!"

"But why?" I gasped.

"Because"—again Mr. Hay grinned like a school-boy— "because Queen Victoria is absolutely convinced that Mrs. Maybrick murdered her husband. There's not the slightest doubt of it in her mind. Do you know the reason she's so sure?"

I didn't, but was eager to learn.

"Because Mrs. Maybrick had a lover," said the Secretary of State. "That was admitted at the trial. And because Her Majesty, Victoria, Queen of Great Britain and Empress of India, is convinced that any married woman who was false to her husband would not hesitate to murder him!"

He let that sink in, grinned again, and then went on more soberly.

"President McKinley has a very sweet and gentle nature," he continued. "He is almost never angry. He never flares into passions as most of us do on occasion. But he certainly let himself go when he read that letter. He felt that he had been doubly insulted. The Queen had not only not replied to his letter herself, but she had let a subordinate reply in a way the President thought was highly objectionable. He goes up in the air again every time he remembers that letter, and he remembers it quite often. Since then," the Secretary of State ended cheerfully, "we don't mention either Mrs. Maybrick or Queen Victoria to him!

"The Prince of Wales got wind of the matter," Mr. Hay went on, while I was taking this in. "He's a born diplomat, and he took a modest hand in the little game. Unofficially we have been given to understand that Mrs. Maybrick will never be pardoned while Queen Victoria lives—but," he added impressively, "the Prince himself has great sympathy for Mrs. Maybrick. He didn't express any opinion of her innocence or guilt; but we *know* that when he becomes King one of his first actions will be to pardon her. In the meantime, she must wait. Unless Mr. Pulitzer wants to lead a lost cause he'd better drop his petition plan."

He stood up.

"Now I'll take you in to the President," he smiled. "But if you value serenity don't mention Mrs. Maybrick to him."

"Of course, I won't. But I won't go in, either," I decided. "I have no other excuse for taking his time. I'll simply fade away."

"Oh, no," Mr. Hay said easily. "You will be glad some day that you met him. Just say a few pleasant words. Give him Mr. Pulitzer's greetings. They've met, and they like each other. He's interested in Mr. Pulitzer's eyes. Tell him about them."

I did. Mr. McKinley looked tired and worried, but he, too, was very kind. Mrs. McKinley, who was an invalid, had been much worse that summer. Nevertheless, she insisted on going everywhere she could with the President. Mr. McKinley was said to carry in his breast pocket, when they two were in public or with others, a large handkerchief to throw over his wife's face when she had her frequent seizures. . . .

It will be remembered that one of the early official actions of King Edward the Seventh, when he ascended the throne of England, was to pardon Florence Maybrick.

One day Gertrude Atherton arrived in New York from California and promptly presented a letter of introduction to Ballard Smith. She was very young and very lovely—a charming embodiment of her own pet heroines—with platinum gold hair, eyes like bits of her California skies, and a strong suggestion of inner fire. She had already written several novels, which were considered very daring in theme and treatment. She told Mr. Smith she was about to write a novel with a newspaper background, and that she wanted to sit around the *World* offices for a time and meet editors and reporters and absorb atmosphere.

We were, of course, in the famous *World* building, then one of New York's supreme attractions for tourists. It was twenty-two stories high, counting the floors in the famous gold dome. My office was in the dome, on the nineteenth floor. It was a crescent shaped affair with two windows and balconies and a thrilling view of the river. Mr. Smith had airily tossed a daily and a Sunday woman's page at me, by this time, to edit in addition to my reporting. I was relieved of detail work and given plenty of help, and he sent me out

only on big cases. He brought Gertrude Atherton to my
office, told me what she wanted, and directed me to see
that she got it.

I gave her a desk and cheerfully invited her to live there,
which she did. She floated about all the offices at will, but
accepted mine as her headquarters. She was clearly fascinated
by the atmosphere of a great newspaper; by the rush and
strain and excitement; by the fact that we all worked both
day and night and never seemed to have time to eat or
sleep. She decided to remain in New York and write her
novel in its proper setting. She engaged a studio apartment
in the Sherwood building in West Fifty-seventh Street,
and she and I began a friendship that has lasted through
the years to the present day.

She had a great many interesting friends and I met them
all. Rose and Charles Coghlan were among them, and Kuhne
Beveridge, and Charles Warren Stoddard. I had as little
time as ever for social affairs, but I often dropped into her
studio parties late at night, or went to her little dinners and
from there back to work till dawn. My special friends on the
World staff were David Graham Phillips, afterwards the
novelist, Bayard Veiller, Frederick Duneka, afterwards general manager of Harper and Brothers, W. O. Inglis, H. H.
Sylvester, Sylvester Rawlings, Augusta Prescott, Anne
O'Hagen, and Grace Margaret Gould. I admired them all,
and I had a special awe of Nell Nelson, who was still on the
World. She was always cordial, but she kept very much to
herself and had no intimates. Her reward was great. She
married S. S. Carvalho, then the *World's* business manager
and ever since then one of William Randolph Hearst's indispensable men.

Most of the members of this group swelled Mrs. Atherton's growing retinue. It was rumored that I was to be the
heroine of her new novel, already named but still to be writ-

ten—*Patience Sparhawk and Her Times*. I was thrilled, and did my best to act like a heroine. My efforts to live up to my imagined obligations must have delighted Gertrude. She chose Morrell Goddard as the hero of the book and described him, as she afterwards put it to me, "even to the bunches on his jawbones." (Mr. Goddard had a singularly firm young jaw.) But when *Patience* came out, the only possible reference to me in the entire novel was one line describing the heroine's home. "Patience lived on Forty-fourth Street, West of Broadway."

That was where I lived. The rest was silence. It was a blow. However, I became reconciled when I read the novel. Patience was a murderess. She and I really had not much in common.

Another friendship made in my *World* days, and which lasted till the death of that friend many years later, was with Mrs. Jefferson Davis. Joseph Pulitzer had married into the Jefferson Davis family, and my first meeting with Mrs. Davis was at a tea in her New York apartment. Like Patience Sparhawk and myself, she "lived on Forty-fourth Street." She was already in her gallant seventies, but from the hour I met her I was under the spell of her charm and magnetism.

Since those days I have learned that she was not as popular with all her southern associates as she was with the devoted group that surrounded her in New York. I have never understood why. I loved her. I had a younger woman's passionate admiration for her wit, her poise, and her courage. Above all, I gloried in her sense of humor and in the dauntless spirit with which she was meeting old age.

Her laughter was the gayest and most contagious I have ever heard. I rarely think of her without recalling it, though in the last phase of her dramatic life I no longer heard it. That was after the death of her daughter Winnie. I have been told many times that she never laughed after Winnie's death, never even smiled. Certainly, I never saw her do either, though I belonged to the little group which made a point of seeing much of her, in the artless delusion that we could cheer her up. She was more or less confined to her apartment in the Hotel Gerard.

I cannot feel that we greatly cheered her, yet she seemed to like to have us with her. Though she no longer laughed or smiled, she was as far removed from a figure of tragedy as a woman could be. She was alone and indescribably lonely, but she was still very much the captain of her soul. The daughter's death had shaken that soul; but the mother's eyes had not lost their steadiness, nor her nerves their poise. She made it plain that she was glad to see us; and in place of the old-time laugh or smile her face took on at certain moments a new look, such as I have never seen on any other face. It was the look with which she greeted us, with which she made us realize that, gravely though she received us, we were always welcome. It was a look that is hard to describe —made up, as I recall it, of acceptance, affection, serenity, and, at times, what seemed the reflection of a soft inner light. I used to watch for that look, and feel my young heart grow warm when I met it.

Mrs. Davis's hotel apartment was in effect a bit of the old South. Her living-room was full of souvenirs of the past. There was a large portrait of her husband in his Confederate uniform; his crossed swords hung above the fireplace; several tattered flags in the background were a part of history. She never introduced any of her friends to any others. She assumed the fact that we were together under her roof, drinking her tea, was a sufficient introduction; as, of course, it was. Her guests were always interesting groups, running to strong contrasts of young and old. The old were men and women whose souls were battle-fields of memories. Most of them were southern and some of them, I was told, had been very close to Mrs. Davis during the years of the Civil War. Against this dramatic background there was always a good representation of young folks—plainly fascinated, as I was, by our hostess.

Occasionally, as it grew late, Mrs. Davis would touch my arm, or give me some other little signal to linger when the rest had left. I was always immensely pleased and flattered by this attention, and by the intimate talks that followed when we were alone. She was entirely conscious of my worshipful attitude, and I knew her interest was not wholly due to my personal charms. I came to her fresh from a desk against which the news waves of the earth were beating. Also, dramatic incidents were happening in the *World* offices, and Mrs. Davis, like most of us, enjoyed "shop talk." I made a special point of storing up for her bits that would interest her. I always knew enough to stop talking when she began; and I would give much to-day if I had been wise enough to make notes of her reminiscences.

It suddenly occurred to me that she ought to write and publish her autobiography. I urged her to do this.

"I'd never dare to," she said. I persisted then and later that she owed the world her own story of her life. This was long before Winnie's death, and while that delicious laugh of Mrs. Davis's was still a running accompaniment to our talk.

One day, when the subject of the autobiography came up again, she straightened with an air of decision.

"My dear," she said, "I'm going to make it clear to you why I can never write my autobiography."

Then she told me the episode of Winnie's pearl pin. Later, with her permission, I put it into a short story, which was published in *Harper's Magazine*. That was largely imaginative. These are the actual facts about the pearl pin.

Winnie Davis, who was lovingly known in the South as "The Daughter of the Confederacy," naturally belonged to many southern organizations. While the Davises were still living in the South one of these organizations presented Winnie with a pin, as a combined badge and souvenir. It was an artistic trifle, bearing a loving inscription and set with a few seed pearls. Winnie was touched by the gift and she became very fond of the pin. For a year or two she wore it constantly. Then suddenly, while they were still living in the South, it disappeared.

Winnie was greatly distressed over the loss of the pin, and her mother sympathized with her. Together they searched the house, the garden, every spot where it could have dropped. They telephoned to friends in whose houses or gardens Winnie had been the day of the loss. They described the pin. It was a gold circle about the size of a dime, and it was decorated with seed pearls. Days passed. No one had found the pin. No one knew anything about it. Winnie's sense of loss deepened. Mrs. Davis advertised for the pin and again described it. It was of heavy gold and encrusted with seed pearls, but valued chiefly for its associations. A generous reward was offered for its return.

There were no results from this effort, either, except the added interest of friends. Winnie and Mrs. Davis continued to describe the pin to friends who came and went. Some one, they thought, might have picked it up without realizing its worth. It was, Mrs. Davis explained, a valuable pin about the size of a silver quarter of a dollar and encrusted with small pearls.

For the next few months the lost pin was a constant topic of conversation in the Davis social circle. Mrs. Davis and her daughter had almost lost hope of recovering it, but they talked about it daily, and again and again they described it to callers. It was larger than a silver quarter, and it was decorated with small but valuable pearls.

As more time went on Winnie and Mrs. Davis were increasingly depressed over their loss, and over their growing conviction that the pin would never be recovered. When they talked it over together they recalled the pin as a heavy gold emblem ornamented by a few perfect pearls the size of small peas. Winnie lost interest in her other jewelry and mourned ceaselessly for her pin. If the subject of other pins came up she and Mrs. Davis recalled the pearl pin almost with tears. Its front, they now remembered, had been covered by half a dozen large and perfect pearls. The pin itself was more a decoration than a pin and was about the size of a silver half dollar. At last their sense of loss became so poignant that mother and daughter rarely spoke of the pin at all, except in private. Then it was only to compare unfavorably the sheen on the pearls of some one's necklace with the luster of the pearls in Winnie's pin.

One morning, more than a year after the loss, Mrs. Davis heard a shriek from the attic. Winnie was not an emotional girl, nor easily frightened, but it was her voice that had shrieked. In a panic Mrs. Davis rushed up the attic staircase. She saw Winnie crouched on the floor beside an open trunk. She had evidently been going over discarded garments which had been in the trunk, and a number of these lay around her. In one hand she held a blouse, and as Mrs. Davis rushed toward her she held this up.

"Mother!" she cried in a strangled voice, "see what's pinned to this blouse!"

Mrs. Davis reached her side and looked. She saw nothing but the blouse.

"There," said Winnie, pointing.

Her mother took the garment from Winnie's hand and looked at the spot her daughter indicated. A tiny dark object was resting against the silk bosom of the blouse. She carried the garment to a window and inspected the object closely. It was about the size of a silver dime, and there were some tiny grayish excrescences on it. Very slowly she returned to her daughter's side and handed back the blouse.

"I remember now," Winnie gasped, "that it was getting warm, and I packed away a lot of clothes and sent them up here—"

Her voice broke. Simultaneously, from two pairs of lips, rose an incredulous cry.

"Can this *possibly* be the pearl pin?"

Mrs. Davis settled back in her chair and gave her climax time to sink in. Then her beautiful laugh gushed forth.

"It's all true," she said. "And I think it proves to you that never, never, *never* would I dare to write my autobiography!"

CHAPTER VII

CARLYLE HARRIS AND HELEN POTTS

ANOTHER mature friend of that period who had adopted me as a protégée was Frances E. Willard, President of the Women's Christian Temperance Union. As in the case of Mrs. Davis, my attraction for her was undoubtedly my *World* connection and the fact that I was not only in touch with the news of the day but with a subterranean current of news that was not published. Miss Willard rarely came to New York without writing to me in advance and making an appointment for tea or dinner. When we met she tactfully drew from my little reservoir such information as she needed. If it wasn't there, I was usually able to get it for her and report later. All the time she made me feel that our brief association was one of the objectives of her visit to New York.

There was nothing insincere in this. She was genuinely interested in youth and enthusiasm. She was even more interested in tapping the human wires she had in every city, and in keeping abreast of significant developments. She was, I think, the best woman organizer and politician then in public life. As a presiding officer over great assemblages of women, such as her own Union and the National Council of Women not even that other human dynamo, Doctor Anna Howard Shaw, was her equal. Miss Willard had a tact, suavity and graciousness the brilliant but forthright Doctor Shaw lacked.

I had often watched Miss Willard presiding over assemblages in Washington and elsewhere in which great issues were at stake and counter currents of feeling ran so high that they would have swept away any other chairman. Miss Willard never lost her poise, her charm, her authority, or her assemblages. I used to think of such meetings when I sat looking at her across her tea-table or opposite her at dinner; and again I was thrilled, as so often before, by this personal contact with great leaders.

One day, after these personal encounters had stretched over several years—for I always dropped my work and hustled uptown for an hour with Miss Willard—she touched on a subject that surprised me. We had been talking of world affairs, and the topic did not seem to fit in. Miss Willard introduced it quite calmly.

"I'm worried about my complexion," she confessed.

She went on to say that she did not believe in cosmetics or other artificial aids to skin culture, but that there must be scientific methods of treating the skin condition which disturbed her. I was no authority on the subject but I knew some one who was. I told her that Harriet Hubbard Ayer, recently appointed "beauty editor" of the *World,* had a thoroughly scientific knowledge of complexion treatment. If Miss Willard wished me to, I added, I would bring Mrs. Ayer uptown to examine her complexion and advise her about it. Miss Willard looked at me as if she were hearing the morning stars singing together.

"Oh, if you *will!*" she breathed.

We made an appointment for the next day, and Mrs. Ayer and I arrived in Miss Willard's hotel rooms on the moment. For several reasons I remember every detail of that visit. For one, it was the last time I ever saw Frances Willard; but in itself it was an impressive occasion. Mrs. Ayer and Miss Willard had never met before. Mrs. Ayer had been a society woman before she lost her money, and she could be either a *gamine* or a social leader as occasion demanded.

Very simply and naturally she gave her best to Miss Willard, and Miss Willard was plainly enchanted by her wit and magnetism.

Having introduced them I slipped into the background and the two became submerged in an intimate talk on complexions. At the end of this Mrs. Ayer promised to send Miss Willard a box of assorted creams and lotions that might help her. (She sent them the next morning.) As we were leaving Miss Willard exclaimed impulsively, and I am sure very sincerely, "Oh, how I *wish* I didn't have to give that talk to-night! There's nothing I'd so love as to have you two girls spend the evening with me!"

I was still in my early twenties, and Mrs. Ayer was in her brave sixties. We were both flattered. Mrs. Ayer, however, was very thoughtful as we walked back to the nearest downtown station of the elevated railroad. Suddenly she said abruptly:

"You're fond of Miss Willard, aren't you?"

"Very," I said.

"Then I'm afraid I'm going to give you a shock." Mrs. Ayer sighed and ended, "That woman can't live a year!"

She had read Miss Willard's fate from the condition of her complexion, which to my eyes had revealed nothing but a becoming pallor. She was right. It was Frances E. Willard's last visit to New York. She died nine months later.

The macabre dance of daily news gathering went on. I had finished my series, True Stories of the News. In addition to my editorial work I was doing murder trials, and other big special assignments. I went to Newport and met Mrs. Paran Stevens. She invited me to a hypnotism party she was giving, in which Donatello, an Italian hypnotist, was to hypnotize some of the most important figures in Ward McAllister's famous Four Hundred.

He did it very interestingly and amusingly, and Mrs. Stevens let me send the story to the *World*. I wrote and telegraphed it that night and it appeared on the first page the next morning—another "beat" on the New York press that warmed the cockles of Ballard Smith's heart. As I have said Mr. Smith had tossed a daily and Sunday woman's page at me to edit in those dragging intervals when I might have been wasting time eating or sleeping between my news assignments. He was a slave-driver if there ever was one, but an appreciative slave-driver and always willing to give me anything in reason I asked for. I had a staff of assistants including Anne O'Hagen, later a brilliant writer in suffrage and civic fields, Grace Margaret Gould, later fashion editor of the *Woman's Home Companion,* Marie Manning, later a shining light of the Hearst publications, and Olivia Howard Dunbar, a clever all-'round reporter who afterwards married Ridgely Torrence, the poet, and thus lived down her strenuous past.

Others came and went. Only a few years ago I was told, by one who said she was there, of a certain luncheon in Paris. Eight American women sat at the table. My name came up casually, and it was revealed that each of the eight had been started by me up the rocky road of her professional life. The group included Zona Gale, Emma Kauffman (later Mrs. Arnold Brunner), Rose O'Neill, Grace Gould, Mary Mullet, Anne O'Hagen—by that time Mrs. Francis Shinn, Mrs. Ayer, and Marie Manning. It's a pretty story and I like to think it is true. But however kindly those women may have felt for me at that luncheon, there were intervals in the old days when the members of my staff must have thought me as vigorous a slave-driver as Ballard Smith himself. Working day and night, as I did, I saw no reason why others should not drive themselves as hard.

I remember Marie Manning—now Mrs. Herman Gasch

of Washington—once asking me pathetically, "Am I always to work fifteen hours a day?" And the story of the time I sent Olivia Howard Dunbar to the Booth-Tuckers is told on Newspaper Row to this hour. One of the charges made against me by that indefatigable band was that I always wanted the news the day before it broke. This tale seems to bear out that theory.

I had heard that a new baby was due at the home of the Booth-Tuckers. The Booth-Tuckers were then enjoying a brief interval in the public limelight as heads of the Salvation Army, while General Booth and the Ballington Booths fought out those little differences of opinion about field work which eventually separated them. I thought the public might be interested in the new baby and I sent Miss Dunbar to the Booth-Tucker home, an hour from New York, to get the story.

From the first Miss Dunbar was not enthusiastic over the assignment. She became less so when she reached the town of the Booth-Tuckers. The weather that day was abominable. The rain came down in icy pellets, and there wasn't a vehicle of any kind to be picked up at the station. Miss Dunbar had to walk a mile or so, sloshing through puddles and having her wet skirts twisted around her ankles by a cold wind, till she reached the Booth-Tucker house on the outskirts of the village. When she got there she observed a depressed gray horse standing at the gate, hitched to a battered buggy, and she gave the animal a glance of sympathetic camaraderie as she passed him. She knew just how he felt. She went up the steps leading to the house and rang the doorbell. No one answered. She rang again and again and yet again. The house was not empty. She could hear sounds of hurrying steps and general activity inside.

At last after repeated ringing of the bell, Booth-Tucker himself opened the door. He was an Englishman, with a

manner usually composed and a personal effect of immaculate neatness. To-day his coat was off, his sleeves were
rolled up. He looked unkempt and almost distraught. Miss
Dunbar told him she was a *World* reporter and that she had
come to get a story and a picture of the new baby.

Booth-Tucker clung feebly to the door-knob, stared at her
an instant in helpless stupefaction, and then burst into
speech. In his agitation his English A's became so broad
that Miss Dunbar could almost have sat down on them.

"My deah young lady," he babbled. "Mrs. Booth-Tuckah
is being delivehed of the child in this houah. You wouldn't
want a picture of the infant befoah its mothah was delivehed
of it—would you, now?"

Miss Dunbar admitted that she would not, and fled back
into the storm. She passed the hour of the return journey
trying to decide whether she would complain of me to
higher powers, or resign, or do both.

I knew all the Booths quite well. In my first year as a
reporter Mrs. Ballington Booth, a wholly charming woman,
had insisted that I should kneel down and pray with her
every time I went to her office in quest of news. When the
Ballington Booths finally seceded from the Salvation Army
to form their American Volunteers, and Evangeline Booth
came over from London to pull the great organization together again, Evangeline put in hours of her first weeks
at work telling me her troubles. She described how she
had soaked her pillow with tears when she was ordered
to take charge of the Army's work in America.

"Ballington and Maud seceded because they were not
willing to obey orders and leave their American work to
head the Army in India, when Father ordered them to," she
said. "I have been the head of the work in England for
years, and it is as exactly as dear to me as the work here was
to Ballington and Maud. But did I rebel when I received

my orders? I did not. We are under military rule. I packed
and came—though I cried myself ill when I was alone!"

I saw much of Evangeline Booth in those first weeks of
her rule here. Then or later I never saw anything more efficient than the manner in which she swept that great army
back into its established fold. The Army loved the Ballington Booths. It wanted to follow them wherever they led. All
it knew about Evangeline Booth was her fine reputation for
efficiency and the fact that she was her father's daughter.
For weeks the Army backed and filled and milled about in
uncertainty. At the end of the struggle Evangeline had it in
line, and the Ballington Booths proceeded to develop their
own fine organization.

In connection with the Booth-Tuckers' baby I remember
going later to a huge mass meeting of the American Volunteers. The youngest of the Ballington Booth babies, very
recently born, attended the meeting in his mother's arms.
Around his little middle he wore a wide sash with the following simple legend inscribed in gold letters:

God's Own

It was time for me to produce another "beat." If I did
not protect myself against it I would be submerged in
World editorial work, which was no part of my own
program. The careless rapture with which I have chron-
icled my little triumphs may have misled the reader as to the
number of them. There were not so many—and one's reputation has to be made anew every day of newspaper life.

I was anxiously looking about for some promising opportunity when Ballard Smith came to my office about nine
o'clock one evening and dumped a great mass of papers on
my desk. He could always put much into a few words. Here,
among those papers, he explained, lay the story that to-morrow morning would electrify New York. No other newspa-

per would have it. It had just been given to him as an exclusive feature for the *World* by his friend De Lancey Nicoll, then District Attorney of New York. What I had to do, Mr. Smith cheerily added, was to go down into that gold-mine of material, dig the facts out of it, and write a four or five column story in time for the first edition of the *World*—which would go to press in just five hours!

Eager as I had been for something "big" in reporting I admit that I was appalled by this assignment. It looked like a two-day job. To go through those heaps of documents, made up of letters and affidavits and signed statements, to classify and read and digest them, seemed to call for at least an uninterrupted day and night of work. And after that to turn out the best story of my life—which was what Mr. Smith had ordered! Four or five columns to be written, while a copy boy waited at my elbow for the pages as they were filled. Mr. Smith mentioned that he and Mr. Nicoll had just dined together—probably for two hours. I reflected bitterly that he could have sent me that material at least an hour earlier. . . . But there was no time to brood over a sense of injury. I tackled the mass of papers—and found in them the grim skeleton of Helen Potts, and the scattered facts that eventually sent Carlyle Harris to the electric chair for her murder.

All the public and I knew about Helen Potts' death before I picked up those papers was that she was a lovely girl of good family, eighteen years old and a student in a fashionable girls' school, who had died very suddenly a few months earlier. Her youth and beauty and the social position of her people had given her death a little publicity. Seemingly there had been nothing unusual about it except the abrupt end of a promising young life. Helen Potts was wept over. Then every one but her friends and family forgot her.

Later, as I now discovered, her mother had found among

Helen's papers and other possessions things that chilled her soul. Helen had been secretly married to a young medical student. Discovery of the marriage had become inevitable. The medical student was not ready for the revelation—nor for the responsibility and support of a wife and family. His letters, found among Helen's papers, proved this. He had no money. He was handsome and charming and clever, and Helen adored him. She suffered from headaches. He had often given her headache tablets. He had given her some the very night she died. Asked about it, several of Helen's fellow students remembered that.

For weeks and months Helen Potts' mother had faced her ghastly problem alone. Helen was in her grave. Would any benefit be gained by a publicity which would throw discredit on her and possibly injure an innocent young man? But if he were *not* innocent! Could Helen Potts' mother let her daughter's murder go unavenged?

In the end the mother had gone in confidence to the District Attorney with her story, and a secret investigation had begun. Helen's body had been exhumed. Enough poison to kill her had been found in her stomach. But the six remaining headache tablets in the box Carlyle Harris had given her had been analyzed at the time of her death, and had been found harmless. Two pills had been taken, to the knowledge of Helen's room-mate. Eight pills had been in the box. All the tablets had been mixed by Helen's husband, young Carlyle Harris.

The past of Carlyle Harris was investigated as thoroughly as the contents of Helen Potts' stomach had been. It was entirely possible that the two pills he had given her that night from that box had contained the death dose, and that the remaining six had been left to do the work they had done so well—the work of allaying suspicion. After many weeks of investigation De Lancey Nicoll had completed a strong case against Carlyle Harris. The young man was to be arrested later that night—too late for the other newspapers to get the story.

I shall never forget that night, or the sensation in New York the next morning, or the long grim drama of the trial. I received much more credit for the story than I deserved. I myself had unveiled nothing. The whole case had been handed to me, as it were, on a tray. All I had given to it was some quick reading, quick writing, and, I hope, some clear thinking.

The trial was one of the most sensational in the history of New York courts. Carlyle Harris was young and handsome, and he went through his ordeal with great dignity and courage. The case against him was purely circumstantial, and from start to finish he protested his innocence. Nevertheless, he was found guilty and sent to the electric chair. As he sat in it, in the final moments of his life, he uttered one of the most memorable valedictories ever delivered against that tragic background.

"Now that I am about to die," he said, "now that nothing can be gained or lost by any statement I make, I wish to repeat for the last time that I die absolutely innocent of the crime of which I was convicted."

It was said at the time that Arthur Brisbane, who was one of the witnesses of the execution, had fainted after seeing it. Mr. Brisbane was then managing editor of the *Evening Sun.* Later he came to the *World* and he and I worked together for three years—he as Sunday editor and I as assistant Sunday editor. During those years we discussed every subject that came to our minds, and many subjects came. I never asked him if that story of his faint was true, but I have always believed it. Under a manner usually rather cold and often forbidding, Mr. Brisbane had one of the most understanding and deeply sympathetic natures I have ever known. It must have been sheer torture to him to see another man put to death.

I can vouch, however, for another striking episode connected with the trial. Carlyle Harris's mother had been in court with her son throughout the hearing. She would have encompassed him like a protecting wall if she could, and she almost did it. Without exception all the reporters of the trial were sympathetic, and considerate of her. On the last day, after the verdict had been reached and given, she presented to every reporter as a mark of her appreciation a copy of one of her books. The book was a treatise on the proper training of the young! Fittingly inscribed, yellowed by age, and no doubt a bit dusty, it still has a place on the shelves of my library.

The panic of 1893 struck the country like a thunderbolt, and Milwaukee was one of its worst victims. Every bank in the city failed, and my father went down in the debacle with most of Milwaukee's other business men. He was at that time a dealer in real estate. He had bought up and was developing huge tracts of land in and around Milwaukee—including a great stretch along the shore of Lake Michigan, which has since become the fashionable residence section of the city. He had foreseen that it would do so; but the real-estate industry died in the panic, and my father lost practically everything he had.

He paid his indebtedness to the last dollar (there was a fine editorial about that in the *Evening Wisconsin*) and prepared to start life over. The shock and strain had been too much for him and his health broke. My sister was to be married in the spring, and I persuaded her and my father and mother to come to New York and pass the winter with me. I had an apartment in the Windermere, on West Fifty-seventh Street. It has since been torn down but it was then said to have been the home at one time or another of practically every writer and artist in town. It was old but roomy and comfortable, and I had an excellent cook. I knew I could give my family everything they wanted—except my society.

So far as that was concerned they saw very little more of me than they would have seen if they had remained in Milwaukee. They were appalled by the hours I kept, of which my letters had told them as little as possible. Now they saw that I was working like a galley-slave. I was off at nine or ten in the morning after a few hours of sleep; at the *World* offices or out on assignments by eleven; in my office again most of the night; and home at two or three o'clock in the morning to drop into bed exhausted and to rise from it and rush to work immediately after breakfast.

I could give them no time and very little attention. But I had plenty of theater and concert tickets for them and made out sight-seeing schedules. On the whole they enjoyed the winter. I was sorry to have them get their first close-up picture of my newspaper life just at the time when they realized their dependence on me—but that could not be helped. They had also the sustaining knowledge that this dependence eliminated that convent dream of mine, if I still dreamed it.

I had not dreamed it very often after I reached New York. I had not seen Mother Caroline since coming East, and she had never again brought up the subject when I did see her in the days before I left. She had extended her tacit invitation. It was for me to accept it or as tacitly ignore it. My mother had still hoped I would return to the music we both loved. Now it was understood that I would continue my career and earn as much as I could. After years of regarding it as a trivial detail the amount I earned had suddenly become important.

The family had a good winter and went back to Milwaukee in the spring. My sister became Mrs. Edward Beyer, and my father and mother settled down in their home, which was all that was left to them from the wreck. My father was full of plans for a fresh start, but the depression was still on and life's thumb was turned down against him. His health failed steadily, and he never got back into the current of affairs, though he lived till 1906.

In the interval it was for me to keep him and Mother comfortable. They were a devoted couple, their old friends were around them, and they had a garden that interested them both. Up till then I had never been interested in money-making. I had been given everything I needed. On the *World* a steadily increasing salary and Mr. Pulitzer's frequent checks kept my bank account in excellent condition. It had never occurred to me to save a penny of my income.

Looking back I can't quite see how I could have spent it, though I remember that I had all my suits made by New York's leading and most expensive tailors. I paid about a hundred and fifty dollars for each suit—a price I have never since paid, even when I was earning twenty-five or thirty thousand dollars a year. Now, money suddenly interested me. I began to look around for ways to earn more. Ballard Smith's brilliant star had faded. Colonel George Harvey was the *World's* managing editor. I didn't know him very well but of course he knew all about my work. I walked into his office, declined the chair he offered me, and, standing beside him, cheerfully asked for an increase in salary.

I can see him now, exactly as he looked then, leaning back in his chair with his hands clasped behind his head—a familiar attitude of his—looking up at me with his characteristic smile. He was very young at the time—in his early thirties, I think. He told me he would look into the matter and that he thought it would be all right. It was, and without any confidences on my part concerning my change of fortune. This was business. I was quite sure I was earning more than I was receiving. Fortunately, Colonel Harvey was sure of it, too. I found the increase in my salary envelop the following Saturday night.

Naturally this brisk incident, added to the Colonel's amazing ability, won my whole-hearted admiration for him, and I mourned him deeply when he left the *World*. His tenure of office there was one of the shortest in the history of the great newspaper. He made a spectacular success, and Mr. Pulitzer was delighted with his new boy wonder. But Colonel Harvey developed a serious case of pneumonia and nearly died of it. After that prolonged illness he had to spend many months in the south of France for convalescence. Even when he had recovered, his lungs were still so sensitive that his doctors ordered him to give up the night work and bad air and nervous strain of a newspaper career. If he didn't, they hinted . . . and shook their heads.

Colonel Harvey talked the matter over with Mrs. Harvey, and years afterwards she told me the full story of his departure from the *World's* staff. I have known many happy married couples, but I have rarely known such deep and quiet love and loyalty as existed between the Harveys. Mrs. Harvey would have scrubbed floors, if necessary, to save her husband the slightest risk or strain. Their love affair had begun in Peacham, Vermont, when they were babies. At the early age of seven "Geordie" Harvey had thrashed another infant of his own age for daring to hover around little Alma Parker, the daughter of the village doctor. From that time neither Geordie Harvey nor Alma had ever thought of another mate. They themselves never seemed conscious that the serene happiness of their married life was anything unusual. They accepted it without question.

As the pair discussed the *World* crisis, Colonel Harvey ended his recital of facts with a simple statement.

"I'll do whichever you say," he told her. "I'll resign, or I'll keep on. We haven't saved much. If I resign we may have some hard sledding before I get another job that brings in what I'm earning now."

"Geordie, you *must* resign," Mrs. Harvey said with emphasis. "You mustn't dream of remaining, at any risk to your health. *Please* resign to-morrow."

He did, but Mr. Pulitzer would not accept the resignation. He suggested a big increase in salary. It was refused. He suggested shorter hours and more help for his managing editor. This suggestion, too, was refused with thanks. It was obviously not practicable. The truth was that while Colonel Harvey would have remained with the *World* if his wife had been nervous over a change, he did not really like the work. He did not mean to make newspaper work his career. His sole compromise was to remain till Mr. Pulitzer could find a successor to him. There was a definite time limit to that—three months, as I remember it.

When Colonel Harvey's last day with the *World* finally arrived, Mrs. Harvey was out of town. She had been called back to Peacham by the illness of her sister. Colonel Harvey was always more or less at loose ends without her. This particular evening he was having some sober second thoughts. It occurred to him that he had taken a big leap in the dark, off a safe and sound plank. Had he perhaps made a mistake? He wasn't at all sure he had not. He was a very generous man and a born spender. He and Mrs. Harvey really had an extremely small reserve. It never occurred to him to look around for some friend who might cheer him that lonely evening. Instead, he did a very characteristic thing. He strolled into Delmonico's, ordered the best dinner he could think of, throwing in a bottle of champagne, and

"We Three"
Colonel and Mrs. George Harvey and Dorothy

settled down to enjoy it. As he was finishing it a hand fell on his shoulder and a familiar voice spoke to him.

"Well, Harvey, how's the big job going?"

Colonel Harvey looked up and recognized William C. Whitney.

"It's gone," he said cheerfully. "After to-day I'm in the army of the unemployed."

"No, you're not," the great financier said with equal brisk-ness. "I'm taking you over right now. Come to my office at ten to-morrow morning and we'll settle the details."

Once more we see on what trifles the shaping of a life may turn. It would never have occurred to Colonel Harvey to ask Mr. Whitney for an opening, Mrs. Harvey added. But there it was. The two men were together for years. Through Mr. Whitney, Colonel Harvey soon knew inti-mately the elder J. P. Morgan and Thomas Fortune Ryan. Among them the three men gave "the youngster" market tips that made his fortune. By the time William C. Whitney died, many years later, J. P. Morgan had made Colonel Harvey the president of Harper and Brothers. Colonel Har-vey mourned for his dead friend as for a brother. His edi-torial tribute to Whitney in *Harper's Weekly* was equaled only, in my opinion, by the simplicity, dignity and feeling with which Mr. Hearst wrote of the death of Arthur Bris-bane. But all this came years afterwards.

The photograph of Colonel and Mrs. Harvey and their daughter Dorothy, reproduced here with the caption "We Three," was taken about the time Colonel Harvey's portrait was painted by John Alexander. There were, of course, those who did not like this portrait, which is really an excellent one. Some criticism of it was made in the presence of Dor-othy, then five years old.

"Well, anyway," Dorothy said fiercely, *"we three* like it very much!"

Colonel Harvey was so delighted by the family solidarity this implied that from then on he usually referred to his domestic circle as "we three." "We three" have all passed from this earth, as Dorothy died in 1937, at the age of forty-one.

At the time Colonel Harvey left the *World* I was still looking about for ways to earn more money. I wrote my first short fiction story (not counting the trifles I had turned out in Milwaukee) and gave it the title "Ruth Herrick's Assignment." It was suggested by another murder trial I had been reporting. I handed it to my friend Gertrude Atherton and asked her to read and criticize it. She had been urging me to write fiction. She was wonderfully kind, and immediately interested, as she would be. Within a day or two she sent me the following note which is still among my souvenirs : *

DEAR ELIZABETH,

Your story is a corker. I experienced a real thrill when the woman came out with her confession. I have sent the story to the editor of the *Cosmopolitan.* God alone knows what editors will do, but this one seems to have better judgment than most and I think he will take it.

The signature was the firm G., the firm A., and the wavering line following both initials which still forms Gertrude Atherton's autograph. The editor justified her faith. He took the story and I felt that I was fairly launched in literature.

Greatly cheered by this episode I proceeded to write some more short stories. In addition to the special reporting I still did of important news and trials, I was conducting the pages I have mentioned and a few more departments tossed at me

* All the letters published in these reminiscences are quoted with the permission of the authors, or with that of the executors of the estates of those who are dead.

from time to time by editors who could get away with it—
Mr. Goddard, Mr. Grozier, Mr. Coates, and others.

One of my duties—to this day I don't know why—was
to keep the Sunday staff together Wednesday and Thursday
nights—the last nights before all the various supplements
of the *Sunday World* were fully made up—and see that
the special artists and writers turned out their work on time.
This was before I was assistant Sunday editor. It was just
one of those things.

I had a big office by that time, and it was well filled on
those nights—the special writers, of course, having waited
till the last possible moment to get at their jobs. There were
eight, ten, sometimes a dozen men and women, all writing or
drawing like mad, smoking like chimneys, and handing their
work to me around two or three in the morning. It was my
task to edit the copy and send it to the composing room, and
to get the pictures to the art department. In the meantime, I
was more or less like a silent teacher in a class-room during
study hours. I had to see that they kept at work—that they
didn't laugh or play or gambol about. One of the artists was
George Luks, some of whose paintings are now in the
great art galleries of the world. I also remember especially
C. Connard, a woman who at that time was doing amazingly
good black and white pictures of animals. She was there
almost every working night and her concentration was a
lesson to the whole assemblage. I doubt if she realized that
there were others in the room.

I was free till the copy began to come in to me toward
morning and it was in that atmosphere of rush and strain
and bad air and sputtering arc lights, and after a day of hard
work, that I wrote my first book. It had occurred to me
that I might use those dragging hours when every one else
was busy. I wrote ten short stories—and called them *Tales
of the City Room*. I had them copied on a typewriter, and

airily took them to Charles Scribner, head of the publishing house of Charles Scribner's Sons. I did not know him. I had no letter of introduction to him. I merely walked into his offices, as I had walked into the *World* offices that first day. I asked for Mr. Scribner, was received by him, and handed him my book. In its preface I explained to readers, as I again explain here, that the City Room of a newspaper is that room in a newspaper office over which the city editor presides, where he gives assignments to his reporters, and where as a rule they do their writing.

The stories were very short, very slight. They were, of course, the impressions and some of the experiences of my first years as a *World* reporter. Many newspaper stories have blossomed along the literary lane since then, but these were novelties at the time. Such as they were they held the heart of my little bottle of life.

Mr. Scribner sent for me in a fortnight and said he would make a book of them.

"But you ought to have them published in the magazines first," he kindly suggested. "I think you could sell every one of them."

I was in too much of a hurry for that. I wanted the book brought out. When would he publish it, I asked. This was October. He said he would bring it out in March, and he did. It had a charming cover, designed by Berkeley Smith, a son of F. Hopkinson Smith. In it Mr. Smith had given the public its first skyline and skyscraper effect in book covers. It showed the gold dome of the *World* building and a corner of the *Times* structure against a background of deep blue sky. When I held it in my hand I was convinced that my fortune was made.

It wasn't, of course, but the little book sold very well and the newspaper reviewers were wonderfully kind to it. With one exception they agreed that it had local color and

the true newspaper atmosphere. The exception was the editor
of a weekly newspaper in some southern village I had never
heard of. He said it was clear that I had never been inside
of a newspaper office. I was heartbroken over this comment.
I forgot all my good notices and sent him a letter on *World*
stationery, giving him my credentials. He apologized, both
in his newspaper and by letter, and in the handsomest
manner.

Before the book came out, however, I had another small
triumph. Up till that time all my work for the *World* had
appeared unsigned. Such reputation as I had was local, and
largely confined to Park Row. Nevertheless, the listening
ear of Edward Bok, always so close to the ground, got some
echo of it. On one of his visits to New York he sent for me
and ordered a series of articles. He was at the old Fifth
Avenue Hotel, and he told me why he always put up there.

He said that when he was an unknown boy he had col-
lected autographs. Many distinguished men lived at the Fifth
Avenue Hotel, or registered there when they came to town,
and he called on them and sometimes secured a little chat
with one of them as well as the autograph he had asked for.
He was always impressed by the hotel's comfort and atmosphere. To him it expressed all there was of luxury and
splendor. Then and there he resolved that if success ever
came to him—and he was sure it would—he, too, would put
up at the Fifth Avenue Hotel and be asked for his autograph.
He kept that promise made to himself. He never registered
at any other New York hotel as long as the old "Fifth
Avenue" existed.

He was at the height of his fame at this time and the
newspapers were having some fun with him. They said he
had cabled to England asking Rudyard Kipling to let him
cut out a line in one story stating that a character in the
tale "tossed down a glass of sherry." They said Kipling had

cabled back "Make it Mellin's Food!" They said a girl had
written to Bok to ask him how to properly leave a party,
and they said Bok had advised her to "make a bright remark
and leave the room under cover of the laughter that followed." They were saying all sorts of things, and Mr. Bok
took them with the utmost good humor. All this was fine
advertising and the circulation of his magazine was growing
month by month.

We had a long talk that day and I was avid, as I always
was, for all he could tell me. We kept more or less in touch
after that, and he used a good deal of my work. But he
never approached the record of his eventual successor, Barton
W. Currie, many years later. In the first months of his
editorship Mr. Currie came to New York to see me, sat in
my Gramercy Park apartment for half an hour, and in that
time ordered eighteen thousand dollars' worth of work from
me for the coming year. So many short stories at a thousand
dollars each. A two-part story to be written around a pet
plot of his own, for three thousand. So many special articles
at seven hundred and fifty dollars each; as many short editorials as I cared to submit at two hundred and fifty dollars
each. Those were not considered especially high rates at that
time, but the total was impressive. It was my misfortune that
year, of all years, to go to a hospital before half the order
had been turned in, and to lose six months of my working life.

My first encounter with Mr. Bok brought me more than
money. The *World* editors were impressed by my début in
the *Ladies' Home Journal*. One of the most up-and-coming
of them, John Tennant, decided off his own bat that if my
name had value there it had value for the *World*. After
that it was signed to my specials unless I forgot to add it,
which I rarely did.

Long afterwards, during my first years as editor of *Har-*

per's Bazar, Mr. Bok again showed his good feeling in a striking way. He had been offered a fabulous salary to leave the *Ladies' Home Journal* and take the editorship of another leading magazine for women published in New York. He had even come to New York to talk about it—not, I am sure, with any idea of accepting the offer, but to see how much the publishers would raise their original bid.

He came to my office to tell me that he had warmly recommended me for the position, and that the publishers were impressed by his faith. They desired to take up the matter with me. Would I make an immediate appointment with them? He warned me that the *Bazar,* as one of three publications published by Harper and Brothers, could never be a big financial success. The advertising would have to be divided among the three and the lion's share would always be given to *Harpers' Monthly* by both publishers and advertisers. Also, in addition to its own expenses, the *Bazar* would have to carry a quarter of the huge Harper overhead. He was entirely right, as it turned out, but at that time I still controlled a large share of the world's optimism. I refused the appointment and the opening, and did not even mention them to Colonel Harvey for several years.

My first New York story, "Ruth Herrick's Assignment," soon came out in the *Cosmopolitan.* It created something of a stir, for a dramatic reason that had nothing to do with its quality and which is explained in the next chapter.

CHAPTER VIII

LIZZIE BORDEN AND THE MURDERS

POSSIBLY I am giving too much space to murder trials in these memories, but the two I include are among the most dramatic episodes in America's crime history, as well as the most widely discussed trials of their day. There was good reason for this in the character and quality of their principals—Carlyle Harris and, later, Lizzie Borden.

Carlyle Harris died in the electric chair, claiming innocence with his last breath. The mystery of the Borden case has never been solved. Lizzie Borden underwent trial for it and was acquitted. The conditions attending the double murder were almost incredible. It was committed about two o'clock on a hot July afternoon in a house situated on a residence street in Fall River—a house which had all its windows open at the time. Neighboring houses stood on both sides of it, not more than a hundred feet away. Passing that house, as various citizens must have done in returning to work after their noonday meal in their own homes on the same street, they should have heard through those open windows even such slight sounds as low laughter or voices raised in ordinary conversation. Yet in that house, and at that hour, two of the most appalling murders of the century were committed—and the murderer has never been found.

The victims were an old man—a wealthy citizen of Fall River named Borden, and his second wife, a few years younger than he was. His two daughters by his first wife, Lizzie and Emma Borden, were the other members of the family. Emma, the younger daughter, was away from home

116

on a visit to friends in a town thirty miles from Fall River. Lizzie, as she told the story, was out in the barn back of the house, brooding tenderly over a setting hen which that day had suddenly declined to set. Thus Miss Borden, she swore, was a hundred feet from the house, from two o'clock till half past two. The old couple, having had their meal, were dozing—Lizzie's father lying on a couch in the living-room, his wife dozing in a rocking chair upstairs. There and then both were murdered with an ax, and with such ferocity that the rooms holding their bodies had become abattoirs. The furniture, the walls, even the ceilings, were thickly clotted with blood.

Into those rooms, she testified, Lizzie Borden came at half past two. She was a teacher in one of Fall River's public schools, and she was loved and respected by her pupils and her neighbors. From those rooms, after a moment of stupe-faction and horror, she claimed, she walked out of the house and across the lawn to the home of her nearest neighbors to give the alarm. Reaching them, the neighbors testified, she was calm, self-possessed, and, as always, absolutely immaculate. She was clad in a light summer dress. I mention her clothing because so much attention was given to it during the trial. She was the neatest human being I have ever seen. She radiated cleanliness like an atmosphere. Throughout the blistering days of her trial, in an August heat that was breaking all records and when the rest of us were wilting in our chairs, Lizzie Borden was invariably as immaculate in appearance as a freshly tubbed and freshly dressed baby.

She was in that court-room on trial for her life because she and her sister were the only human beings who would gain by the old people's death. Emma Borden was out of it. The family of her distant hostess could and did account for every moment of her time the day of the murder. Lizzie had been at home, so Lizzie Borden must have committed the murder. So reasoned the authorities of the State of Massachusetts. By that murder the Borden sisters would inherit several hundred thousand dollars. The old man was a miser. He had been niggardly and a martinet with his daughters. All they had were their small salaries as teachers, and he had made them pay him a large part of those as board. The relations between the daughters and their stepmother had not been cordial. There had been no quarrels, but there was watchful remoteness on both sides. Plenty of evidence here, the State of Massachusetts held, to put Lizzie Borden on trial for murder.

On the other hand, the defense of her was passionate and prolonged. There was, to begin with, her fine record, her character. She was a torch-bearer, an upholder of high standards of life. She was a good teacher, a loyal friend, a good neighbor. Even aside from all this, the defense held, no woman but a giantess would have the physical strength to commit those appalling murders. Moreover—and here was the telling point—any one who committed them would have been drenched with blood.

It was a trial filled with drama. The prosecution advanced its theory. The woman had stripped to the skin, had committed the murders while nude, had bathed and redressed after them, and hastened to the neighbors. Even the jury looked aghast at this, and the three old judges on the bench, who had known Lizzie Borden since she was a child, turned their tired eyes on her with deep sympathy. So did almost every spectator in the court-room. But neither sympathy nor attacks aroused any response in Lizzie Borden. From start to finish of that terrible ordeal she seemed as aloof as a Buddha image in its temple—above the tumult and the tragedy, unconscious of the life-and-death conflict that went on around her.

Things happened in that court-room which would have shaken a weaker soul. Lizzie and her sister had enjoyed just one "good time" in their lives. They had saved and economized until they got enough money together to go to Europe one summer in the cheapest way. They had kept to themselves on the voyage home, because they were rather low in their minds over the return to the grim atmosphere of their father's house.

But Lizzie made one friendship on that voyage. She met and liked a woman from the far West, and talked to her freely. Years later that woman traveled across America to testify at Miss Borden's trial that Lizzie had confided to her, on their last night at sea, that she was sick at heart over the dreary prospect of reëntering her prison. I could have strangled the creature as she sat in the witness chair, feeling important and smugly manufacturing her little strand of the rope that might hang her fellow-voyager. My fellow reporters felt the same way. We looked at Miss Borden to see how she took it. That was part of our job. She was not taking it at all. Her thoughts seemed far away. Apparently she was not even hearing that flat, monotonous voice.

I was, I think, the only woman reporter in the court-room the day the old man's skull was put in evidence. The reporters around me were for Miss Borden as one man— convinced of her innocence, showing the conviction between the lines of their reports, and burning with sympathy for her. I was as sure of her innocence as they were, but at first I refused to give them my opinions. Night after night, when the trial was over, we all sat out on the little balconies of the hotel, in an atmosphere like the exhaust from a mighty engine, and talked the case over. If Miss Borden had not committed the murders, who had? An escaped maniac? The crime seemed the work of one. A gorilla? A gorilla was indicated, by the appearance of those rooms. *The Murders in the Rue Morgue* came cheerily to mind.

I had a room with a balcony. The night we had been discussing gorillas I woke from a restless doze at three o'clock in the morning to see a gorilla standing framed in the open French windows. But it was only the big night watchman, who had climbed up there to show me how easy it was. He explained that it wasn't safe to sleep with open windows so easily reached from the street, only one story below. He mentioned maniacs, and the fact that the Borden murderer might still be at large in the woods near Fall River. I rose hastily and closed the windows.

As I have said, the old man's skull was brought into the court-room by the defense lawyers. The purpose of the exhibit was to show the terrific force of one blow that had split the head diagonally from the top down through the left jawbone. No woman, the defense held, had enough strength to deliver that blow. The skull was resting on a small oblong board, and the split jaw had been fastened in place with a piece of wire. Miss Borden's leading lawyer, Judge Robinson, held the skull high, that the jury and the spectators in the court-room might see it. Then the very walls of the room seemed to lean forward to look and listen. For the wire slipped, and the old man's jaw sagged back and forth in a grisly suggestion of speech. Spectators caught their breath and then exhaled it in a gasp that swept the court-room like a great sigh.

"The old man is trying to testify," I murmured to my friend Julian Ralph, who sat next to me.

"What's he saying? What's he saying?" Julian gulped. I was so shaken that I gave myself away.

"He's saying that she's innocent," I answered, and Julian looked his relief. All the newspaper men had been afraid that being a woman, and therefore without man's great natural sympathy, I would show a bias in my reports that might divert some of the current of popular feeling which was sweeping toward Miss Borden.

I still believe that Lizzie Borden was innocent. So, at the time she was acquitted, did her judges and her jury. But strange things happened as the years passed. Her neighbors, at first so loyal in their belief in her, began to avoid her. In the end she and her sister moved to another town. A large part of their inheritance had gone to pay the expenses of her trial, but the sisters still had enough to live on in comfort. Then Emma became insane.

If the general testimony on that subject is true, Lizzie never again allowed her sister to see or to be seen by any of her old friends. Neither did she send her to a sanitarium or engage nurses for her. She kept her in their new home till Emma died several years later. She herself nursed Emma —devotedly they admit, giving her practically all her time, going nowhere, remaining almost as much a prisoner as the unbalanced patient. There was plenty of gossip about *that*. Why, their old friends asked, was no one but her physician allowed to see Emma? What might Emma have babbled if she had been given the opportunity to talk? Lizzie Borden must have heard of these speculations, but she remained as unmoved by them as she had been unmoved by the testimony in the court-room.

My real reason for bringing up the old case is my own unfortunate connection with it. In what I wrote of Lizzie Borden during her trial, I probably showed, as my associates did, faith in her innocence. But, as it happened, not long after her acquittal my first New York magazine story —the one Gertrude Atherton had mothered—appeared in the *Cosmopolitan Magazine*. It had the title "Ruth Herrick's Assignment." It had no more to do with Lizzie Borden than it had to do with Tommy Tucker. But it was the story of a woman on trial for murder, who in a moment of nervous collapse confessed her guilt to a woman reporter. The trial was going the woman's way. The prosecution was weak. It was already clear that the woman would be acquitted. The reporter's problem was whether to betray the prisoner's confidence, give her newspaper a great "beat" and send the murderess to the chair, or to wipe the confession from her memory, "let down" her editor and her newspaper, and save a criminal's life. The murder had many extenuating features. Ruth Herrick kept the secret, and the woman was acquitted.

Published at any other time the story would not have attracted much attention. Coming as it did, soon after the Borden trial, and with my reports of the trial fresh in the public mind, it was immediately suggested and then generally assumed that Lizzie Borden had confessed her guilt to me, and that I had let her off. Even the managing editor of the *World,* then James Farrelly, sent me this note:

"*So,* Ruth Herrick, *that's* the kind of a reporter you are, is it?"

That story had been written before the Bordens had been murdered. In vain I pointed this out, privately and publicly. All the conditions of the murder were wholly different from those of the Borden case. It was her husband my guilty heroine had sent to his grave—under conditions which made the grave a very fitting place for him. It was useless to explain all this to persons determined to cling to their "drama."

Less than ten years ago, at a reception, I overheard one woman telling another that I had "saved Lizzie Borden." There are those who still believe it, and who cock a knowing eye at me when I deny it. But again and, I hope, for the last time, I explain that I never saw Lizzie Borden outside of the court-room, and that I was never less than twelve feet away from her as we sat in that stifling torture chamber.

She could hardly have shouted a confession to me through that fetid air. Moreover, Miss Borden was not the type of woman to confess anything to anybody.

She outlived Emma by many years, but she is now dead. After her death the old barn on the Borden place in Fall River was torn down, on the theory that the murderer's ax, which had never been found, might be discovered somewhere among the barn's foundations. It was not.

I hope I have shown that life was not all murder trials in those days, but possibly I would better underline the point. We also had prize-fights in the news, and the greatest of these was the fight between John L. Sullivan and James J. Corbett, in which Corbett defeated the old champion. That fight was arranged by the *World's* sporting editor, George Dickenson. Mr. Dickenson, who was immensely popular in the sporting world and thoroughly deserved to be, held the stakes for this fight, and the details of it were arranged in the *World* offices.

I don't remember why my desk happened to be next to Mr. Dickenson's during those few hectic weeks, but it was; and the two fighters with their groups of followers were constantly coming and going around us. Mr. Dickenson introduced them both to me, and John L. Sullivan and I promptly proceeded to lay the foundation of a pleasant friendship. For one reason, Arthur Brisbane, who had just been lured to the *World* by Mr. Pulitzer, was devoted to Sullivan. For another, there was something about the great champion that I liked. He was a spectacular figure, and an appealing one. He always went about with a retinue as large as a king's, and it was said of him that he had never broken faith with any man.

Mr. Brisbane's devotion to him dated from a nice little episode in London several years before this contemplated fight. Sullivan had been invited to give a boxing exhibition before the Prince of Wales, later Edward VII. He accepted and made a suggestion.

"I'd like to have me frien' Art'ur Brisbane there," he said.

The gentlemen in charge of the boxing affair explained to the fighter that this was the Prince's affair, not Sullivan's, and that the only guests at the boxing match would be those invited by the Prince himself. There could be no exception to this rule. Sullivan nodded.

"Aw right," he said simply, "then I don't box!"

There was considerable excitement over this announcement. Mr. Brisbane, then London correspondent of the New York *Sun,* naturally wanted to send an exclusive story of that match to his newspaper, and Sullivan knew it. The Prince of Wales was annoyed. He wanted to see the match. Sullivan's backers were also annoyed. They wanted the fighter to have the world advertising a match before the Prince would give him. Both sides argued and pleaded. Sullivan merely reiterated his little refrain.

"If me frien' Art'ur Brisbane ain't there, I don't box!"

In the end he had his way and Mr. Brisbane got his story. Billy Inglis told me the tale to explain the affection between the two men, who were as different as two human beings could be. Mr. Sullivan put the matter to me much more simply.

"Me an' Art'ur Brisbane is frien's," he mentioned.

He always stopped at my desk for a few words, or for a longer chat, when he came to see Mr. Brisbane or Mr. Dickenson. He told me of some of the things he said Corbett's crowd was trying to "put over" on him in connection with the fight. My sympathy was all with him. Occasionally, when an excited discussion was in progress at Mr. Dickenson's desk, and I couldn't help overhearing it, Sullivan and I would exchange a look of intimate understanding. On one occasion he assured me in the presence of a delighted group that if I "ever had any trouble wit' any guy" I had only to mention it to him, John L. Sullivan.

We were all "rooting" for Sullivan, all convinced of his coming triumph over Corbett. On the night of the fight, those of us who had not gone south to see it got the reports of it at our desks round by round as they came in over Mr. Dickenson's special wire. Mrs. Corbett had been invited to come to the *World* offices and hear them, too. She must have been struck by the passionate enthusiasm for Sullivan felt by all those around her. But Sullivan was knocked out in the eighteenth round.

He got up bruised, bleeding, and still almost unconscious to bellow his last message to the sporting world—a manly message congratulating his victor and wishing him well. I remember that at the finish Mrs. Corbett said casually, "Oh, goody, goody," and "me frien' Art'ur Brisbane" was in tears.

Memory throws its high lights on another episode of that decade. I may not be giving these chronicles in the order of their happening, but it must have been somewhere near this time that I passed a day at Upper Red Hook, New York, with Mr. and Mrs. William Jennings Bryan. Mr. Bryan had come East to press his presidential campaign and Mrs. Bryan had come along to admire him while he did it.

She was a nice woman, simple and sincere, and a devoted wife. What I remember about her most vividly was that she was wearing her first silk petticoat and was quite set up by it. We were all wearing silk petticoats then. They were as ubiquitous as silk stockings are now. Mrs. Bryan's rustled beautifully as she walked, and this delighted her.

Mr. Bryan was a warmly human and friendly man, and

he had a personal magnetism that was never turned off. But in Upper Red Hook at least he made the same type of mistake J. Sloat Fassett made in New York when Fassett took off his coat and addressed an audience in his shirt sleeves.

Mr. Bryan was too informal with those simple New York farmers. He climbed down to their level, and they heard and resented the descent. A certain general store in Upper Red Hook was the pet rendezvous of the farmers of that region. They gathered around the big stove in the center of the store, swapped yarns, and talked politics. Mr. Bryan joined the circle. Enthusiastically but misguidedly, I think, he swapped yarns and talked politics with them as man to man. They liked his talk and they liked him; but they did not like his extreme informality. Possibly they would not have liked Abraham Lincoln's. However that may be, they decided, and a number of them told me so, that this country needed at its head a man with more dignity than Mr. Bryan had. Upper Red Hook voted against him.

CHAPTER IX

"ME FRIEN' ART'UR BRISBANE"

MR. BRISBANE'S arrival in the *World* offices created a sensation on Park Row. He had been a spectacular success as managing editor of the *Evening Sun,* and it had been thought that no human power could lure him from that newspaper. But Mr. Pulitzer had his little ways. He made Arthur Brisbane editor of the *Sunday World,* appointed me assistant Sunday editor, and we worked together in that relation for three years—the most interesting and educative period of my ten years on the *World.*

We had two very small connecting offices high in the gold dome of the *World* building. Later, a very able and attractive young Englishman, Horace Green, joined us as special staff writer and rewrite man; but he was usually out of the office.

Writers were not then as fond of the word "glamorous" as they have since become, but it would have fitted Mr. Brisbane very nicely. He was the young Napoleon of journalism. Though still in his early thirties he had already made a reputation here and in England. He was the wittiest and the most brilliant talker I had listened to up till that time, with the exception of Colonel George Harvey, and he was extraordinarily handsome. He was very tall and perfectly proportioned, and he had a head and face to make a sculptor's fingers reach instinctively for clay. Throughout our three years of close association in those little offices, working fifteen hours and more a day, I never saw in him the slightest suggestion of personal vanity. He had other characteristics, both great and small, which made him, all in all, the most interesting of the thousands of human beings I have known.

I have sometimes wondered why I did not fall in love with him. Most girls in their twenties would have done so, I think. Yet, after all, there were good reasons for my immunity. One of these, of course, was the terrific drive of our work. Another was my own basic and lifelong prejudice against any combination of office work and sentimental dalliance—a prejudice Mr. Brisbane and the other fine men I have worked with obviously shared. I had not, however, escaped some unpleasant experiences in the casual meetings of my days and nights as a reporter. Against the background of my convent life the stares and winks and "passes" I occasionally encountered seemed horribly degrading. There was a period when I was wretched over them—when I felt that they not only smirched me but that, in a way, I might be responsible for them. Possibly something in me drew them out!

I was living through this phase, and was very unhappy over it, when I met Margaret E. Sangster, poet and at that time editor of *Harper's Bazar*. She was already in her sixties and looked them—mature, motherly, very gentle, and very sweet—the type of woman who exhales an actual aura of goodness. Through her I also met a friend of hers who is still living. I will call her Miss Blank. She was about sixty and a lovely Madonna-like creature. She had the same effect Mrs. Sangster gave of carrying a lily in her hand. I had an immense admiration for them both, and I still cherish it.

One day, when they were lunching with me at the old Hotel Astor on lower Broadway, I observed that Mrs. Sangster's usual serenity had been ruffled. She looked disturbed, and even annoyed. This was so unusual that Miss Blank asked the reason for it. Mrs. Sangster explained. She had

had a most unpleasant experience that morning, she said, with a man who had come into her office. He was about her own age, and she had known him pleasantly for several years, but he had suddenly gone amorous.

I looked steadily down at my plate. Her story seemed to me extremely amusing. To the twenties the sixties are very close to the end of life. I could not picture passion against their bleak background. Her friend, however, was immediately sympathetic. She, too, had undergone such a shock, quite recently. They talked it over. I sat silent, but by this time my young heart was singing a roundelay. If those two wonderful women, at their age, were still subjected to these experiences, surely I need not blame myself when such shocks came to me. After that, I didn't. I learned a special technique in meeting and checking them.

There were not so many of them, after all—nothing like the number our heroines of fiction have undergone in the big cities. I was not often annoyed even at night, when I constantly went home from the *World* offices at three and four o'clock in the morning. Naturally I went alone. It never occurred to me or to any one else that I needed escort. I could ride on an elevated train most of the way. I usually lived several blocks from the station, and of course I had to walk that distance.

While I was on West Forty-fourth Street I walked a block from the Forty-second Street station to Broadway, and two blocks up Broadway. Then I had only to walk one rather dark block west on Forty-fourth Street. When I lived at the Windermere I had to make a little trek up Ninth Avenue, and then East. That was dark and rather forbidding. A certain stunning young Irish policeman, who was on that beat and of whom I still cherish grateful memories, took it upon himself to meet me at the foot of the elevated station whenever he could do so, and determinedly escort me to my door. He did this during one of our great New York blizzards. It took us from half past three o'clock in the morning till four to fight our way through the storm and snowdrifts to the Windermere, and my feelings during the interval were mixed. I was immensely grateful to him, but rather humiliated over my need of help.

My one really unpleasant night encounter during that time was a ghastly one, which took place when, like Patience Sparhawk, I was still living "on West Forty-fourth Street." I had come down the steps from the elevated station at about quarter past three in the morning, moving very briskly and obviously going somewhere in a hurry, as was my habit. Before I could move half a dozen feet a cab drove up to the curb and stopped, and the driver leaned down ingratiatingly. He was so close that he could have touched me.

"Cab, Miss?" he whispered. "Get in. It won't cost you anything."

I was startled by this and looked first at him and then at the cab. A man in evening dress sat in it, his face pressed against the glass of the side window, his eyes staring out at me. We occasionally hear some one described as looking as if he had been "buried and dug up again." This man looked exactly as if he had been through such an experience. His head was a death's head. Its color was indescribably horrible—yellow, with an undertone of green. Nothing about him moved—not even his eyes, which were small black balls sunk far back in their sockets. He was precisely like a dead man, staring at me through the glass of his coffin lid.

I made a swift gesture of refusal and horror and hurried past the cab. The driver whipped up his horse and followed, keeping close beside me at the curb.

"Get in, Miss," he reiterated. "It'll be worth while. *Get in!*"

It was a nightmare. The street was dark and deserted. I

would have appealed to any one in that moment, but there was not another human being in sight. I began to run. I put the width of the sidewalk between us, and ran on. The driver kept pace with me till we reached Broadway, while the thing inside stared out at me immovably. Later and ever since, I felt certain that the man in the cab had really been dead, and that the driver had not yet discovered it.

At last the blessed lights of Broadway shone ahead. It was far from the rainbow way it is now, but there was a good showing of arc lamps, paling before the advance of dawn. With a gulp of relief I swung into Broadway. The driver stopped, hesitated, and then continued west along Forty-second Street. Five minutes later I was at my own door, then safely inside, with that door barred against the universe.

During my three years on the *Sunday World* with Mr. Brisbane I made this pilgrimage four times a week at three or four o'clock in the morning. Part of my work was to make up the *Sunday World* in the composing-room. This kept me busy from late afternoon to dawn every Wednesday, Thursday, and Friday night, and on Saturdays till about midnight. Then I had to make way for the special news sections of the Sunday edition. When I began this make-up work the compositors were still setting type by hand, and putting it into the forms a pinch at a time, as it were. One of our men, Fred Muller, could sometimes slide a whole galley of wet type into the form without "pi-ing" any of it, but if he failed most of the column went to pieces. The great composing-room was a busy place on those nights. I had various "make-up" men in front of me, on the other side of the empty forms between us, which it was their job and mine to fill according to the "dummy layouts" I held in my hands. More than a hundred men were laboriously setting type around us, by hand, letter by letter.

Then the linotype machine came in, during those three years, and the work it had taken a hundred men to do could be done on the machines by twenty. Our printers were stunned by the innovation, and all my sympathy was with them. The younger compositors learned to operate the linotype and swung quickly into the methods of the future. The old fellows—the most independent class of workers in the world—fought the change as long as they could. They lost their fight, lost their jobs, and drifted through the country looking for work in the small offices that could not yet afford the expensive machines. In the meantime, we were passing through a difficult transition period in the *World's* composing-room. Rebellion and nervous strain were all around me. The men who had consented to operate the machines sympathized with their associates, and showed it in various ways—usually by making two or three new mistakes while ostensibly correcting one.

I stood over the forms from late afternoon till almost dawn. Then I went home, fell into bed exhausted, and was back at the office by eleven the next morning to repeat the record.

Just once in those three years I turned my back on duty for a few hours. One Thursday afternoon I coolly handed the dummy pages to Fred Muller, and went uptown to Carnegie Hall to hear Teresa Carreno's first New York piano recital after her years of absence in South America. Muller told inquiring executives that I had a headache and was taking a few hours off. I had never had a headache in my life and I have not had one yet; but the explanation was as good as any other.

I always needed music stimulation. I had promised my mother to get in an hour a day of piano practice, whatever happened. I was keeping the promise, but with some difficulty. The only hour I could be sure of was the one immediately following my return home at night. So far as I was concerned that was quite all right. The music and the change of position always rested me. But I had a dark suspicion that my neighbors might not share my enthusiasm over music toward dawn. There was only one neighbor in the next house, in a room on the other side of the wall between us, who could be seriously disturbed. I was prepared to stop instantly if any one pounded on that wall.

No one pounded, but after two years of this night practice I received the report of my neighbor. She was an old lady who had just died. Obeying one of her last requests, her nurse came to me to thank me for that music. For many years the old lady had been a victim of insomnia. My one-hour nightly recitals had been a welcome break in the monotony of lying awake staring into darkness. She had looked forward to them and enjoyed them. I wish I had known it then!

Mr. Brisbane's hours were also erratic. Sometimes he would be at his desk all day and all night; sometimes he would not appear for two or three days if he happened to be writing at home or investigating uptown some subject he planned to write about. He had not yet begun his famous editorials. Those came after Mr. Hearst had swung him over to the *Journal*. But he wrote a great many special articles, often a full page in length: and whatever subjects he chose he put into them everything he happened to be reading or thinking about at the time.

His articles always created a sensation. I remember a page he wrote about Chicago which split that great city wide open. He read everything that seemed interesting to him, and he remembered and quoted everything he read. I never knew another such memory as his. In dictating to his secretary he would tell her to quote so many paragraphs from such and such a book, on about such and such a page. He was almost invariably right in these casual directions—or so nearly right that she could find the extracts he wanted by turning a page or two.

This was where my education came in. I, too, had been a reader all my life. I was still reading everything worth while I could get hold of, in every spare minute I had. I humbly followed Mr. Brisbane's lead. My convent education had been good as far as it had gone. It was a small, firm ground-work to build on. My task now was self-education. I read everything Mr. Brisbane read or advised. He was interested and talked to me a great deal when we had time. He also tried out a number of his pet theories on me. Incidentally he gave me a post-graduate course in human nature. He was full of extraordinary characteristics and contradictions. When he was especially interested in anything he gave him-self up to it completely. It amused him, I remember, to start in the *Sunday World* a Page for Men. He wrote most of it himself, and during the first weeks it appeared he gave his entire time to it. He hardly seemed to remember that there was a *Sunday World*. It was worth all his time, however, for it was an amazing achievement—the forerunner of his famous editorials.

On those occasions when I departed from the office at four in the morning, leaving him still there, I was sure to find my desk covered with little notes from him when I got back the next morning—scraps without envelops, each pinned separately to the roll-top desk, and looking like a large flock of white butterflies that had just lighted. He jotted down on single sheets any instructions or suggestions that occurred to him, one at a time and as fast as he thought of them—and he expected to have every one of them attended to the minute I opened it. I never heard him utter an oath, and in the entire three years we worked together there was never the slightest shadow of unpleasantness between us.

His sympathies were intense, and easily stirred. He would help any one in trouble. But he was capable of an icy and lasting anger against individuals who failed him, and he had a personal "black list" that grew to startling proportions. When he had lost faith in a man he didn't want him to come around at all. This was sometimes embarrassing, when I had not lost faith in that man—but Mr. Brisbane's instructions were always followed.

His extraordinary sympathy for human suffering made him pick up some strange gauntlets. He developed a deep interest in Maria Barberi, during her first trial for murder. She was convicted, and he wrote an article that undoubtedly won her second trial and her ultimate acquittal. She knew this and so did every one else. The day she was acquitted she came directly from the court-room to the *World* offices to thank him, followed by a pageant of enthusiastic Italians. Mr. Brisbane had a telephone message that the procession was on its way, and he fled before it like a startled hare. He buried himself up in the obituary department, leaving me to entertain the delegation and receive on a deeply reluctant cheek the tears and moist kisses Maria Barberi had meant for him.

In manner Mr. Brisbane often seemed very cold and detached, but I have never known anything more beautiful than his devotion to his brother Fowler, and to his sister Mrs. Thursby. (He was unmarried at that time.) Fowler, who was an invalid, spent a good deal of time in our offices, basking in the warmth of his brother's presence which seemed an elixir of life to him. He had several acute attacks of illness there, and Arthur brooded over him with an amazing tenderness. I also knew Mrs. Thursby quite well.

Both she and Fowler plainly considered their brother a super-man, and they had good grounds for the belief.

It was during this time that one of Mr. Brisbane's intimates told me of Arthur's devotion to his father. I had already realized how deeply he cherished the memory of the elder Brisbane, who had been a distinguished socialist and a member of the noted Brook Farm Colony of Massachusetts. It was from him that Arthur received and developed throughout his life his interest in and understanding of the manual laborers of the world, and the power of writing to them and for them as he did. He was, he felt, carrying on his father's work, and doing it in the way his father would have approved.

The friend added that when the elder Brisbane died Arthur was only eighteen or twenty years old. He would not allow hired hands to perform the last services for the old philosopher's body. Alone, he himself prepared it for the grave; alone he carried his dead father downstairs and laid him in his coffin.

Looking at him as he raced into and out of the offices with his superhuman energy, his immense vitality, his seeming coldness and remoteness, his air of physical and mental aloofness from all except those nearest and dearest to him, it was hard to picture Arthur Brisbane as saving the life of a poor emigrant girl out of sheer pity for her; as fainting at Carlyle Harris' execution; as weeping over the downfall of his friend and worshiper, John L. Sullivan. He seemed by turns ice and fire. He could be implacable, and he could be understanding to the core of his soul. He had hours of irresistible charm and gaiety, and hours of black depression.

Long after our three years of professional association had ended and he was with Mr. Hearst's forces, I continued to meet him frequently. I lunched with him and his sister, Mrs. Thursby, visited their home at Hempstead, Long Island, and frequently met Mr. Brisbane at the week-end parties of Colonel and Mrs. George Harvey at Jorjalma. It was very interesting to see the changes in him as time passed, and as his fame and income grew. Arthur Brisbane was becoming a very rich man.

In the old days he had been more or less indifferent to money. It had been merely a convenience to provide what he and his dependents needed for safety and comfort. His income was large and he spent it liberally. He would gamble on anything and everything, and at the drop of the hat. Now, he was accumulating—buying New York land right and left, building up a fortune. Mr. Hearst, always generous to his employees, advised and helped in this accumulation. When Mr. Brisbane bought the deserted village of Allaire, in New Jersey, and planned his country home there, he offered me ten acres of land if I would build a summer cottage on it. If I chose to build the cottage of field-stones, he said, he would contribute the stones—of which his land had all too many. He wanted to establish a summer colony, and was making the same offer to other friends. Allaire seemed to me a bit too far from New York for daily commuting, and I could not follow up the opportunity.

Increasing prosperity did not atrophy Mr. Brisbane's sympathies. They remained as active as they had been in his youth, as he proved when he rushed to the defense of Mary Baker Eddy, in her eighties. A small but powerful group of her followers held her incompetent, and was trying to get control of her business affairs and those of her church. Mr. Brisbane was at once interested in the case and decided to look into it. He went to Boston to meet and to talk to Mrs. Eddy. He was then a very big man in the American newspaper world—probably the biggest. Mrs. Eddy had never even heard of him. She accepted him as an ordinary reporter and throughout their interview she addressed him firmly and repeatedly as "Young man." However, she evidently liked him, and realized that she could trust him. She talked to him very frankly, giving him her side of the controversy and incidentally convincing him that she was wholly capable of handling her own affairs and those of her church. He subsequently downed her opponents so promptly and thoroughly that they were never heard from again.

As it happened, Mr. Brisbane came to the Harveys' country place for the week-end following his visit to Mrs. Eddy. I was a fellow guest there, and he told me in detail his experience with her. At the end of their interview, he said, she suddenly sat back and looked at him.

"Young man," she told him very impressively, "I am going to do something for you that I have not done for any one for years. I have made a rule not to do it. I have refused fortunes to do it. But to-day I am going to give you a treatment."

Mr. Brisbane took the treatment, and he took it with the utmost respect. As he described it I realized that he had been deeply impressed by it. My own feeling for Christian Science is merely the respect I hold for the honest convictions of others. I showed my surprise at his obvious satisfaction over that treatment.

"It did impress me," he admitted slowly, "and Mrs. Eddy herself impressed me still more. She's really an amazing woman!"

The episode had an aftermath. Mr. Brisbane and I drove back to New York Monday morning with Colonel Harvey. It was a seventy-mile run and Colonel Harvey, who liked fast driving, had instructed his chauffeur to make good time. The Colonel seemed to have a special control over the roads between New York and Jorjalma, which he traveled so often. Policemen, springing forward with lifted hands to stop the racing car, would recognize its owner, turn the gesture into a salute, and say with a forgiving grin, "On your way, Colonel!"

We were traveling at about fifty miles an hour—very high speed for those days—and Mr. Brisbane did not like it. He had a strong prejudice against fast automobile driving. Colonel Harvey was sitting in the front seat to stimulate his chauffeur. Mr. Brisbane and I sat together in the tonneau.

"Do you see that tree over there?" Mr. Brisbane asked me, indicating a tall pine in a field we were whizzing toward. "If a tire bursts at this speed, you and I will be under that tree in another second with our necks broken!"

I saw that he was really disturbed.

"What are you afraid of?" I asked cheerfully. "Haven't you just had a treatment from Mrs. Eddy? Don't you realize that you're immune from danger?"

He surprised me again.

"Why, that's so," he said thoughtfully. "That's so!"

The reminder evidently comforted him, and he rewarded me by being a very amusing companion during the rest of the journey. He was one of the five best talkers among the men I have known. The others were Colonel Harvey, Poultney Bigelow, John à Becket, and Frederick Duneka. The best woman talker I have known is my friend Josephine Daskam Bacon—to whose verbal flow I have listened with delight for thirty years. Frances Hodgson Burnett comes next, with Mrs. Edward Ringwood Hewitt and Doctor Anna Howard Shaw as close "runners up."

But I am far ahead of my story. At the time I began to write of him here Arthur Brisbane was still the Sunday editor of the *World*. I must add one more reminiscence of those days before I quote his later letters. Mr. Brisbane and I were, as I have said, high in the *World's* dome. The *World* building was still one of the show places tourists felt impelled to visit when they came to New York. The Spanish

Duke of Veragua was one of these visitors. American newspapers had discovered that the Duke was a lineal descendant of our benefactor, Christopher Columbus. They published columns about the Duke and he was received everywhere with considerable éclat. Arthur Brisbane met him at a New York dinner and invited him to come to the *World* offices the next morning to see the building and the view. Both were sufficiently eye-filling, and the Duke was impressed. He was also a great gentleman, wholly without humor, but gracious and agreeable.

Mr. Brisbane and I showed him around, and I brought out the Spanish I had inherited from my grandmother. We were standing on one of the dome balconies, looking down at the midgets on the street twenty-two stories below us, when Mr. Brisbane was suddenly moved to give the Spaniard an idea of the speed with which our American journals print the news.

"If you should regrettably fall from this balcony to the street," he put it, "I think we could get out an extra edition of the *Evening World* announcing the deplorable event just about the time you struck the sidewalk!"

The Duke took a full minute to absorb this theory. When he had done so he was like Queen Victoria on another memorable occasion—"not amused"!

I am quoting one of Mr. Brisbane's later notes to show how closely he followed the careers of his old friends and how natural it was for him to send them a line of encouragement. This note concerns a short story of mine, "Bart Kennedy, Genius," which had just been published in *Scribner's Magazine*.

April 10, 1908

MY DEAR MISS JORDAN,

You may be interested to know that Mr. Von Utassy, who runs the *Cosmopolitan*—in my opinion he is the best magazine man in the country—tells me that your short story about the greenhorn who finally invented the hatpin is the best short story —what he calls "the best seller"—that has been published in any magazine for a couple of years. Sometimes it is good to get an outside, unbiased opinion of our own work, and so I send you this "trader."

Yours sincerely,
A. BRISBANE

The Spanish-American War developed while I was still with the *World,* and I passed that summer on Governor's Island, in New York Harbor, with Mrs. Benjamin Gilman, the wife of Captain Gilman of the Thirteenth U. S. Infantry. I could commute to and from the city on the Island ferry, and the new experience was deeply moving.

The Thirteenth Infantry Regiment was one of the worst sufferers in the battle of San Juan Hill. Very few of its officers survived. Captain Gilman got home on the hospital ship *Relief* and I went down the Harbor with Mrs. Gilman to meet him. He lived only a week or two and, as the casualty lists came in, the Island quarters of officers and enlisted men alike were places of tragedy and mourning.

Mrs. Gilman collapsed after her husband's death, and I had to attend to the details of the funeral. I knew nothing about military funerals then, but I learned all about them that summer. My first aide in connection with Captain Gilman's funeral was a singularly handsome young lieutenant with a tragic history. Several years before the war an intoxicated soldier had stumbled into the lieutenant's quarters one night, and the lieutenant had awakened and shot him. The young officer was held blameless. The man had no right in his quarters at three in the morning, and was apparently burglarizing. He was really on a drunken quest for more whiskey. But the lieutenant had smashed nervously after the shooting, and had carried into his recovery a nervous obsession that the dead man was always with him. He heard his victim dogging his footsteps by day, felt him crawling into his bed at night. He was normal in all other respects, a fine officer and a brilliant one. He had gone to Cuba hoping to be killed. He had repeatedly flung himself in the path of death. But he had survived, while his friends died around him. Now, in black despair, he was back on Governor's Island, helping to bury them.

He was a somber figure of that summer, and the Colonel of the Regiment was another. The Colonel had been terribly wounded during the charge up San Juan Hill and had lain on the battle-field all night before he was discovered. He, too, had carried an obsession into his convalescence. The moment darkness fell he heard the voices of dying men around him, calling for water or begging for death. He could not remain in darkness. When, after his return, he came over in the hot summer evenings to talk to us, we had to hang out little lanterns on our dark veranda, that he might see the points of light. The Thirteenth Infantry, which had started up San Juan something like a thousand strong, was reduced to about eighteen men who alone answered the first roll-call after the battle. Not all the others were dead. They were wounded, or they were in field hospitals with yellow fever or dysentery. Lieutenant William Shipp, the husband of my life-long friend, Margaret Busbee Shipp, was among those killed in that battle. Margaret, by the way, was one of the four most charming women I have known. The others were Mrs. Otis Skinner, Mrs. William D. Barbour, and the Marchioness Lagergren.

Gilbert Parker, not "Sir" Gilbert then, visited New York while he was basking in the warmth of his first success, *Pierre and His People*. Mr. Parker had just returned from the Canadian wilderness where he had undergone thrilling hardships he loved to describe. He and John à Becket and I struck up a lofty friendship. Mr. Parker liked to sit before my fire and thrill Jack and me with tales of the nights when he lay on Canadian snows in a sleeping bag in a temperature of forty or fifty degrees below zero. Then he would go out into my hall, get into huge galoshes and thick overcoat and ear-muffs, and plunge into the perils of a New York winter night when the temperature was fifteen or twenty degrees above freezing point.

I never understood those ear-muffs and galoshes, and Mr. Parker never explained them.

CHAPTER X

PEAKS OF FRIENDSHIP

JOHN À BECKET, one of the best friends of my newspaper days, had returned from London about this time
and joined the staff of the *Sunday World*. He had a roman-
tic history with a tragic finish, and there was an element
of tragedy all along his human way.

His original plan in life had been to enter the Catholic
priesthood. He had almost completed the entire course of
training for the greatest of all Catholic Orders—the Jesuits
—and was about to take his vows when he realized his basic
unfitness for the vocation. I am sure his preceptors and
other associates must have discovered it long before he did,
and that they left it to him to realize the truth in time. He
was the gayest, the most debonair, and one of the most
delightful of men; but he had in him none of the material
of which Jesuits are made except his fine classical education
and his lasting devotion to his faith.

When he came out into the world after his long years
of study he was as unfit as a baby to meet the problems and
the buffetings of normal life. As it happened, one of his first
friendships was with S. S. Carvalho, then, I think, managing
editor of the *Evening World*. Mr. Carvalho was at once
interested in the brilliant young man, and gave him a situation as editorial writer on the *Evening World,* at forty
dollars a week. It was, in one way, an ideal position for the
novice, but it ruined him. He reported for duty in the *World*
offices between nine and ten o'clock in the morning. He wrote
one or two short, good editorials, and at one o'clock he went

blithely to his luncheon, his day's work done. His salary seemed a large one to him, for he had never handled money and had no sense of its value. Moreover, his tastes were simple. He lived comfortably and buoyantly and made friends on every side. He was convinced that this was the individual's struggle for existence, of which he had heard so much, and that he was earning his living by the sweat of his brow.

His work was so good that after a year or so Mr. Carvalho sent him to London as assistant to Tracy Greaves, then London Correspondent of the *World*. This assignment, so wise and well-meant from Mr. Carvalho's viewpoint, destroyed John à Becket's last chance of being a real worker. His salary was increased, his work was largely of the social nature for which he had a special flair, his hours on duty were what he chose to make them. He was more than ever convinced that he had only to blossom and exist.

After two years in London he was recalled to New York by Mr. Carvalho, who was convinced, with considerable reason, that he was too easeful in his experience abroad. John à Becket came to the *Sunday World* as a "space writer," with no regular salary, and to be paid only for what he wrote on order.

To evolve ideas for "specials," to suggest them to the editors, to go forth and get the facts he needed and write them up in vivid style—all this was wholly out of his line: but it was what he had to do to keep his job. If he had been forced to do it when he first emerged from the Jesuit cloisters he might have made a success of it, though he was a born play-boy. But several years of ease and affluence had made the real fight for existence intolerable to him and even impossible. He made a failure from the start, though Mr. Brisbane and I did our best for him. For the rest of his life he lived from hand to mouth, writing only when he was in desperate need of money, idling as long as that money lasted, cherishing a little grudge against life, but carrying it philosophically; always gay, always outwardly cheerful, always the most amusing of companions.

Up till the time of his death, thirty years later, he was my best man friend. During the first year of our acquaintance I had assured him I would be the mother he needed so sorely. He was much older than I but he accepted the relation, and called me "Mother" to his last day. He always addressed my mother as "Grandma," and my "adopted sisters" Miss Prescott and Miss Cutler, of whom I shall write more later, as "Aunt Harriet" and "Aunt Martha." He became knight errant to the family. Having little else to do he was ready for escort duty anywhere at any time.

He carried on my personal education from the point where Arthur Brisbane had laid it down. He insisted that I should write more for the magazines, and he read my outpourings with ruthless eyes and brain. Most of what I know about writing he and Mr. Brisbane built on the foundation Sister Ethelbert had laid. He dined with me several nights a week and put in much time coaching me on various subjects. He held me sternly to my religious duties, if my work threatened to make me neglect them. He called for me every Sunday morning to escort me to early Mass, no matter how late I had worked the night before.

I remember that one Easter morning toward the end of March he arrived in a howling blizzard. But it was Easter and he had mysteriously acquired a spectacular new suit of very light gray, brilliant new tan shoes, a blue tie and a pearl-colored hat. Always a child at heart, and wishing to dazzle me with this splendor, he had not put on an overcoat. I was then living on Stuyvesant Square, and I had secured the privilege for us both of attending Mass at a little convent chapel on East Fifteenth Street. It was only a few blocks from my home and no cabs were available, so we plowed there through the snowdrifts and the storm. By the time we reached the convent Jack's new finery was so soaked and bedraggled and his expression so utterly woebegone that after one horrified glance at him I dared not look again. I buried my face in my hands and resolutely kept it there. That morning I must have received credit from the Sisters around me for a devotion I certainly was not feeling at the time.

Jack was deeply interested in music and would have kept me at the piano as rigorously as my mother had done if I had allowed it. Together, for many years, we went to all the New York concerts of the Philharmonic and the Boston Symphony orchestras. He liked to feel, and he certainly said a hundred times in the course of those years, that our friendship was like that of Madame Récamier and Chateaubriand. He frequently quoted the story that Madame Récamier's neighbors could set their watches by Chateaubriand's punctual arrival at her home at four o'clock every afternoon. I am sure he regretted that my professional and social engagements prevented any such record for him.

He was occasionally critical about these other engagements and especially about the frequent presence of another bachelor friend, Charles A. Conant, the economist, on the family hearthstone. Charles Conant was in every way the opposite of John à Becket—very successful, very serious, author of many solid and solidly written books on finance, expert adviser on finance to his own and foreign governments. The gold dollar of the Philippines was called a "Conant" in honor of him, as he had established the Philippine currency system. He wore a "Conant" on his watch chain, and rather expected me to festoon myself with the pretty coins. He had absolutely no sense of humor. He and

John à Becket disliked each other intensely, and each spent considerable time pointing out to me indirectly how little there was in the other. Both came down through the years with me, two of the best friends a woman ever had, till the hours of their tragic deaths.

Charles Conant's lack of humor was conspicuously illustrated at a Sunday evening tête-à-tête dinner I once had with him. That morning I had run across one of his articles in the *Atlantic Monthly*. I read it casually and discovered to my surprise and chagrin that it was so technical I was not clearly following it. I read it a second time, slowly and deliberately, and made its contents mine, knowing it would please Charles to have me praise it intelligently. However, a less worthy impulse came upon me that evening. We were dining at Delmonico's. The food was good, but the atmosphere was rather heavy. So was Charles. Never sprightly, he had a bad cold that night and didn't care who knew it. In his quiet way he held a low opinion of the intellect of women and of the nature of their knowledge of economic and world affairs. In our conversations, extending over so many years, he constantly instructed me when I was discoursing from the conversational tower of pure reason. This had always annoyed me. That night I suddenly took revenge.

"Charles," I began, when it had become clear to me that the occasion needed a lighter touch, "I've been thinking a lot to-day about the economic conditions in the Philippine Islands."

Charles looked worried.

"Yes?" he murmured uncertainly.

"I'm only a poor weak woman," I continued, "and you haven't had more than a quarter of a century to work on my brain, so it's not very well developed yet. But don't you think the real situation over there is—" and I handed him a brisk synopsis, in my own words, of his premises in the *Atlantic* article.

Charles looked startled.

"Why—yes—it is," he admitted, blinking at me.

"All right," I went on. "Of course, I don't know anything about it, but isn't it possible that such conditions might lead to—"

I reeled off the gist of the second part of his article, while Charles listened in growing discomfort.

"Is that all nonsense?" I asked cheerfully, "or do you agree that there may be the germ of an idea in it?"

"Why—yes," Charles murmured faintly. "I—I do agree."

"Then," I said, "if that's so, why isn't the solution—" And I brought forth the conclusions and suggestions in his article.

"Am I really thinking, Charles?" I ended anxiously. "Or do I just think I'm thinking?"

"You're really quite right," Charles brought out slowly. His position was difficult, but he rose to it gamely. "At least, I agree. As—as a matter of fact, I said very much the same thing in an article I've recently written."

"Yes," I told him happily. "I read it this morning."

I have rarely seen a man cheer up so suddenly.

Many years later I had a final and very different conversation with Charles Conant. He had been in Cuba on some government business, and telephoned me one morning that he was just off the steamer and had come up to New York to consult his physician. This was just before America's entrance into the World War, and it happened that I was giving a dinner at the Colony Club that night in honor of the Baroness de Seidlitz of St. Petersburg, friend of and lady-in-waiting to the Czarina. The Baroness had recently landed in New York and had brought among others a letter of introduction to me from Maurice Francis Egan, then

American Minister to Denmark. I mentally rearranged the table, added Charles to the list of dinner guests, and postponed any questions about his health till we met that evening.

He arrived promptly at five minutes to eight, immaculately dressed as usual, looking very pale, but otherwise cheerful and normal. I seated him opposite me at the table with the Baroness at his right, and he devoted himself to her and to his other neighbors. He had a strong sense of social obligation and could always be counted on to carry his full share of dinner conversation. I remember thinking as I looked across at him that he was doing especially well that night. The Baroness was an attractive woman of the world, and Charles Conant was a gallant man who knew his Europe well.

I, too, was interested in the Baroness. She had promptly confided to me that she had come to America on a secret mission for the Czarina, and she had thrown in the secret for good measure. Briefly, the mission was to see our American Secretary of State, then Robert Lansing, and ask him to suggest an armistice to the Central Powers. America, still neutral, was to throw her full weight behind the proposition, and the Empress guaranteed that Russia would immediately swing into line with her—which would inevitably end the war. It was well known that the Czarina's opinion had great weight with her weak husband, but her strong pro-German sympathies were not yet fully realized here.

Through my friend Mary Harrison McKee I had succeeded in getting an appointment for the lady with America's Secretary of State, and I was seeing myself as at least a pawn in world affairs. The Baroness had brought over with her, as a secretary, a singularly handsome and charming young Norwegian of fine family, who sat at my right at dinner. He was gay and witty and I was delighted with

John à Becket
From the painting by Edward Quinn

Charles A. Conant
From a photograph

Henry James
From a photograph

Arthur Brisbane
at thirty-five

him. He sailed for Russia a few weeks later, and, the Baroness told me long afterward, was never heard of again.

After America had entered the war the real sympathies of the Czarina were realized in this country, and her friend the Baroness de Seidlitz was regarded with caution. Her credentials were carefully gone into by our government, but she convinced the investigators that she was all she claimed to be and that she had acted in good faith. She herself had been born in Vienna, of a Polish father and a Hungarian mother, had been educated in France, and had married a Russian nobleman and become a striking figure in Russian court circles. She seemed strongly pro-Russian from start to finish. She passionately assured me that, of the many lands and peoples she had intimately known, Russia was beyond all question the most delightful, and sophisticated Russians were the finest human types. She had a long talk with Mr. Lansing, but she afterwards admitted to me that he had not taken the Czarina's proposition very seriously. Certainly nothing came of it.

My other dinner guests left the club-house a little after eleven o'clock, but Charles Conant waited to escort me home. We sat down in a corner of the club lounge for a brief chat, and I asked at once what his doctor had said that morning.

"He gave me quite a shock," Charles told me gravely. "He says I have a cancer of the stomach and that I can't live more than six months!"

When I could get my breath I gasped out that he must see other specialists—several of them, at once.

"Oh, I've done that," Charles said. "I've put in the day being overhauled by half a dozen of them. They all agree."

We talked a long time. When we parted an hour later, at the door of my home in Gramercy Park, I felt that I had not said enough of what was in my heart. I went to my desk and wrote Charles a long letter which I mailed before I went to bed. I don't remember what I said, but I shall always remember the first sentence of Charles's reply to that midnight outpouring. He began,

"It is worth being ill to get that letter from you this morning!"

He returned to his work in Cuba, and died there within six months, "in harness" as he wished to die.

The passing of John à Becket was equally tragic in a different way. He was found dead in bed one morning from asphyxiation caused by a defective gas stove in his room. It was not a case of suicide and was not so considered for an instant, even by the police. Every condition proved it an accident. His deep religious conviction in itself would have forbidden suicide. His door was unlocked, his windows were open. He still loved and enjoyed life, and he had come into a little money and was unusually prosperous at the time. He had passed the previous evening with his close friend Joseph E. Willard, afterwards American Ambassador to Spain, and had been in high spirits.

As it happened, the day of his death was an unusually gay and care-free one for me. I had given the morning to my little god-daughter, Deborah Bacon, because it was her birthday. She and her mother, Josephine Daskam Bacon, and her older sister and I had spent several hours in the Bronx Zoo, and had then lunched at Delmonico's. I remember the merry laughter with which our friend Mrs. Pearce Bailey heard my selection of the restaurant; but I saw no reason why the children's mother and I should not have a really good luncheon while the infants consumed the simpler food suited to their tender years. Their luncheon ended with ice-cream and a birthday cake with five candles on it, which Deborah preferred to light herself. She had just lit her candles—a merry game—and was intrepidly

attacking the job of cutting the cake, and making a mess
of it to a running accompaniment of laughter and advice,
when a big clock near us struck one.

I reached my downtown desk at half past two, to find
that half a dozen imperative messages had come to me
during the morning from the little Italian hotel where John
à Becket had lived. Something serious had happened. I was
to go there at once. I went. The manager had found him
dead about ten o'clock that morning, while I was wrestling
with Deborah's questions at the Zoo. It was now after three.
A number of Jack's other friends were already at the hotel
when I got there. They were about to send him to an "undertaking parlor."

As my apartment was the nearest approach to a home
that Jack had ever known, I had him sent there and went
back, stunned and dazed, to get ready for him. Nothing
happened until after midnight. Then, about half past twelve,
three men appeared carrying tall candlesticks, candles, a long
wicker basket which they placed at my feet, and the coffin
and its supports. When these latter had been put into
position I said to the men,

"You may bring Mr. à Becket upstairs now."

They stared.

"There he is," one of the men said, and pointed to the
wicker basket.

We had been stepping over and around it as we came
and went. It was my first and last experience with that form
of receptacle for the dead. When my friend had been placed
in the coffin the men left. There was nothing for me to do
now but to light the candles at his head and feet. . . . I was
alone—I had insisted that my family should leave me alone—
and I was in a nightmare. All this simply could not be
happening. I would soon wake up. . . .

As I lit the last candle a tall clock in the corner of

the room struck one. The sound, and the shock of the sharp contrast it suggested, brought me out of my nightmare and back into realization. So had that clock up at Delmonico's struck, exactly twelve hours before, while Deborah was cutting her birthday cake. I saw first the picture of that happy little group, then the shadowy room I was in, with the light of the flickering candles falling on my friend's dead face. I knew what had happened. . . .

John à Becket's funeral was held the day before Christmas. After the Requiem Mass at St. Francis Xavier's Church in New York, we took him out to a great Catholic cemetery on Long Island, and left him there in the midst of a blizzard equal to the one he and I had struggled to church through on that Easter morning so long ago. He was extremely comfort-loving. As I turned away I could almost hear his voice crying out to me,

"Oh, Mother, *don't* leave me in this desolate spot!"

When I reached home Martha and Harriet had decorated the apartment with holly and mistletoe and exuberant red bows. They felt that a change of atmosphere and mood was needed. My desk was piled high with the mail I had not had time to open for three days. It was made up of hundreds of cards, from friends all over the world, wishing me a Merry Christmas.

CHAPTER XI

ANNIE PECK AND MRS. AYER

TWO of the most important women on the *World* during my final years there were Harriet Hubbard Ayer and Jeanette Gilder. Mrs. Ayer was our beauty specialist, and there could not have been a better one. Miss Gilder, the sister of Richard Watson Gilder, poet and editor, was herself the editor of the *Critic,* then New York's leading literary monthly. She came to the *World* offices two or three days a week to write specials and do book reviewing. Both women were thirty years older than I was, but they were wonderfully kind to me and I was devoted to them.

Mrs. Ayer was a tragic figure. She had been a Chicago society woman, rich, popular, magnetic, and really beautiful in her day. Mr. Ayer lost his money and then disappeared, while Mrs. Ayer went into business and retrieved the family fortunes by putting on the American market lotions, creams, and other beauty aids. Something of her character and quality are shown by her attitude toward the husband who deserted her. She had never criticized him. When he crept back to her in the days of her business prosperity—weak, broken, and a dying man—she took him in and had him nursed and cared for till the end.

A long time after that she was legally committed to an asylum where she remained for several years. When she was finally dismissed and declared sane she was penniless. She secured a job on the *World,* worked there day and night like the rest of us, and was one of the gayest and most gallant spirits on the staff. At first she was in the back-breaking and heart-aching situation of the "space-writer," whose published work does not bring in a large income. Later, of course, all that was changed. Mr. Pulitzer recognized her ability and saw to it that she was properly paid. But in the beginning she usually wrote seven or eight columns a week, representing fifty or sixty dollars earned, and later showed me her "string" of published material, representing less than twenty-five dollars to be paid her on Saturday. I could offer only moral support. She was working on the daily edition, and I was still on the *Sunday World*.

What I write of her here is her story as she told it to me, seated by my library fire one night after she had dined with me. I have never heard the other side of that story, if there is one. But I believed her then implicitly, and I still believe her.

She brought with her some of the legal papers in her case: THE STATE OF NEW YORK *vs*. HARRIET HUBBARD AYER, lunatic.

I was still in my twenties, and I remember the cold chill that slithered along my back as I read that heading and then looked at the brave, poised woman before me. She was one of the sanest human beings I have ever known. Her humor was delicious, her courage heart-lifting, and her mental balance seemed perfect. I knew her for years, and never changed my opinion on those points.

Her conviction, as she explained it that night, was that she had been put away by a small group of men who were scheming for control of her business affairs. After she was in the asylum her friends were told that she was in a mental state which grew worse with the arrival of visitors. She described in detail her first night at the institution.

She had been taken to it on the pretext that she was going for a drive, and she had no idea where she was till the doors clanged shut after her and she was put in charge of a robust woman attendant. The woman took her to a private room, silently helped her to undress, and put her to bed. She had refused to answer Mrs. Ayer's questions and her first remark, other than casual orders about the undressing, was made after her patient was between the sheets.

"Now, you," she said briskly, "bring your hands out from under those bedclothes and leave them on the bedspread where I can see them. And don't try any tricks with me, for I know them all. Sleep, if you can. It's the best thing you can do."

She then turned off all the lights in the room except that of a reading lamp, sat down beside the bed with a book and a box of pecans, and read and ate pecans till dawn.

The end of the story was cheering and very dramatic. Mrs. Ayer's friends obeyed orders and remained away from the institution, believing that this was best for her. No letters she wrote were mailed, no letters sent her were received by her. But she made new friends in the asylum, and one of these was a New York man who periodically and voluntarily came there for the treatment of inebriety. He was quite sane between drinking bouts, and he roamed around the grounds of the sanitarium as he chose, and left it when he was ready to go. Mrs. Ayer was never allowed in the grounds except with an attendant, and even then she was not permitted to talk much with other patients. The New York patient, almost ready to leave after one of his brief visits, stopped near her one day, stood beside a flower bed with his back to her, and began to hum a French song while he bent over the flowers as if examining them in detail.

"I am very sorry for you," he sang in French. "If there's

any way I can help you when I get out, I will do it. If you have any friends outside who will help, too, write their names and addresses for me and drop the paper into the big clock in the assembly room. Don't write anything but names and addresses. I will understand."

Mrs. Ayer, who spoke and understood French as well as she did English, listened with a pounding heart and singing nerves, but gave no sign that she had heard him. Later that day she managed to drop her list under the weights of the eight-day clock. Her new friend found it there and kept his promise. He looked up her friends at once. An immediate investigation was started, and Harriet Hubbard Ayer was examined and declared sane.

"I should be in that asylum still if it hadn't been for that man," she ended simply.

Her interests were in other hands. She had no money to go to law about them, and no wish to do so. She had had enough of law. She joined the organization known as the Daughters of the Eastern Star and clung to it for years as to a life-line.

"They will never let me be put away again," she told me.

They never did. Harriet Hubbard Ayer worked to the end of her life and died early in the nineteen hundreds after a few days' illness of pneumonia. Jeanette Gilder went to her home a few hours after her death and was so struck by the beauty of that dead face that she sent Ernest Haskell, the artist, to make a sketch of it for the *Critic*. It proved afresh, each time one looked at it, that death had given back to Harriet Hubbard Ayer the great beauty of her youth— and something more.

One of the most amusing episodes of my years on the *World* was connected with Annie Peck, the mountain

climber. I still like to think of that when I am especially
low in my mind.

Annie Peck was then America's most distinguished mountain climber, and in her day she had scaled most of the
difficult mountain peaks of this earth. She left our troubled
world only a few years ago, and I am sure she died gallantly. She was then old and ill, and her work was done.
But she was a born fighter, and in her long life she had
fought more than mountain peaks and glaciers and crevasses
and sudden avalanches. Probably she would have liked to
keep on fighting, in an existence that now offers so many
opportunities to valiant souls like hers. She was a philosopher,
however, as well as a climber of mountains, and she was
deeply interested in the mysterious peaks of the world beyond this. To her, I am sure, death was merely another
adventure—her greatest and her last. She had faced it
too often to fear it. Her one regret on that final journey
would be, I suspect, that she could never return to tell her
friends about it.

My most vivid memories of Miss Peck date back to the
year she climbed Mount Popocatepetl in Mexico. She was
not a business woman. Money meant nothing to her except
as a means to the end of her climbing expeditions. Very
literally she lived for climbing, and she reached her peaks
of life only when she reached the tops of the mountains
she was scaling. Her full moments were those when the
climber pits skill and experience and even life itself against
nature's greatest hazards, and wins out.

Mountain climbing is an expensive pastime, especially
the sort of mountain climbing Annie Peck did, which took
her to the ends of the earth and to the dim heights of
Himalayan peaks, including the Jonsong and the Queen Mary
peaks of the Karakorum Range, twenty-four thousand feet

above the sea. When she could do so, she had her climbs financed by others, though she never asked more than the actual expenses of her expeditions. Her rewards were the fight to reach the top, and the thrill of that fight.

When it occurred to her to climb Popocatepetl, the idea also struck her that she would ask the *Sunday World* to finance the adventure. Popocatepetl is an uneasy volcano, without any elements of repose. At that time it had been constantly erupting streams of fire and lava, and the habit had discouraged climbers. No woman had yet reached the top. Miss Peck was sure she could do so, and that she could write an absorbing account of the achievement.

Arthur Brisbane was still the editor of the *Sunday World* and I was still his admiring assistant. Nelson Hersh was also on the editorial staff, and Miss Peck put her project before the three of us with her characteristic enthusiasm. It would be a brilliant feather in the *Sunday World's* cap, she assured us, to have its banner planted on that terrific peak. The achievement would interest the whole world and reflect glory on its backer. The *Sunday World* should have the exclusive story—on condition, of course, that it paid for Miss Peck's outfit, her fares to and from Mexico, her hotel bills there, the wages of her guides, and any other actual expense of her climb. She asked nothing, wished nothing, for herself.

Mr. Brisbane was immediately interested in the project. Mr. Hersh was acquiescent, but less enthusiastic. My own reaction was the modified zest of the editor who would have to do most of the detail work connected with the feature. The matter was settled before Miss Peck had talked ten minutes. She went out triumphant, with her contract and a good advance payment in her pocket.

I saw much of her, and learned to like her immensely, while she was getting her outfit during the weeks that followed. In some ways she was incredibly naïve and unworldly. There hung about her something of the remote atmosphere of the heights where she was most at home. It was plain to us, and we assumed it was to her, that the nerve-racking perils of the climb would be what most interested the public, and that these must be dramatically played up in her story—*if* she survived to write that story. Personally, I had visions of her feet pressing forward over red-hot coals, of her clutching hands grasping molten rocks.

In our preliminary advertising we did ample justice to the appalling risks of the expedition. These advertisements began to appear soon after Miss Peck had got her equipment together and joyously departed for Mexico. As we bade her good-by we wondered if we would ever see her again. We even wondered—and this thought is one of the last to lodge in the minds of newspaper editors—whether we were justified in letting a woman take such risks.

Letters soon came from her. She was established in an attractive hotel at the foot of the volcano, waiting for good weather. There were many delightful persons at the same hotel. She dwelt on their charms. The greatest of these seemed to be that they were all passionately interested in her forthcoming climb. Many of the more intrepid of them told her they envied her, and added that they wished they were going with her. To these Miss Peck, in the exhilaration of her high project, made the obvious laughing response.

"Come right along," she said.

At last she sent us the date fixed for the climb. The weather had cleared. She added that climbing conditions were as nearly perfect as she could expect them to be.

It was at this point that we really let ourselves out on the matter of advertising that climb. Mr. Hersh took charge of this end of the work, and the late P. T. Barnum could have learned much by studying his methods. New York held its breath as it read his outpourings.

The climb was to be made on a Thursday. Miss Peck promised to put the story on the wires the same night, that it might be in ample time, with its illustrations, for the Sunday supplement that carried the account of the unparalleled achievement, and which must go to press on Friday. I had visions of Miss Peck reposing on the brinks of lava streams just long enough to write it.

That Thursday I was at my desk in the *Sunday World* offices all night. Mr. Brisbane had been called out of town to an important conference with Mr. Pulitzer. Most of the Popocatepetl material was already in the forms. There were stories and legends about Popocatepetl itself. Stories about previous efforts of other famous climbers to reach the top. Stories about Miss Peck's mountain-climbing career, of which this scaling of fiery Popocatepetl was the glorious climax. The leading story, of course, was to be Miss Peck's vivid recital of her appalling difficulties, her hair-raising perils, her final triumphant climax.

The night hours crawled on. At last, toward morning, the story began to come in over the wires. As it came it was brought to my desk page by page. I was to edit it and rush it to the composing-room as fast as it arrived. I grasped the first pages with hands that shook. Miss Peck was safe, or she could not have sent her story. But what had she gone through, what had she suffered, what injuries—perhaps permanent—had she sustained in that fiery hell?

Between the telegraph-room and my desk a boy rushed back and forth bringing me more of the "copy." I read on— and sat transfixed! Shock and incredulity swept over me in waves. For this was Miss Peck's story, told with the utmost simplicity:

She had started on the climb at daybreak. The weather

was perfect. In the gray light of early dawn she had been surprised and pleased to find half a dozen of her fellow guests waiting for her in the hotel lobby—to see her off, she assumed. They left the hotel with her, and accompanied her to the point where the climb began. Here a sad little episode had occurred, which Miss Peck described with womanly sympathy. A boy of fourteen, the son of one of the guests who was with the party, was sternly sent back to the hotel by his mother. The boy had protested, had entreated, had finally wept. He, too, wanted to climb Popocatepetl. But his parent was firm. The climb would be too arduous for one of his tender years. Draggingly, with hanging head, the boy turned back.

The rest of the party went on with Miss Peck. She realized now that they all wore stout boots and climbing costumes. It dawned on her that they had taken seriously her casual invitations to be with her on the climb. The first part of the ascent was made on horseback and was very easy. When the horses were left behind it became clear that she was to have the gay companionship of her traveling acquaintances as long as they could stand the gaff. At midday they were still with her. It developed that they had brought luncheon-baskets.

They made tables of the rocks, which were only comfortably warm, and they sat around these tables and enjoyed their ample luncheon. Popocatepetl was on almost incredibly good behavior. It belched no fire at them, it sent forth no rivers of lava. In the words of the rural reporter, "A pleasant time was had by one and all." Miss Peck still expected to lose her escort as the climb grew more difficult, but the little party of five or six remained intact. All of its members were happy and comfortable. No clouds of fire blocked their way. No hot coals burned their feet. One woman, whose stout shoes were new, was slightly inconvenienced by that fact; but her motto, too, was "Onward." Climber, guides, and escort toiled steadily toward the peak.

In the late afternoon, while the setting sun was making an effective panorama of the mountain and its background, the party came within reach of its goal, the crater. It was at this point, Miss Peck admitted, that she was surprised. On that crater, outlined against the evening sky, was a small and lonely figure. At first no one knew what it was. Even Miss Peck didn't know. But as they drew nearer, and Miss Peck got out the *Sunday World's* banner to plant it on that dizzy height, she recognized the waiting object. It was the little boy whose mother had ordered him to return to the hotel. He had doubled back, had found a shorter route, had got in advance of the rest of the expedition, and had finally planted himself on the top of Popocatepetl as a human banner, waving a triumphant greeting to later comers.

Miss Peck ended this artless recital with a simple comment. "We were all amazed," she admitted.

Not one of them, I am sure, was as much amazed as the assistant editor of the *Sunday World* was when she read that account. Across my desk lay a proof of Mr. Hersh's latest advertisement, announcing the *Sunday World's* representative's triumph in mountain climbing. I stared at it for one helpless moment. Then I took the complete set of pages into Mr. Hersh's office, dropped them before him, and sat down to watch his reaction as he read them. He had a very expressive face, but I am quite sure that never before or since did it express so much. At the end of the reading, when he was able to articulate, he spoke in a strangled voice.

"You're going to fix this thing, aren't you?" he asked.

"Of course," I agreed.

I went back to my desk with that story. I took out the picnic party, the lunch baskets, the joyous stroll up the mountain side, the pleasant camaraderie. Last of all, and with the most poignant regret, I took out the little boy on the crater. I sent Annie Peck to the top of that fiery citadel dauntless and alone. I made the *Sunday World's* banner of triumph wave in the evening breeze. But then and later I sympathized deeply with Miss Peck's disappointment over the published version of her adventure.

"I thought you would want the *facts*," she said sadly and with mild surprise. "Of course, I see your point. As it turned out, it wasn't really a difficult climb at all. Popocatepetl's behavior that day was miraculous. There had never been anything like it."

She sighed. "I do wish you had left in that nice little boy!" she ended.

In the final months of 1899, J. P. Morgan, the elder, appointed Colonel George Harvey president of Harper and Brothers. The first working day of January, 1900, I followed the Colonel to the Harper offices on Franklin Square to take up the editorship of *Harper's Bazar*.

At the time of my resignation I was in charge of the *Sunday World's* two most important departments—the four-page Comic Supplement, and the eight-page Editorial Forum. The Comic Supplement was famous as the home of the "Yellow Kid," whose existence there was the origin of the expression "yellow journalism." The Editorial Forum was our most dignified "high brow" department—the space in which great minds of Europe and America set forth their theories on the leading issues of the day. Those two departments made an odd tandem for editorial driving—but I always had plenty of variety in my *World* work!

In connection with my change of occupation, Mr. Pulitzer gave me three surprises. On receiving my resignation he did not reply with the letter of approval and good wishes for success in the new field, which I had confidently expected. Instead he wrote a letter to Colonel Harvey reproaching him for taking me away from the *World*. This was a strikingly different attitude from that of my friend William Van Benthuysen, then managing editor of the *World,* in our last interview.

"I could raise the Harper ante," he said, "to an extent that might keep you with us. I'm not going to do it. You deserve the big chance the Harper job will give you, and I want you to have it. Go to it—with my blessing!"

I wrote again to Mr. Pulitzer, mentioning that I had expected, and had reason to expect, a better feeling from him than that his letter to Colonel Harvey revealed. I had worked for him faithfully for ten years.

This letter had an immediate effect. Mr. Pulitzer softened and sent his head secretary, Dr. Hosmer, a man I liked and admired, to the *Bazar* offices to ask me if I was really happy in the change.

I was exhilarated by the visit and told Dr. Hosmer I felt as if I had died and gone to heaven. Mr. Pulitzer didn't like that remark. He immediately showed his resentment, I was told later, by cutting me out of his will. He had made a will, it seems, leaving ten thousand dollars to every employee who had worked on the *World* for ten years or more. My little joke cost me that amount. It was an effective operation on a sense of humor frequently too keen for my own good, but both the sense of humor and I survived it. When Mr. Pulitzer died during my ten years with Harper and Brothers I was one of the former *World* editors who was invited to his New York funeral, and I went.

That funeral is an undying memory. The final services were held in St. Thomas's Church, on Fifth Avenue and Fifty-third Street, the Christian Church of which Mr.

Pulitzer, though born a Jew, was a member. Most of his former editors were especially invited to attend these final services.

They accepted the invitation almost to a man, and twenty-four hours before the funeral they poured into New York from every part of the country. They came from California, from Texas, from Kansas, from Maine. When those in charge of the services realized how large the gathering of former *World* editors was to be, they arranged to have the group meet at the Gotham Hotel, two blocks above St. Thomas's, and join the funeral cortège at the church door. The editors were to walk down Fifth Avenue two abreast, in solemn and dignified parade, and fall into line for the march into the church directly behind the coffin, the family, and the then-present *World* staff.

It was an excellent plan, and it would have worked out beautifully but for the fallibility of human nature. At the Gotham the former editors of the *World,* now a highly impressive gathering in numbers and personality, naturally found themselves engaged in something like a family reunion. Fellow workers who had not seen one another for a quarter of a century, and who may not have cared much for one another during their old-time association, were overcome by the unexpected pleasure of this reunion. They smote one another's backs; they patted one another's shoulders; they almost embraced.

While the reunion was still at its height they were ordered to leave the Gotham, form in twos, and begin their march to the church. It was very hard to secure and hold their attention. The maneuver of getting them out into the street revealed more dear familiar faces to those earnestly looking for them. It had dawned on the newspaper men that most if not all of their former associates were in the crowd around them. No game of hide and seek could be more fascinating than the discovery of favorite individuals in that throng. Joyously and heartily the ex-editors lent themselves to this diversion. Every individual had the most gratifying success in his efforts. Whoops of delighted recognition filled the air.

"Jim, you tow-headed fraud, put it there!"

"Hi, Dick, wait for your old pal!"

Happy pairs, reunited after decades, danced together on the pavement. Orderly lines, held for a moment, broke up in confusion. Reminiscences were yelped from one ex-editor to another. Men ran up and down the lines, seeking some one they hadn't yet found.

With perspiring brow the Master of Ceremonies vainly tried to whip the broken lines into some sort of order. It was an impossible task. The reunions and the glad outcries of recognition were at their height when the former editors reached the entrance of St. Thomas's Church.

Before it stood the empty hearse. The coffin containing the body of one of America's greatest newspaper editors was slowly being carried into the church. For a moment the approaching procession failed to see it. Eyes were still seeking old friends in the crowd, hands were being grasped, backs were being slapped. Personally, I remember being especially impressed by my reunion with E. A. Grozier, then editor of the *Boston Post*. In our *World* days Mr. Grozier and I had always respected each other, but we had certainly never been on the terms which spectators must have suspected who saw us now. Mr. Grozier used to check up my expense accounts, and was quite fussy about them, objecting especially to cab fares and necessary tips to maids and porters. All this was forgiven. Our reunion seemed one of the high moments in life, and Mr. Grozier, usually an unemotional man, appeared to feel just as I did about it.

Around us equal expansiveness was being shown. Those figures that had suddenly come back through the mist of the years took on a strange radiance. It was all natural and human and terribly annoying and embarrassing to the Master of Ceremonies. He and his aids began to push and shove the ex-editors into place. The ex-editors didn't even observe their efforts. They saw nothing, heard nothing, but their friends of former days.

At the right and left of the steps leading up to the church the newspaper photographers were gathered, their cameras focused to snap the stricken band of ex-*World* editors as they sorrowfully approached. They took one look at the bright faces of Mr. Pulitzer's former reliables, and their nerveless hands dropped to their sides. It takes some doing to check a newspaper photographer in the midst of his professional activities, but the tableau of those waving hands in the advancing mob, the sound of those cheery outcries, did it. This was not one of those pictures which emphasize the dignity and impressiveness of the last honors paid to a great man. Very literally, the photographers fell back. Several took pictures as personal souvenirs. Long afterwards I saw one of these. Without its Fifth Avenue background it would have served very nicely as a snap-shot of Old Home Week in Haynesville Center.

The Master of Ceremonies, now reinforced by additional desperate aids who had grasped the situation, swung the editors into line by sheer physical force. The editors gasped, blinked, and caught on. They saw the coffin with its escort of distinguished pall-bearers disappearing through the entrance of the church. They heard the solemn notes of the great organ rolling out to the Avenue to meet them.

Something like an electric shock swept the ranks of former employees. Every pair of shoulders straightened, every smile disappeared. Lines formed as if by magic. Reverently, two by two, with bent heads and eyes and hearts full of memories, the men and women who had formerly helped Joseph Pulitzer to build his *World* followed their dead chief into the crowded church.

In connection with my change from the *World* to the editorship of *Harper's Bazar* I also made a radical change in my living arrangements. I moved from West Forty-fourth Street to an apartment on Stuyvesant Square, and I took in two friends who optimistically thought they would like to live with me.

I was not sure this was a wise experiment. They were both delightful girls, or I would not have considered it at all. But I had lived alone for ten years, and it was my own adaptability to the new conditions that I doubted. The recruits were Harriet Beardslee Prescott, a graduate of Mount Holyoke College and already head of the catalogue department of Columbia University Library, and Martha Hill Cutler, a graduate of Smith College, then studying art in New York. We had been close friends for several years, and we decided to try life together for a summer.

Even for that short interval we protected ourselves by various stipulations. Each of us had her own profession, her own friends, her own interests. It was understood that each would continue to live her life in complete independence of the others. If I wished to give a dinner they would dine out. If they wished to give a dinner I would arrange the meal and the details and also tactfully fade from the picture. If, in the autumn, any or all of us wished to separate the separation would take place with the utmost good feeling on all sides.

Now, in 1937, that association and understanding have existed for almost forty years. My sister Alice says the brilliant success of the experiment is due to the fact that Harriet and Martha have such beautiful natures. This is true. They have become her sisters, too, and they were daughters to our mother up till the time of Mother's death.

CHAPTER XII

"THE LADY OF YADDO"—AND OTHERS

IN my youthful arrogance I had assured my father and mother, when I left Milwaukee, that in ten years I would be the editor of *Harper's Bazar,* or of *St. Nicholas* or the *Youth's Companion.* I made good that prediction with hardly a day to spare, and because Colonel George Harvey, who knew me and realized that I was at least an indefatigable worker, had become president of Harper and Brothers.

My experience with Harper's was what I had so unwisely described it to be in my message to Mr. Pulitzer. I had died and gone to heaven. I must admit, however, that I had my hours of fellow-feeling for the little girl whose mother had promised her heaven, and who, dazed by the effulgence of the picture drawn, wistfully asked if she could occasionally pass a Saturday afternoon with her little friends in hell. I had been living in an atmosphere where the news of the world broke over me like pounding breakers. The contrast of the academic calm of Harper's sometimes depressed me.

My first lesson in the relative tempo of the two offices came the day I took up the new job. I was the third editor of the *Bazar.* Mary L. Booth had conducted it very successfully from its beginning up till the time of her death twenty-two years later. Then Margaret E. Sangster had been in charge for ten or fifteen years, till Colonel Harvey became the new head of Harper's.

Running true to the best editorial traditions, I began with the unexpressed but firm conviction that the efforts of my predecessors had left much to be changed. The

171

Bazar was then a weekly. From the first I planned to make it a monthly, but that would take a little time. The current issue, however, was before me, almost ready for press. I tore it to pieces and started out to make it over, with about two days before me for the job. My first concern was with the illustrations. Picture-processing takes time. I hastened to the downstairs office of a young Mr. Demorest, then the head of the mechanical end of the art work, with hands full of illustrations I wanted processed immediately.

"What's the quickest time you can make on these pictures?" I asked him. "I'd like to make up the new pages as soon as possible."

What I really wanted was to make up the pages late that afternoon. The feat might have been possible on the *World*.

Mr. Demorest looked at the pictures, then at me, and made a calculation. His brow was corrugated by the violence of his mental efforts. It was subsequently corrugated every time we met.

"Lem' me see," he brought out thoughtfully. "This is Tuesday, ain't it? You can have these a week from tomorrow!"

It was at this moment I fully realized that I was in a new atmosphere—a literary atmosphere, given up to quiet living and high thinking. Mr. Demorest did rather better than he had promised; but the strain on him was so great that he offered me a confidence which became part of the annals of Franklin Square.

"Miss Jordan," he said on this second occasion, "I ain't makin' no excuses for bein' late with me work, for I know they don't go. But I give you me word I got so much to do that they's times when I leaves this place feelin' noivous!"

Among us, I suspect, the four recruits from Park Row— Colonel Harvey, Frederick Duneka, Arthur Chandler and I —made the whole Harper staff feel "noivous" in those first days of reorganization, and we ended by "feelin' noivous" ourselves. I myself felt especially "noivous." High-geared human machine that I was, I could not adapt myself to the deliberate Franklin Square pace, nor to the notion of evenings and Sundays and holidays all my own. I put in a full day's work at the office, and then took manuscripts home and read them most of the night. I passed Sundays and holidays planning the changes in form and content the new *Bazar* was to have. Colonel Harvey had his hands full. In his reorganization he made Frederick Duneka general manager of Harper and Brothers and Arthur Chandler head of the advertising and promotion departments. We were, in the vernacular of the day, "a close corporation"; there is little question that in those first weeks we became prominent features in the worst dreams of our Harper associates.

However, we finally struck a happy medium of pace between the frantic rush of the *World* offices and the soporific calm of the literary atmosphere, and everybody was happier. From that time on my injudicious boast to Mr. Pulitzer was justified. I was doing work I loved, in an atmosphere of harmony; and I was meeting frequently and intimately many of America's most luminous literary figures.

The first of these was Henry Mills Alden, who had then edited *Harper's Magazine* for more than forty years. He sat in a tiny cubby-hole partitioned off the magazine's main office. It was barely large enough to hold him and his desk and chair, with an extra chair for one visitor. The retreat had a window, which Mr. Alden largely obscured by piling manuscripts and books high on its sill. There he sat, eight and nine hours a day, a great god in the American literary machine, his beautiful old head bent over his manuscripts, his brilliant brown eyes undimmed by time. A cigar was constantly in his mouth, its ashes falling into the welcoming ridges of his waistcoat. In that detail he was like Colonel

Cockerill. The two men had other points of resemblance. Mr. Alden was the kindest, the gentlest, the most benignant of human beings—a man who dwelt on one of the high plateaus of life. Everybody at Harper's loved him, and the four recruits immediately found themselves in full accord with that devotion. Colonel Harvey was like a son to Mr. Alden, and the older man repaid him with an affection and loyalty very beautiful to see.

Mr. Alden's first wife had died a few years before we arrived at Franklin Square. She had been an invalid for a long time and was said to have undergone thirty operations. How her husband had retained his serenity and his philosophy during that drawn-out torture for them both it is hard to imagine. Now he had married again, and of this second marriage a nice little story was told.

Meeting Mr. Alden one day at the Century Club, Richard Watson Gilder, then editor of the *Century Magazine,* said to him, "By the way, Alden, I sent a charming little southern widow to you six months ago with a letter of introduction. She was a poetess named Ada Foster Murray, and I thought her work was good. Did you ever do anything for her?"

"W-ell," Mr. Alden said thoughtfully, "I *married* her."

They had not been married long when Colonel Harvey came to Harper's. He discovered that Mr. Alden had never been to Europe. He immediately sent the pair to Italy for a belated honeymoon, which was also the first long vacation the old editor had ever been given. Before the Aldens sailed Colonel Harvey discovered that in the big Alden house at Metuchen, New Jersey, there had never been a study, or indeed much privacy of any kind, for the editor. Now, with three unmarried daughters of his own there, and his second wife's four children, there was much less than before. While the honeymooners were enjoying their enchanted wanderings Colonel Harvey had one room of the Alden house made over

and furnished as a large and beautiful study—a surprise for
the bridegroom when he returned. Mr. Alden was enraptured
with it, but I doubt if he was ever in it alone. Certainly there
were never less than three or four persons in it when I was
there, which was quite often. The entire family used it as a
living-room.

Mr. Alden's youngest daughter was Annie Fields Alden.
She and I became close friends and I often visited her. I had
never met the first Mrs. Alden, but I liked "the charming
little southern widow" very much, and we, too, became
friends. She was as sweet and as gentle as Mr. Alden himself, and even more transcendental. When in the course of a
few years it became evident that Annie, child of Mr. Alden's
heart and flower of his flock, must die of the same disease
that had killed her mother, Mrs. Alden met the tragedy
with a fortitude and philosophy that were as sincere and
deep-rooted as they were trying to the other members of
the family. Annie told me in her last months that when
they were all striving to adapt themselves to the first shock
of the knowledge, Mrs. Alden went about the house ex-
claiming, "What is death? Only a dear friend." Annie
added that after some days of this Mr. Alden finally crashed
down to earth and exclaimed, unpoetically but very humanly,
"For God's sake, Ada, *shut up!*"

One of my most vivid memories of Henry Mills Alden
brings him back as he stood by Annie's coffin on the day of
her funeral.

"Isn't she triumphant?" he asked me.

The death of this daughter was perhaps the greatest sorrow her father had ever known. But he stood at her grave
with head and shoulders unbowed, the cold wind stirring
his white hair, his luminous brown eyes on the distant hills,
remote alike from time and place.

I returned from the funeral just in time to speak at a

dinner given that night by the New York Women's Advertising Club. The subject assigned me was "Woman and Her Latch-Key," and the speech was expected to be exhilarating. Instead, it was the worst public address I have ever made. It must have been one of the worst any one ever made anywhere. I was very fond of Annie Fields Alden. . . .

It is only fair to Mrs. Alden to add that when death came to her, many years after her distinguished husband died, she met it with the same high philosophy she showed when it approached others. She died in 1936. A short time before her death she had tea with me in my New York apartment and cheerfully told me her call had come.

"The doctors say I can't live many months," she put it. "What difference does that make? I'm over eighty. I've had a good life, and I'm ready to go."

She had come to me in the midst of one of New York's mid-winter blizzards, and she mentioned that she was taking a six o'clock train for her daughter's home in the country.

"But how are you going to get to the station?" I asked, anxiously. There was a sheet of ice over the city.

"Oh, I'll just slip down in the subway," Mrs. Alden chirped.

"You certainly will, if you go there," I agreed. "You will slip all the way down, from the top step to the bottom."

When she left I put her into a cab, paid and tipped the driver, and gave him money to deliver her into the hands of a porter who would see her safely into a seat on her train. She protested that all this was absurd.

"I could get to that train without the least trouble," she insisted.

She would certainly have attempted the feat, and no doubt would have succeeded. I never saw her again. She died six weeks later, in a heart attack. She was a gallant figure to the end, leaving this world almost as casually as she would

have left a room—with a door open behind for her friends
to follow.

While Mrs. Humphry Ward's novel, *Lady Rose's Daughter,* was appearing serially in *Harper's Magazine,* Mr.
Alden was intensely interested in it. There was considerable
discussion in the editorial rooms, and even some strong feeling, about the finish of the story. Most of us were disappointed in it. Mr. Alden did not share that emotion. I can
still see him on the day the final instalment reached him from
England, hastening across the big counting-room of Harper's
to Mr. Duneka's desk, waving the manuscript in his hands
and crying aloud as he came,

"Jacob gets her. Jacob *gets her!*"

The rest of us were not so happy. That Mrs. Humphry
Ward herself shared our doubts of her novel's climax was
proved by a confidence she made later to Agnes Repplier,
during the English novelist's first visit to this country. Miss
Repplier told me the story, which also throws a high light
on that dark abyss which should have been the home of Mrs.
Ward's sense of humor.

"I told her frankly I was disappointed in the end of that
book," Miss Repplier began, "and *what* do you think the
woman said? She said, 'My dear Miss Repplier, no one
knows better than I do that the end of *Lady Rose's Daughter*
was a literary mistake. No one knows better than I do that
a woman like Julie would *never* have been happy with Jacob!
But to tell the truth, my dear, I was in such a run-down
nervous condition at the time that I simply dared not face
the terrible emotional strain which would have attended an
unhappy ending!' "

I met Mrs. Ward several times during her visit, and I
went to the much-discussed luncheon Colonel Harvey gave
for her. There was a delicate question of precedence on that
occasion, for though Mrs. Ward was the guest of honor, the

Duchess of Marlborough was also at the luncheon. The Colonel put his problem to Mrs. Ward and she—who loved duchesses so much—solved it with true British common sense. Following her advice the Colonel put the Duchess at his right at the table and Mrs. Ward at his left. I greatly admired Mrs. Ward as a novelist, but much as I liked her books I always faded away from her actual presence as swiftly as I could. Never before or since her coming have I met another person as serious as she was.

Colonel Harvey frequently entertained members of the British nobility, and he knew a great many of them. Mrs. Harvey told me that one night, after his Harper days and while he was American Ambassador to Great Britain, the Colonel took six English duchesses to a London music-hall! While he was still with Harper's he gave a luncheon in New York to the Countess of Warwick, better known as King Edward the Seventh's "Babbling Brooke" (she was Lady Brooke when the King first met her). On the day of the Colonel's luncheon she had a cold, and felt in need of sympathy. To each of the guests, as we were presented, she made the same remark.

"I've a simply atrocious cold. Do you ever have colds? They're most unpleasant, really!"

I heard her say that six times. Gertrude Atherton, who had returned from London with the literary laurels placed on her brow by leading critics there, and who was at the luncheon, assured me I had lost count. The correct number, she thought, was sixteen. Certainly that remark seemed the only one the great lady made that day, as she wiped her weeping eyes and moist little red nose.

Subsequently she gave a lecture, for which I was a patroness. It was delivered in Carnegie Hall, and I met my obligations by taking a box and giving a party. My guests, a light-hearted and irrepressible lot, had expected, I think,

FIVE FRIENDS OF THREE DECADES

Mrs. Spencer Trask   *Mrs. Edward Ringwood Hewitt*

Mrs. Arthur Murray Dodge

Mrs. James Robert McKee   *The Marchioness Lagergren*

some interesting revelations about London social life. The Countess, however, confined herself strictly to the remote history of England and the early Warwicks, when she talked at all. Most of the time she was on the platform she seemed looking about vaguely for the pages of her manuscript. She read the lecture from these, and apparently was reading it for the first time, as she had great difficulty in making it out.

When she finished a page she cast it from her to the floor of the stage. Unfortunately other pages she had not meant to drop slipped down at the same time, and were so hard to distinguish among the mass on the floor that she lightly ignored them. At the end, when she disappeared from view, she made her way through a carpet of fallen pages that crackled like autumn leaves in Vallombrosa. Two of my young friends were playing "patticake" when I gave my attention to my guests; and so far as I could see most of the occupants of other boxes around us had been carrying on low-voiced but interesting chats. Every seat and box in Carnegie Hall had been sold, but the Countess's lecture was not regarded as a success.

Colonel Harvey had made new contracts with Mark Twain and William Dean Howells, and Mr. Howells had promised to put in a day or two at Franklin Square every week. We built a nice little office for him in a corner of the *Bazar's* big editorial room. He mentioned that in English offices tea was served every afternoon between four and five. On that hint we also served tea, and I adapted myself to another sharp contrast between the present and the past.

Mr. Howells was as popular among us as Mr. Alden was, but in a different way. He was magnetic, sophisticated, surprisingly practical and deeply understanding. He was as immaculate in his appearance as Mr. Alden was careless, and he had a charming manner and a worldly smile. When at the end of my first year with Harper's he learned that I was to pass my five weeks of vacation in a first visit to Europe, he was immediately interested.

"Select the most congenial friend you have, to go with you," he began.

"Oh, I've done that," I cried happily.

"And *then*," Mr. Howells ended impressively, "leave her at home!"

"What countries are you going to see?" he wanted to know, while I was getting over the shock of this.

I mentioned that as I would have only three weeks on land I must be satisfied if I saw *all* of France, England and Germany. I very nearly did it, too, by swift traveling. Following thirty-eight subsequent voyages across the Atlantic I picked up some threads of interest necessarily overlooked during that flying inspection.

Practical as Mr. Howells was in many ways, he could ride the clouds, when he chose, as buoyantly as his life-long friend Henry Mills Alden rode them. He could also firmly fix his attention on subjects that did not really interest him. Dining with him one evening in his New York apartment, as one of a quartette that included his daughter Mildred and James Lane Allen, I found the dinner conversation confined entirely to birds, because James Lane Allen knew a great deal about them. We all learned most of what he knew.

Mr. Howells had a nice but sometimes acid humor. On another dinner occasion, when he had been carving a turkey laboriously for twenty minutes, Mildred thoughtlessly asked for a second portion before he had been able to serve himself. Her father handed back her plate with a sigh.

"Maybe there's a pin in this," he said hopefully.

Both Mr. Howells and Mildred disliked music. They had no ear for it whatever, and it actually annoyed them. Colonel and Mrs. Harvey had a box for the opera during those years, and were as hospitable with it as they were in their home.

Mr. Howells accepted their invitations to the opera several times, and sat through the performances with a hurt expression.

"The opera is wasted on me," he confided to a common friend. "I'd rather go to a boiler factory!"

The friend tactlessly repeated the remark to Colonel Harvey who said forgivingly, "We'll invite him to a boiler factory some time."

During my early years with Harper's my father died, and his death was the great blow of my life. Notwithstanding his instructions to me to lean on no one I had always leaned on him. With his going I felt adrift in the universe.

Mother waited a year, till she had sold our old home, and then came to New York to live with me. Her coming meant another readjustment in living conditions, so I moved into a larger apartment, on Gramercy Park. Harriet and Martha, firm fixtures in my life by this time came too, of course, and shared my enthusiasm in getting ready for Mother. She was then sixty, in perfect health, and as active and independent as I was; but in some way I had convinced myself that she was old and feeble and must be tenderly guarded. On this point she gave me my first lesson the day she arrived.

She was traveling on the Pennsylvania Railroad. It did not occur to me that I could meet her in Jersey City and walk her casually into the ferry-boat to New York. Instead I myself crossed in the ferry-boat to Jersey City in a cab, that I might have the cab close to the train and get the exhausted old lady into it at once. Then the cab would go directly onto the ferry-boat, and off the ferry-boat in New York and on to the new apartment, with no change and no strain on mother's venerable legs and nerves.

The train was a long one and a great number of passengers left it in Jersey City. To my horror I could not find my mother among them. I darted here and there in growing anxiety. There was no sign of her. I confided in the driver, waiting patiently on the cab.

"I can't find my mother!"

"There's a lot of passengers. She'll be along pretty soon," the cabman yawned.

"But," I cried, "she's sixty years old!"

The cabman, who was about twenty-two, almost fell off his box.

"My God," he exclaimed, and jumped down to my side.

Together we frantically searched the throng till the last of the train's passengers had disappeared into the waiting ferry-boat. Then it occurred to me to telephone to the apartment. Mother was there, the cook told me, having tea and toasted English muffins and strawberry jam in front of the living-room fire, with Martha and Lena, my devoted maid, in close attendance on her. Mother had cocked a casual eye at Jersey City, had not seen me, had slipped onto the ferry-boat, and was the first passenger off the boat and into a cab on the New York side. Her foregathering with Lena that day was the beginning of an association of twenty-eight years between them. Thenceforth Lena devoted most of her time to my mother till the end of Mother's life.

Mark Twain (Samuel Clemens), who often came to the office, was a frequent member of week-end parties at Jorjalma, the Harveys' country home. I can see him still, as vividly as when he was among us, dressed in one of the white linen or white flannel suits he always wore, with his white hair forming a halo around his splendid head and his dark eyes shining with mischief. He was as impish as a bad boy, and we never knew what he would do next.

One evening I put him beside May Sinclair, the English novelist, at a dinner I was giving. It was Miss Sinclair's first visit to America, and she was the most silent guest we had ever had from any shore. The favorite indoor sport of literary New York that winter was the effort to draw Miss Sinclair out. No one succeeded. She had just published her novel *The Divine Fire,* which was having a sensational success in England and America. Like the rest of us, Mr. Clemens was fascinated by the amazing contrast between the passion and power of that novel and the personality of the prim, tucked-in little woman who had written it. That night he did his best to make her talk. He himself had never been more entertaining. But Miss Sinclair took Mark Twain as she took every one else—almost in silence.

At end of the dinner, when we were leaving the men alone, Mr. Clemens escorted Miss Sinclair to the dining-room door. Having opened it for her he stopped, faced her, and fixed his brilliant eyes on hers. With the greatest solemnity he put his fingers to his lips and produced a long-drawn, sibilant "H—u—s-s-h." Then he went back to his place at the table. As we passed into the next room together Miss Sinclair stared at me, and spoke at last.

"Now, why did he do *that?*" she asked. "I hadn't said a word!"

Which reminds me: The last time Rebecca West was in New York I asked her when Miss Sinclair would pay us another visit. The answer threw an interesting side-light on the secret of our attraction for foreign visitors.

"Why should May Sinclair come to America?" Miss West asked, in genuine surprise. "She can't lecture!"

Here's my favorite story about Mr. Clemens. One day he made a call on a distinguished literary woman he was meeting for the first time. He came home beaming. He told Mrs. Clemens he had enjoyed the call immensely. But his wife was gazing at him in consternation.

"Oh, Samuel," she gasped, "you forgot to put on a tie!"

Mr. Clemens seemed depressed by this oversight. He went at once to his room and looked over his entire collection of ties. He selected the handsomest and packed it carefully in a box. Then he added his card and sent the box to the lady. On the card he had written, "Sorry we couldn't come *together.*"

It often happened that Mr. Clemens and I were at Jorjalma for the same week-end. I took an early train back to New York Monday mornings, so I usually breakfasted alone; but occasionally Mr. Clemens, who could not sleep late, was moved to come downstairs and join me. Personally, I like silent breakfasts at seven o'clock. Mr. Clemens discovered this, so he invariably started a profound theological argument. When he had tied me into a hard knot, as he always did, he was happy. He had no belief in an existence beyond this one. He discovered that I had, and the fact fascinated him. One morning toward the end of his life he said during one of those discussions,

"You may be interested to know that I have only a short time left on this planet, and that I'm getting ready for the transfer. I'm practising with an aëroplane every morning, and with a parachute every afternoon."

During another of those breakfasts I decided to divert his mind from theology by talking about Yvette Guilbert, the Parisian singer. She was then singing in New York and I had heard her both here and in Paris. From theology to Madame Guilbert was a long step, but we took it in our stride and Mr. Clemens asked me about a certain song she had made famous. It was the wonderful song with which Yvette Guilbert could always chill the nerves of her audience —the song about the old French peasant woman and her devoted son.

The son was finally lured away by a siren. He forgot his

mother and left her alone, helpless and suffering. The siren
was still jealous of her. She demanded that, as proof of his
love, the youth should kill his mother and bring her the
mother's heart. He obeyed and ran back to the charmer,
carrying the heart between his hands. In his haste he tripped
and fell, and the heart rolled on the ground. As it rolled, his
mother's feeble voice came from it.

"Oh, my son," it wailed, "hast thou hurt thyself?"

I told Mr. Clemens this story. It gripped his imagination.
He monologued about it for half an hour, and often brought
it up in our later talks.

A frequent and surprising discovery made in those days
was that fine minds can often be interested and diverted
much more easily than small ones. In my frequent visits to
Europe as time went on I always made a point of passing a
week in Munich for the music. While I was there, usually in
August, I visited the great toy factories of Nuremberg and
brought back for my eighteen god-children large collections
of interesting mechanical toys, which were not on sale in
American toy-shops till just before Christmas. When these
were especially interesting I took them out to Jorjalma to
exhibit them there. I have seen them hold the attention of
able minds for hours at a time. Once I held up the work
of Harper's for almost an entire morning by exhibiting to
Mr. Duneka, Major Frederic T. Leigh and Mr. Chandler a
new German talking-picture-book I had brought back. One
looked at a picture of a donkey and it brayed. One looked at
a bird and it sang. One hung over a child's picture and it
squeaked "Mamma." My idea was that we might get up a
similar book for sale in America. The cost of making it
here proved prohibitive; but those three men played with that
book for two hours, making all the machinery work and
wearing the ecstatic grins of little boys.

When I came to Harper's I was thirty, but all my new

friends thrilled me as deeply as my journalistic encounters with the great had done in my early twenties. It still seemed incredible that I was meeting constantly, and in such friendly fashion, the men·and women whose books I had read with awe during my childhood and school days. Through the Aldens I saw much of Mary E. Wilkins, who also had a home in Metuchen. Through Gertrude Atherton I had met Kate Douglas Wiggin in the *World* days. Both were California women. Then I rarely had time to follow up a friendship, however intriguing. Now Kate Douglas Wiggin had married George C. Riggs and was living in New York. We began a friendship that endured till her death. Through her my circle widened and took in other authors outside the Harper fold.

It was at her home I first met my beloved Frances Hodgson Burnett, but our close friendship did not begin till years later. The first meeting occurred during one of Kate's evening receptions. Mrs. Burnett and I got off in a corner together and talked steadily for two hours. I had read every book she had written up till that time, and there was nothing Mrs. Burnett liked better than to talk about her work.

Later, when we had become almost inseparable, she told me that when her family found her wholly lost in a book, her face radiant with interest, they knew she was reading something of her own! Both she and Mrs. Riggs had an attitude toward their work that was singularly childlike and artless. They were fascinated by what they wrote. Mrs. Burnett always took the stand that her writing was a sort of fairy gift, for which she deserved little or no credit and which therefore she could discuss and admire almost impersonally. Mrs. Riggs had no such notion. She had worked hard and she had won her spurs. She saw no reason why she should not love her literary children, and she did.

One of my vivid memories of Kate Riggs is connected

with a luncheon she gave when her most popular book, *Re-becca of Sunnybrook Farm* was published. She had a dozen friends at her table. Beside the plate of each was an auto-graphed copy of the book, as a souvenir. That was charming, and after the luncheon Kate announced that she would read to us her favorite chapter of the book—the one in which Rebecca decided to obtain a wedding ring for a woman who sorely needed one.

It was a delightful chapter, very tenderly written. We all gathered in the living-room, prepared to listen to it with full appreciation. But the author, who had always taken her own work very seriously, was particularly obsessed by this chapter. She was actually overcome as she read it, and punctuated the reading with emotional gulps. Her de-voted sister, Nora Archibald Smith, to whom Kate was the elixir of life, was immediately and equally overcome. Together they choked and wiped their eyes while the rest of us looked and felt self-conscious. We were deeply in-terested, but we had no inclination to weep.

Unfortunately, the situation struck me as rather amusing. With lips and jaw firmly set I gazed sternly before me. I was getting along very creditably when I suddenly met the eye of a fellow guest. I hardly knew the lady, but we must have been kindred spirits. Something electric passed be-tween us. The next instant the face of each of us was buried in her handkerchief while our shoulders shook con-vulsively. I thought all was lost. Kate would never for-give us.

Kate was reading on, however, and Nora, glancing across at us with wet eyes, happily diagnosed our symptoms as the same as her own. Both she and Kate bade me good-by that day with special tenderness.

Kate entertained largely and very delightfully. She was constantly having charades, tableaux, spinster parties and other diversions. Her husband, a charming man, was the only man at her first spinster party. She made him appear as the tail of a kite.

She was always an amusing talker, and never more so than at one luncheon when she told her guests of a day in her childhood when she had broken seven of the Ten Commandments. We passed the rest of the luncheon hour guessing which Commandments Kate had broken and urging her for details.

She died in her sixties at a nursing home in London. Mrs. Arthur Murray Dodge, who called there a fortnight or so before Kate's death, was the last of our group to see her. A few months before that, and just before Kate sailed, Mrs. Burnett and I, attending a matinée performance of *Will Shakespeare,* saw Kate sitting alone, directly in front of us. We effected a change of seats with a stranger next to us, and during the remaining intermissions of the play Kate and "Fluffy" (Mrs. Burnett) exchanged tragic confidences about their health.

Life at Harper's became increasingly pleasant. Part of my job, a very important, stimulating, and delightful part, was to keep in social touch with authors. I had to drop my night manuscript reading and my holiday work over plans and "dummies" to do this—and that was an excellent thing for me. In a different way I had been overworking as much as on the *World* and, of course, there were still some trying experiences.

I had changed the *Bazar* from a weekly to a monthly magazine, and had also changed its size—to the anguish of its loyal little group of old subscribers. It seemed to me that every member of that group wrote me a letter of protest. But the group was too small to be considered vital in our brave new plans. The problem of the *Bazar,* however, was

exactly as difficult as Edward Bok had warned me it would
be. It not only had to carry the entire expense of its mechanical and editorial make-up, but in addition to these it had
to carry one quarter of the entire running expense of the
great Harper firm and its big factory. I had many sleepless
nights over this. I could put my finger on all the other expenses and decrease them. But my quarter of the vast "overhead" was chalked against the *Bazar* as a lump sum I was
expected to accept without comment.

Still, the work was absorbing and life with gracious gestures was constantly giving me new friends. One of the most
radiant of these was Mrs. Spencer Trask—who wrote, very
rarely but always exquisitely, under the name of Katrina
Trask.

Mrs. Trask was one of the half dozen most remarkable
women I have known. She was the wife of Spencer Trask,
the banker, and an invalid during the ten years I knew her,
suffering from an organic heart ailment that finally killed
her. She had everything but health—beauty, great personal
magnetism, a sort of genius, and an irresistible personal
charm. When I passed my first week-end with her, at her
home in Tuxedo, she was still able to dine with her house-
guests and remain with them through the evenings. Soon
after that she was wholly confined to a suite of rooms on
the second floor of her superb house, Yaddo, in Saratoga,
where she lived in the splendid isolation of a queen, giving
her friends the hospitality of her home but seeing only one
of them at a time and—theoretically—for short periods.

Friends who came to her for week-ends were warned
not to be alarmed if Mrs. Trask suddenly had a heart attack,
and never to feel themselves responsible for it. Such attacks
came constantly, we were assured. Mrs. Trask wore around
her neck a small gold whistle, whose summons, if she had
breath to blow it, would bring help from every part of the

great house. If she became unconscious, anybody with her was to give the signal. She was, of course, never left alone. She carried her invalidism as a banner in battle. No one ever heard her complain. Her interest in life, in other human beings, and in the arts, was the interest of a fine brain and a flaming soul.

On my first evening with them she and Mr. Trask had a dozen house-guests, including three who subsequently became my intimate friends. One of these was Mrs. James Robert McKee, the daughter of Benjamin Harrison. The other two were a newly-wed and very lovable young couple, Mr. and Mrs. Morgan Goetchius, of Tuxedo. There were also two composers—Arthur Nevin and Arthur Farwell. Both were writing Indian operas at the time, and they played extracts from these after dinner. Then we all gathered around the huge fireplace in ·the great hall, put the lights out, and told in turn the most blood-curdling ghost stories we could remember. Mrs. Trask's story especially chilled our blood. I went to my room at midnight with a vivid memory of it. Before I was undressed there was a tap on my door and Mrs. McKee walked in.

"Hello, neighbor," she said cheerfully. "I heard you moving about. Are you sleepy?"

I was not, and I was very glad to see Mrs. McKee. We settled down for a long talk before my fire. I told her about that Cape May interview with her mother, years before, and of all it had meant to me then and since. Mrs. McKee listened with tears in her eyes. Her mother had been dead for many years, and she adored her memory. That talk laid the groundwork of one of my longest and finest friendships.

This was the first of many week-ends with Mrs. Trask, but the only one in which she joined her house-guests. After that often I visited her in her home at Saratoga, and at her camp on an island in Lake George. At Yaddo, she could no longer come downstairs. Instead her guests visited her, one at a time, in her rooms overlooking the far-away hills.

She was like several other invalids I have known—determined to do so far as she could whatever she wished to do, and succeeding by force of will power and a dauntless courage. She often kept me with her for hours, talking half the night or more. On one occasion she held me till three o'clock in the morning. I had no wish to go. I was thrilled and fascinated; but, of course, I made repeated efforts to leave, in anxious consideration of my hostess.

When I left at three o'clock I was mentally alert, but physically very tired. I had put in the day at my office before taking the last afternoon train for Saratoga. Before I was in bed there was a knock on the door. Mrs. Trask had sent Miss Pardee, her life-long companion, to my room with a little package she wished me to have that night. It contained a very beautiful ring—a star sapphire set in diamonds—which she had had Tiffany make especially for me. It has been on my finger ever since, and will remain there while I live.

Katrina Trask had a royal way of doing things. Another time I found on my dressing case a corsage bouquet fastened by an exquisite diamond pin.

I cannot imagine a more enchanting or brain-stimulating companion than she was. She was unique in her capacity for starting unusual verbal games. Once it amused her to assume that we were Greek women of two thousand years ago, treading fields of asphodel and talking of contemporary interests as we walked. She expected immediate return of her verbal ping-pong shots, and her interest in others rested to a large degree on their response to this demand. This called for mental briskness, for one never knew what she would start next.

She was carrying on a lively correspondence with her friend Carmen Sylva, Queen of Rumania, during those

years, and we were occasionally modern Rumanians as well
as early Greeks or Egyptians. It was the past and the men
and women of the past that most interested Mrs. Trask.
She never admitted that she believed in reincarnation, but
I always suspected that she did. She had a language of her
own that she dropped into in moments of excitement. Nobody
understood it, but it sounded fascinating.

All this, of course, had to be put over with actual genius
to make it interesting. Badly done it would have been deadly.
Mrs. Trask played her various rôles with a brilliance that carried a companion with her, if the companion had it in her to
respond. If she had not there were no more games and few
week-ends at Saratoga for her. Mrs. Trask would have made
a really great actress. She could throw herself into any part
with her whole heart, and at a moment's notice.

Naturally, she had strong dramatic interests. She wrote a
play called *King Alfred's Jewel,* and suddenly decided that
she would have a private performance of it at Yaddo, her
Saratoga home, with Thomas Mott Osborne, the civic re-
former, as Alfred, and with me as the Queen. She told me of
this during a visit to her Lake George camp. That was another superb setting for her. Its tents had tapestried linings,
and a small army of servants helped her to live the simple
life against this dreamlike background. All the comforts of
her town houses surrounded her, and a wonderful set of
chimes welcomed her friends to her island.

She took a vast interest in the proposed play, and went
to great expense for Mr. Osborne's costume and mine.
His came one week-end while we were both at the Camp.
That night he put it on. Then, as a surprise to Mrs. Trask,
he secured a boat, rowed to her camp, and stood up in the
boat in the moonlight, serenading her. He was a very handsome man and the effect was superb. Mrs. Trask was enchanted. This was illusion after her own heart.

We never had the performance of *King Alfred's Jewel*, which was to have been given at Yaddo during the following Christmas holidays. Just before those holidays Spencer Trask —a mighty man whose emblem was the pine tree, and who had adored his wife throughout their life together—was killed in a railroad accident.

The life-long associate of the couple had been Mr. Trask's friend and partner, George Foster Peabody. The devotion of the three, each to the other two, was unique and beautiful. No one who knew them was ever blind enough or small enough to misinterpret it. In his will Mr. Trask had appointed Mr. Peabody co-executor with Mrs. Trask. Some years after her husband's death Mr. Peabody married Mrs. Trask, to continue the care and protection Spencer had given her. She lived several years in this devoted and unselfish companionship; but her love of life and her spirit of gaiety had died with Spencer. She ceased to have house parties, but she did not forget her friends, as these letters show:

YADDO

With all my heart I bless you, my dear Miss Jordan, for your very beautiful letter so full of comprehension and interpretation of my book, and for the wonderful tribute you give it which is like tonic to my heart.

That book does not seem like a literary work to me. It was the passing on of a Vision that had been vouchsafed to my own soul and I trembled lest the Vision should be blurred in the transmission. The verdict of your clear sight, which I especially value, gives me new courage.

I have been wanting to write to you of many things, but writing has been the one thing that has been impossible. First, of course, I wanted to give you my profound thanks for what you have done for me by your letter. Then I wanted to speak to you of a great change which has come into my life. Perhaps you have heard it from others but I wanted you to hear it from me.

I have told you in the past about the great financial stringency that has been pressing upon me since my husband left me. At last it has become so serious that I am obliged to close this beloved home which is a very part of myself.

I move out the end of this month to a little farmhouse on the place.

Of course, I hate it—but I would be unworthy of my philosophy if I could not prove it. The practical details of the readjustment have kept me more than busy and that is why I have not written all the letters that I have had in my heart. . . .

Peace be with you,

KATRINA TRASK

YADDO

Though everything is pressing and life is calling to me on *every* side, I must stop one moment, My dear Ladye, and send a deep and joyous response to your exquisite story in the August *Harper*.

You have struck a clear, true note of humanity which must meet an answering response in every heart.

I have thought of you often and wondered how and where you are. Now I know how you are. Since I read this story I know that all is well with you. That being so, the where does not so much matter.

In the midst of our strenuous life, with the echo of shrieking shells, and the vortex from international complications, to find a story like yours is like being in a tangled jungle and coming upon a clear, fresh, crystal spring.

Peace be with you,

KATRINA TRASK

CHAPTER XIII

HENRY JAMES AND THE LONDON SEASON

ONE of my most delightful new friends was Margaret Deland, whose novels and Doctor Lavender stories were then among Harper's most popular fiction. I admired her immensely. The highest compliment I ever received was the one Mr. Alden gave me when he once predicted that I would some day succeed to Mrs. Deland's literary laurels. He was all wrong about that, alas. Even Henry Mills Alden had to make occasional mistakes.

I was writing a good deal at that time—*Tales of the Cloister* and the *May Iverson* stories, most of which were published serially in *Harper's Magazine*. Mr. Alden liked them—largely, I suspect, because their convent background was so new to him. The tales also helped to keep alive my own interest in convent life—not that any help there was needed. I sometimes eased the increasing strain of an overfull professional and social life by taking the midnight train for South Bend, Indiana, and passing Saturday and Sunday with two new convent friends I had made—Sister Mary Rita and Mother General Perpetua, both of the Order of the Holy Cross. They were wonderful women, and I needed those quiet days in a convent atmosphere as much as I had needed rest and change on *The World*. There I had failed to get them. Now I could have them, but not as often as I wished.

The New York professional and social games were strenuous. I was rarely at home over week-ends. I passed most of these at Jorjalma, and the rest with other hospitable

195

friends who had country homes near New York—Mrs. Spencer Trask, Mrs. Adrian Joline, Mrs. Selden Bacon, Mrs. McKee and many others. One week—the record week—I had eighteen Friday-to-Monday invitations. A few of them were from friends who really wanted me. The great majority, as always, were from generous and gregarious couples who enjoyed entertaining and liked to be surrounded by cheerful guests. I was a cheerful guest, even when I had to bring manuscripts with me and read them late at night after everybody else had gone to bed.

About this time Katherine Cecil Thurston's novel, *The Masquerader,* was running serially in the *Bazar.* Mrs. Thurston had written some short stories for the *Bazar,* and I had suggested that she try her hand at a novel. She did, and two interesting ribbons of memory tie up that package.

The story attracted unusual attention even as a serial, but the most striking letter of the great number I received came from a dying woman. She wrote that she could live only a few weeks longer and that she was deeply interested in Mrs. Thurston's story. She longed to finish it before she died and she asked if I would send her the rest of the novel in proof or manuscript form. I sent her the proofs, and then passed on her letter to Mr. Duneka, knowing he would be interested in it both as a tribute to our fiction and as a human document.

Unfortunately Mr. Duneka was away from the office that day, making one of his frequent visits to Mark Twain. A bright young man on his staff read the letter and was stirred by the advertising possibilities in it. Without consulting anybody else he had it put into print and broadcast throughout the country as a special literary bulletin. On a sober second thought he used only the writer's initials, but she and I were equally outraged by this breach of confidence. She wrote me a stricken and reproachful letter that added to my regret and humiliation. It was a long time before Mr. Duneka, himself equally regretful, could soothe me.

When the serial publication was finished and the novel was coming out in book form, Mr. Duneka and I had another spirited encounter over *The Masquerader*. We were very good friends, but we had worked together on the *World* and neither of us had any awe of the other. The discussions between us were always extremely frank. I asked Mr. Duneka how large the first edition of *The Masquerader* was to be.

"Five thousand copies," he said.

It was no affair of mine how many copies of *The Masquerader* were published in book form, but I immediately went up in the air. I reminded him of the unusual attention the serial had received while it was running, of the fact that every one in the office was reading it and was thrilled by it, of its present popularity in luncheon and dinner talk.

"You ought to publish a first edition of twenty-five thousand copies at the very least," I ended. "You could safely publish fifty thousand."

Mr. Duneka looked at me thoughtfully.

"Doesn't it ever occur to you that you can be wrong?" he asked. "*I* realize that I can be wrong sometimes. But then, *I'm* very modest."

Annoyed by this remark I assured Mr. Duneka that I could distinguish him from a violet at a single glance, and Mr. Duneka retorted that it was because he was so much more modest than the violet that I could. Then he delivered his ultimatum. He would order a first edition of ten thousand copies of *The Masquerader;* and the unsold copies would be stacked in heaps in my office to teach me not to be so cock-sure.

I was so often wrong that it is pleasant to remember that I was right about *The Masquerader*. It swept the country and broke all records of the period. While I was still reminding Mr. Duneka of this I went to Boston for a weekend with Margaret Deland and bought all rights to her *Awakening of Helena Ritchie,* which had an almost equally big sale. This sort of thing was not a part of my regular job. I threw it in as an extra. In my experience with Mrs. Deland it was also a labor of love. She was, and is, an amazingly big-hearted, big-souled woman with a most lovable personality and a gorgeous sense of humor. She gave a Boston tea for me Saturday afternoon at which I met for the first time another friend, Alice Brown.

The friendship between Miss Brown and me did not burst into bloom as rapidly as most of my new friendships had done. On the contrary, from the first a barrier rose between us, small but firm. It was a nice little barrier, prettily covered with the flowers and vines of good manners; but it was something I could not get over. I regretted this and was also artlessly surprised by it. All I ask of my friends is a reasonable amount of understanding, interest and entertainment, for which I am prepared to offer as fair an exchange as I can.

It was hard to understand Miss Brown's continued aloofness. She fled like a startled hare when I drew near. Once I actually saw her do it, at a reception to Ellen Terry, when she took sanctuary behind that august figure. I did not know then, and I have never learned since then, what was back of it. Miss Brown would tell me to-day, if I asked her, that it was shyness. It wasn't. That barrier, intangible but steadfast, remained between us for twenty years. Then my mother died, and Alice Brown wrote me one of the most beautiful letters I received. The barrier went down with a crash I could distinctly hear. From that time—seven years ago— Miss Brown and I have been the best and most understanding of friends. A strange experience. I shall never know why that barrier went up—or down!

On the Sunday of my week-end with her, Mrs. Deland had at luncheon the rarest souls of Boston's Brahmin literary group—including Julia Ward Howe, Thomas Wentworth Higginson, and—I think—Thomas Bailey Aldrich. Most of the guests were over eighty. When we were alone again Mrs. Deland remarked tentatively that I might have enjoyed a younger group more. The remark hurt. The meeting with that group was then and has remained one of the high lights of my literary experience—and I was aghast over Mrs. Deland's tacit suggestion that I had not appreciated it.

Two little episodes of her luncheon remain with me. We were talking about a recent edition of *Who's Who in America* —which apparently was filled with names my distinguished fellow guests had never heard of. Mrs. Howe suddenly spoke to me across the table.

"Miss Jordan," she said, "why shouldn't you and I write a book on What's What in America?"

I agreed and suggested that we start it before breakfast the next morning. Through two of her daughters, Florence Howe Hall and Maude Howe Elliott, I often met Mrs. Howe in New York after that, and several times heard her repeat her Battle Hymn of the Republic, as she was usually urged to do in any group she joined.

Mrs. Deland's luncheon was given in March. There had just been a heavy snowfall in Boston, followed by a quick thaw. While we were still at the table that day a small avalanche of snow fell on the extension roof of the dining-room. It made a mighty crash and the few younger guests were startled by the unexpected sound. Mrs. Howe, Mr. Higginson, and Mr. Aldrich merely raised their eyebrows and looked smilingly surprised over the unnecessary excitement of the others. Their calm was impressive.

A few months later I gave a New York luncheon for Mrs. Deland with Kate Douglas Wiggin, Gertrude Atherton and

Frances Hodgson Burnett among the guests, as well as Jane and Mary Findlater of Scotland. The Findlater sisters had just collaborated with Kate on a little book called *An Affair at the Inn,* and were making their first visit to America as her guests. My luncheon was at Delmonico's. If I may say so the food was extremely good. All the guests seemed to appreciate it except the Findlater sisters. Each picked delicately at a roll and neither ate anything. Kate cast an occasional despairing glance at them and later confided her sorrow to me.

"They won't eat a mouthful of anything they're not used to," she told me, "and my cook doesn't know how to make their Scotch broths and porridges. I've set every known American dish before them in vain. They've starved at my table. I've said to them, 'Haven't you even any curiosity?' But they *haven't,*" she finished with a deep sigh.

Mrs. Deland's letters, of which I had many, were always a delight, holding as they did the very essence of her personality. I kept them all, and I have dropped a few of them into the pages of this book to emphasize my point:

35 NEWBURY STREET,
BOSTON

DEAR MISS JORDAN,

It is perfectly useless to try to tell you what a tremendous boost your letter of the 7th gave me. . . . I am immensely cheered and helped by everything you said of my story! In fact, I am ready to say that you are the people, and wisdom will die with you. There are few things I want to do more than to believe in Helena—and when I read your letter I did believe in her—for a while, anyhow. The reason I have bored you to death by whining about it so, is that I have not been able to make the people in the story living creatures, and that was why I ventured, humbly, to say that if I had had another year to work on it I thought I might have made them live. But maybe I could not.

Anyhow, I thank heaven for what life there is in them, and

I am also grateful to my friends for alleging that they can see it without using opera glasses. You can imagine how much I value Colonel Harvey's good opinion, and I am impressed by the mental and moral stimulus which my publishers have so generously given me, every man Jack of them. Mr. Duneka wrote the kindest letters, and when I saw Mr. Alden in February he, too, was most encouraging.

Of course, he put his finger on one awfully weak place, which I have since patched up. He also told me candidly that the danger in the book was preachiness. After that I was on my guard to shut out the Shorter Catechism. Still, it slops over once in a while, and becomes didactic. Anyhow, the thing is done, and you like it—and I like you, but not in consequence of your literary appreciation, dear friend. . . .

When do you go abroad? And where do you go? If fate takes you to Madrid, do look out for Mrs. Elliott, who is there having the time of her life, hobnobbing with kings and queens and court artists, and sich. Her letters to me have been perfectly superb, bubbling over with vitality and beauty. I hope she will not try to lick her impressions into shape too soon. I may be mistaken, but I have a theory that emotions need to hibernate in the soul for a while before they can express themselves in literature which shall have at once vitality and distinction. I wrote something like this to her, but my comment was made only because some of the work she sent me betrayed an embarrassment of riches. If it had not been so good, it would have been better. However, she has got the real stuff. If she can put into shape, as I believe she can, the extraordinary situation in Spain, showing the *Zeitgeist*—the new wine in the old bottles, the modern thought confined in the methods and manners and traditions of a thousand years ago—she will produce a really great piece of work.

Forgive the long letter, and believe me,

Most gratefully yours,
MARGARET DELAND

35 NEWBURY STREET, BOSTON

MY DEAR MISS JORDAN,

I am much disturbed not to have sent you the paper which I promised you three weeks ago. When I promised, it was a little more than half written—and I thought it was going to be simple enough to finish it up. But Mr. Deland has been ill ever since that time, with an attack of rheumatism, which, although it is not serious, has been very engrossing to me, and I have not added one line more to my paper. I will try and get it into shape for you before I go abroad the middle or end of June. ...

Thank you for the quotation from the letter. Yes, it is a help to me. I feel the subject so much that I am a little doubtful as to my ability to write about it, because there is so much danger of being morbid. To tell you the truth, *I am afraid of life:* and while my theories are fine, and lend themselves to essays, I confess that I am somewhat like the boy who whistles when he passes the graveyard to keep his courage up. I don't quite believe my theories! ...

Very sincerely yours,
MARGARET DELAND

TUESDAY—76 MT. VERNON STREET

DEAR EDITOR,

Your letter gave me so much pleasure and made me so glad that I came to see you—altho' I think I had better never come again, lest you find me out!

I have just come back from the Pit whence I was digged— its name is Pittsburgh, and the suggestion of Hell is not bad. It is an awful and splendid place; the apotheosis of hideousness —but an apotheosis for all that. Miles of coke ovens flaring in the gloom, miles of furnace sheds, cavernous black depths where points of electric light twinkle far up in the shadows, or showers of red sparks crash out from under hammers, or a living serpent of a white hot steel rail goes sliding over the black floor. And through it all, little gnomes moving and working day and night. It is all power and squalor and potentiality, and I am mighty glad I don't live there!

I read the "Voice in the World of Pain," the night I got back. I am so glad you wrote it, for the conviction in it will help people; and besides, artistically, it made cold shivers run down my back—and I am grateful to anybody that can do that. I do hope I may see you again soon. Aren't you to be anywhere in Yankee Land this summer so that you can look in on me at Kennebunkport, in Maine?

Cordially yours,
MARGARET DELAND

SUNDAY—KENNEBUNKPORT, MAINE

DEAR MISS JORDAN,

You might not think so—considering that I have not acknowledged it—but that letter of yours about my illness, gave me a lot of comfort. In the first place, it was kind of you, with a thousand and one things to do—to write it; and then its friendly courage was a brace.

I am better—in fact I am compelled to say that seven pounds, carefully lost, have returned; and I am apprehensive that they will bring seven others more wicked than themselves. The only thing that bothers me is a queer, unreasonable fatigue. It seems as if some spring had been cut. I hope you do not know the feeling. It interferes with work—in fact, I can't work. I hope to begin soon—but at present, if I whisper the word, Mr. Deland glares. He rules me with a rod of iron—as you said he would; but I thrive under it. Are you going to be in this part of the world this summer? If you are, will you come to Kennebunkport? If you say yes, all shall be forgiven. I refer to your conduct last summer.

I suppose the reason I am bowled over, nervously, is that the necessity of the operation was very suddenly revealed to me, and there were several days of the apprehension of malignancy. Did you read a story of mine called *The Stuffed Animal House?* I know now that it is true. The sudden confronting of Death is a profoundly shaking experience. To be sure, it turned out to be a mistake; but while it lasted it changed life.

It was all a deep experience; and part of it was the dearness and kindness of friends—as witness your letter.

Cordially yours,

MARGARET DELAND

35 NEWBURY ST., BOSTON

DEAR MISS JORDAN:

You are a very good-natured editor, and you shall have one, or possibly two, papers before I sail for foreign parts. I have begun one of them already. . . .

I think you are right in what you say of grief. . . . The sting of grief is regret: and yet regret is the measure of our ideals. I suppose human nature could not afford to be without it. In

a certain way, it is the price that Love pays for loving; but it
is sometimes a frightful price, and I have long felt that I
wanted to say what I do truly feel. Let us remember to be kind,
because if we have to remember that we have been unkind, life
will be unendurable. I rather fancy that this is what acquaintance with grief means. It is a warning to daily living.

I would be so glad if I might have another glimpse of you
before we both take our departure. Won't you tell me where you
are to be in Europe, so that if I am anywhere in your neighbor-
hood I can come and knock at your door?

Cordially yours,
MARGARET DELAND

In the same mail with this letter, as it happened, came one
from Mr. Howells, dated from the Villa Lamberti, in San
Remo, and breathing nostalgia. The last line explains the
nostalgia. Mr. Howells would not have been homesick if his
daughter had been with him. After a few paragraphs on
business matters he goes on to say:

... We are in the loveliest air and under the sunniest sky.
But it is not the Italy of old, because I am not the Howells of
youth. At times I am hungry for home, but we shall stay the
winter, probably.

I wish you had a moment to send me some news of James, if
you have any. He promised to write, but I know how it must
be with him.

My daughter is in Florida, but we expect her here next week.

Yours sincerely,
W. D. HOWELLS

Another of my favorite friends of that period was James
Huneker, the distinguished music critic and reviewer. He
was also among the most interesting men talkers I have
known. He always called me Brünhilde, and some of his
letters to me are included in the biography of him published
after his death. He was a close friend of Edward MacDowell,

and I remember all too vividly one story he told me about the composer.

The two friends took frequent country walks together. During one of these MacDowell remarked that he could locate a hidden spring by using a witch-hazel switch. When Huneker scoffed, MacDowell found a witch-hazel switch and proceeded to prove his claim. He found the spring. He enjoyed the little triumph, and often referred to it afterwards. Then Huneker began his European wanderings. When he returned to New York the first news he had of his old friend was that MacDowell was failing mentally. Huneker went at once to see him. Because of the long association of the two men Mrs. MacDowell led him to her husband's room, and left him there alone with his friend.

The big room was furnished as a nursery. In the center of it MacDowell sat, surrounded by toys. There was a large drum before him, and in his hands was a brilliantly painted trumpet. When Huneker entered he was alternately beating the drum and blowing the trumpet, or absorbedly doing both. He paid no attention whatever to his visitor, and the picture was so tragic that Huneker walked to a window and stood with his back to the room trying to control his emotion.

Suddenly a hand touched his shoulder. He swung 'round, to find MacDowell standing beside him, his face alight with interest. ·

"Do you know," he crowed, "I can find a hidden spring with a witch-hazel switch!"

Then abruptly the light of intelligence went out. The composer's features twisted and his expression was that of a lost and frightened baby. For another instant he stood still, trembling, and looking at his old comrade. Then, abruptly, he went back to his place on the floor, picked up his drumsticks and his toy trumpet, and filled the room with discords.

I was now going abroad every summer, meeting many interesting men and women in many lands, having all sorts of varied and interesting experiences. One of those I remember most clearly was that of Wanda and the mermaids.

I met Wanda during a voyage to Spain. She was an engaging child of six, who seemed as free from supervision as the breezes that swept the decks. She came and went among us as she chose, equally at home with the passengers or on the Captain's bridge. She was a wise child who had her own ideas on most subjects and expressed them with startling freedom. I suspect that she had lived most of her little life in European hotels, foregathering with the types she met there. She spoke English, French, and German, and she had a staggering vocabulary that included many verbal gems from other tongues.

Notwithstanding her sophistication Wanda liked fairytales. She discovered that I could tell them and we became fast friends, each of us equally indifferent to the new theory that such tales have unfortunate effects on youthful minds and slumbers. Personally I have always had a special interest in mermaids. I passed this on to Wanda, who immediately and passionately shared it. Together we peopled the ocean with mermaids, and I am sure that Wanda rather expected to see them climbing up the sides of our ship.

When we were midway across the ocean one of the worst storms of years struck the Atlantic. It was a mighty thing, of wild winds and engulfing waves. The decks were awash and the passengers were urgently advised to remain below. Most of them did so, because they were seasick and had to. Wanda and I were among the few who remained on deck. Wanda was deeply concerned about the mermaids. She wanted to know exactly what was happening to them in such a tempest. The storm was now at its height, and their plight seemed serious to her.

I agreed that it was. I suggested to Wanda that the storm had probably tied a hard knot in every mermaid's tail. Intrigued by the charm of this picture as it came before me, I added that all the mermaids we were especially interested in—those who had figured in our stories—might be sitting this minute in a row on the bottom of the sea, looking at the knots in their tails and feeling terribly low in their minds. Wanda was both fascinated and depressed by the suggestion. Did the knots hurt? Not in the least. They were merely extremely inconvenient, and cramped a mermaid's style.

Wanda went up to the bridge to find out whether the Captain was prepared to do something about those tails. He was in his cabin, however, and the first mate was on the bridge. The first mate took a lively interest in the problem, but before he and Wanda could settle it the biggest wave of the storm came along. It engulfed the great ship, tore off part of the bridge, and carried Wanda and the mate away on its crest. The officer had just time to grasp the child's wrist with his left hand before they were swept over the broken bridge with the shattered timber around them. By what seemed a miracle they were not carried overboard. They landed on the deck below, shocked, badly bruised and choking, but without a serious injury in either body. The mate had a rub-down and a change of clothes and went back to his job. Wanda was taken to the ship's hospital for a thorough going-over and was then put to bed, from which she sent an immediate and imperative summons to me.

The doctor, and a parent of Wanda who suddenly appeared from some mysterious bourne, objected to any visiting. Wanda had experienced a great shock and must be kept absolutely quiet. But Wanda persisted, and rolled and tossed in her bed till they sent for me. What Wanda imperatively needed, it then appeared, was to know whether, if she had kept on going with the mate, she would have reached the bottom of the sea and discovered those mermaids' with the knots in their tails. And would she have been able to help untie the knots? In short, Wanda was feeling a sense of frustration. She was convinced that she had missed a great opportunity, both for observation and for social service, and she could not endure the knowledge.

She was vastly relieved to learn that the wave which had almost carried her off the ship had at the same time untied the knot in every mermaid's tail. The mermaids were extremely comfortable now, and were keeping very quiet indeed because their doctors had ordered it. Much cheered by this reassuring picture, Wanda went to sleep.

The peak of my European experiences came when Mrs. Harvey invited me to go abroad with her for three months as her guest. Five weeks had been the limit of my previous visits—two weeks on the sea and three on land, the three devoted to earnest but abortive efforts to see most of Europe in that time. The prospect of three months made me breathless. We put in six weeks in Paris, with side jaunts through the château country, and finished with six weeks at Claridges in London, at the height of the London season, meeting Colonel Harvey there. Characteristically, he had planned a large dinner for the night we arrived: and he immediately told me he would seat me next to Henry James.

That evening was, I think, the most interesting of my literary life. There were twenty-four guests at the table—an especially brilliant group including some of the most distinguished men and women then in London. I remember only Henry James and Mr. and Mrs. George Leveson Gower (pronounced Loosen-Gore). Sydney Brooks told me that Mr. Leveson Gower was the "nephew of two-thirds of the British nobility and the cousin of the rest," and that Mrs. Leveson

Gower was a daughter of the eighth Earl of Monson and one of the reigning beauties of London. They are both still living and Sir George has succeeded to the title of his father, who was said to be the original of Mrs. Humphry Ward's "Lord Lackington" in *Lady Rose's Daughter*. Henry James and the Leveson Gowers were close friends.

The next day Mrs. Leveson Gower, of whom I saw a great deal while I was in London, told me Henry James had said all sorts of nice things to her about me. Mrs. Leveson Gower was an unusually charming woman, but I remember her particularly because of the interest she took in the pleasant friendship that developed between Mr. James and myself. She gave a large dinner for Colonel and Mrs. Harvey a few evenings later, and firmly placed Mr. James and me side by side at her table. The Harveys were given more than a dozen brilliant dinners in the next six weeks, to which I, being their guest, was also invited. Mr. James was at eight or nine of those dinners and invariably—goaded on by Mrs. Leveson Gower—our hostesses placed us side by side.

The absurdity of the situation was all that saved it from becoming annoying. Fortunately, we each had a sense of humor; but if that little flame of friendship had not been the real thing our friends in London would certainly have killed it among them.

It survived, however, and it had started in the most beguiling way. In the beginning Mr. James must have been flattered by my thorough knowledge of his novels. I had not only read them all, many of them several times, but I remembered each of them in detail. One of the little gifts some fairy gave me at birth is a freak memory. I not only remember the books I read, but for years afterwards I can quote complete passages in them. I have known only one other person who could do this to the same degree. That was Arthur Brisbane. He remembered the book passages most striking and most worth while, however; while my memory's store-room is cluttered with all sorts of useless furniture.

However, I could and did remember Mr. James' novels so vividly that I could have passed an examination on them anywhere. I had no thought of impressing him with the fact, but he promptly discovered it and I think he set a few traps for me. We talked about his books through most of the dinner. When the men returned to the drawing-room after dinner Mr. James came to me at once—and we settled down to a talk on the general problems of the universe, which continued till the end of the evening. After this sturdy start our friendly liking survived even the well-meant efforts of our friends to kill it by over-culture.

Colonel and Mrs. Harvey and I met Mr. James almost everywhere we went, and we went to dozens of interesting houses and places. I learned all sorts of things about Mr. James. The strangest was that in appearance he was not in the least literary. That had been almost a shock to me. One of my earliest impressions of him had been gained from a photograph showing him resting his head on his hand and looking as if he had written all the literature in the world. I found him a rather over-plump man in his sixties, quite bald and round of face, who would have been classified by an intelligent person who did not know him as a successful lawyer or banker of the old school. It was not until that first dinner was half over, and he suddenly turned and looked at me very closely, that I realized the strange power of Henry James' eyes. They made me feel in those instants as if he had read me to the soul—and I rather think he had.

I learned other things about him. That, incredibly, he was extraordinarily shy. That his habit of hemming and hawing and repeating a sentence two or three times was largely due to this shyness. I had originally diagnosed it for Colonel and

Mrs. Harvey as a quest for perfection : instinctively bringing out the perfect sentence the first time; repeating it more deliberately to test every word the second time; accepting it as satisfactory the third time, and triumphantly sending it forth as produced by Henry James.

One example of this has been a feature of my intimate monologues ever since. I can still produce it word for word, with the exact timing and every intonation of Henry's voice. Henry Savage Landor was a fellow guest at one of those gay dinners of our London season, and I had asked Mr. James if he himself accepted literally Mr. Landor's recital of his incredible experiences in Tibet. Mr. James reflected an instant over this problem and then delivered his verdict.

"Eliminating—ah—" he said, "eliminating, ah-h— eliminating nine-tenths—nine-tenths—nine-*tenths*—(slowly) -of-of-of- (very fast) of what he claims (slowly) there is still—(fast) there—is still—there is still—(faster) enough left (pause) enough left (pause) to make—to make—to make (very fast) a remarkable record (slow) a remarkable record—ah—ah—(slower)—a re-markable re-cord!"

There is no exaggeration in that quotation. It is a typical example of Mr. James' ordinary method of speech. He almost never changed a word in his verbal gropings, and the intelligent reader will observe that every word in the sentence was the word which best expressed Mr. James' meaning. And (as always) those seemingly fumbling, groping phrases held, when complete, deep food for reflection.

I soon learned, however, that when Mr. James was deeply interested these little affectations of speech fell away. He spoke always with rare and exquisite use of words as the tools of his trade: but he talked naturally and simply, and often with beguiling humor and an odd exuberance.

At times he also talked with an extraordinary candor. Once he told me of a young disciple of his who insisted on sitting at his feet—where, I inferred, he was very much in his great master's way. Mr. James grew so weary of having him there that he pulled wires and found an opening for the youth in Canada—a country far removed from Mr. James' feet.

"I went to see him off," Mr. James ended exuberantly. "I was afraid he would discover how delighted I was to see him off. I shook hands with him again and again. Then, at the last moment, just as the train was leaving the station, I emptied all my pockets and gave him every penny I had with me."

Mr. James stopped and looked at me with the wide grin of an impish little boy. "I had taken pains not to have too much money with me!" he ended.

Another time he described to me his sole meeting with Thackeray, when the latter was making his first visit to America. Mr. James was an infant of six at the time, clad in a new suit decorated with shining brass buttons.

"They covered me as stars cover the sky," Mr. James said. "I was dazzled by them. I expected Mr. Thackeray to be dazzled, too. But my buttons amused him, and he laughed. It was a terrible experience for me. I have never forgotten it—for in that moment I experienced my first sense of disillusionment."

Mr. Landor, the explorer, whose claims to fame Mr. James had summed up so accurately, was also a frequent fellow guest at these London dinners. He had just returned from his expedition to the "forbidden city" of Lhasa, where, by his accounts, he had been captured, tortured, and very nearly blinded and killed. London society appeared to be made up equally of those who believed Mr. Landor and those who did not. He was very entertaining at dinner one night when we sat side by side.

He began by explaining that human beings are brought into the world with certain primitive instincts—a legacy from past ages. Properly developed these would be invaluable aids in after-life. A baby, left in a room among strangers, will instinctively reach to the person it feels it can trust. But, Mr. Landor sadly pointed out, the first thing we all do is to ignore and thus in time destroy these instincts. We often instinctively recognize a man as an enemy in first meeting him, and just as often we end by ignoring that instinct and making a friend of him. In one way or another we always pay the piper for the blunder. He himself, Mr. Landor added, always cultivated and followed his instinctive feeling about others.

For example, he said, when he formed his expedition to penetrate Tibet to the forbidden city of Lhasa, he had chosen as head man of his guides and porters a native that no one else seemed to trust. Again and again, from all sides and sources, he was warned that this man was not reliable. If engaged, Landor's advisers were sure, that native would destroy the success of the project. But the explorer's instinct, on which he always relied, convinced him that the guide was all right. He engaged him. And, Mr. Landor added triumphantly, *that* was the man who had saved his life at Lhasa, with appalling risk to his own.

Mr. Landor gave a tea for us in his big studio, whose walls were festooned with sketches and photographs of himself and his expeditions. Many of these showed his difficult ascents in the Himalayas, and I was greatly struck by his garb. The pictures represented him as a human fly, pasted to the sides of peaks twenty thousand feet above sea level, or hanging by an eyelid, as it were, over abysses thousands of feet below him. Wherever he hung or clung he was always clad exactly as he was clad at the party he was giving that day—in a blue serge sack suit, with a nice shirt and collar and tie, and brightly polished shoes. I expressed some surprise over this.

"Oh, that's the way I always dress," Mr. Landor airily explained. "Summer or winter, in the tropics or at the north pole, I dress exactly the same. I never wear anything but a blue serge suit, shoes and socks, a shirt, a collar, and a tie."

I asked if he didn't add an occasional sweater or a bit of woolen underwear at the top of the Karakorum Range, for example, twenty-five thousand feet above sea level. Mr. Landor looked pained.

"I never wear underwear of any kind," he assured me. "See!"

He bent and pulled the leg of his trousers far above the knee. His other guests came closer. They expected, I think, an exhibition of scars he had brought back from the tortures at Lhasa. There was no underwear in view.

"No woolen shirt, either," Mr. Landor cried gaily, and tore open the bosom of his starched linen shirt-front. There was nothing under the linen shirt-front but Mr. Landor.

David Munro, who had come to London with Colonel Harvey and who was also at the tea, always claimed that this was the most entertaining exhibition we had attended during that memorable London season.

A dinner given by Mr. and Mrs. Edwin Abbey was the most interesting of the long series. I sat at Mr. Abbey's left. He had recently painted the picture of the Coronation of Edward VII, and all the members of the royal family had posed for him, singly and in groups. He told me a great deal about them. He began the evening by telling me that Emperor William of Germany had a cancer of the throat, like his father, and could not live two years.

"I have it on the highest authority," he added. "Not the King's, but some one much closer to Emperor William than Edward VII is."

He talked a great deal about the royal sitters. Queen Alex-

andra had been really distressed by the painting of one of
Edward's legs, he said, and made the artist do it over.

"You must surely have observed," the Queen murmured
reproachfully to Mr. Abbey, "that the King has an unusually well-shaped leg. You have not done it justice."

The present Duke of Windsor was in the Coronation
picture and was therefore one of the sitters. It was the cus-
tom of Mr. Abbey to make original black and white sketches
of his sitters, and then to paint them on the large canvas.
He asked each of the royal sitters to autograph these
sketches, which were for his own collection, and they were
all very gracious about doing so. Little Edward, who was
just learning to print letters, was very much set up at being
asked to sign his portrait. He seized the sketch and the pencil,
and beginning close to the right margin of the picture,
made a huge EDW. Then, to his chagrin, he discovered that
he had used up all his space.

He looked at those around him. They were watching him,
but at a sign from his grandfather they remained silent.
Little Edward, however, had now thought of a suggestion
himself—a typically kingly one. He asked Mr. Abbey to
make a new sketch and leave more room at the bottom of it.
His grandmother, Queen Alexandra, pointed out that this
would be a great deal of trouble for the artist, and could
not be done. "Davy" must think of some other way of sign-
ing his name on the sketch.

The small boy's lips quivered. For an instant he looked
ready to burst into tears. Then he seized the pencil and
printed above the big EDW a very small *ard*. The sketch,
with this signature, is one of the treasures in the Abbey Collection. The episode reminded me of an inscription on one
of the old headstones in a New England cemetery.

"Lord, I am Thine," had been the dead woman's triumphant choice as her epitaph. Here, too, space had given out—

this time by just enough for one letter. The abridged version, old and mossy now against the marble, still meets the startled eye. "Lord, I am Thin."

At the Leveson Gowers' dinner I met Sir George, a really delightful old gentleman whose interest in America, however, seemed confined to the harnessing of Niagara Falls. He was quite deaf, but he wished to know all about those falls. They happened also to be the subject that always held Arthur Chandler's attention in his hours of leisure. I had often listened while Mr. Chandler discoursed on the falls at great length, and I had not always been interested. I was grateful to him in that hour for the information I shouted at Sir George, and to which the other dinner guests were forced to listen. It was certainly more accurate than it would have been without the helpful memory of Mr. Chandler's monologues.

Mr. Howells and his daughter Mildred were also in London that season and we met frequently. But my greatest interest continued to be Mr. James, who was always turning up. We invariably greeted each other with enthusiasm and a cheerful camaraderie that no intelligent person could possibly mistake for any warmer emotion than a pleasant friendship. The silly gossip about us died. It was revived later, however, when Mr. James returned to America to write his impressions of his native land after a quarter of a century of absence from it.

He found it greatly changed and was pained by many of the changes, which seemed to have borne out his worst forebodings. I was having some eye-trouble and eye-tests at this time, which meant that I was at home for a few days and moving in dimly lighted rooms. Mr. James frequently dropped in to sit in this gloaming with me, and I shall always remember his understanding sympathy.

Incidentally, he poured forth his first vivid impressions

of American life. He disliked America's noise, the sloppy
speech of its people, their bad manners and frequent rudeness.
As an instance of the rudeness he gave me a first-hand account of an experience with a young brakeman. The brakeman was passing through a railroad car in which Mr. James
was a passenger. The author stopped the lad and asked at
what hour the train would reach a certain city. The brakeman looked at him, and passed on without replying.

"And that," Mr. James sadly ended, "was the end of an
association which, although so brief, I had fondly hoped
might be so pleasant."

Most of all Mr. James objected to what, in an impassioned moment, he called our "damned orchids." He seemed
shocked by the oath even as it fell from his lips, but he made
it clear that the "damned orchids," which he seemed to be
finding on every luncheon and dinner table where he sat as
a guest, epitomized to him America's tendency toward vulgar
ostentation.

In his turn he supplied Americans with a few disappointments. He remembered clearly and fondly the fine old literary
guard of Boston and New York, but he had no knowledge
of or interest in the literary new-comers. While he was
here I gave a reception for him, to which I invited his
available old friends, as well as our best group of up-and-
coming young writers. The names of the latter meant nothing
to him, and his hearty handclasps did not comfort them for
the revelation conveyed by his vague smile. Some of the
writers, both old and young, resented this. In presenting them
to the Master I pronounced each name with almost piercing
distinctness, but usually in vain. Hamlin Garland was so
affected by the unbroken calm with which his name was
received that he broke out earnestly, "I'm *Hamlin* Garland,
Mr. James!"

"A-h—h," said Mr. James, and shook hands all over

again, smiling cherubically. There is a story that when Miss Wilkins was introduced to him very impressively as "Miss Mary E. Wilkins, the *author*," Mr. James brought out the smile again and said kindly, "Ah, you *write?*"

I never believed that one.

My Gramercy Park apartment is diagonally across from the Players' Club. Mr. James dropped in at tea time one afternoon, as he had a pleasant way of doing, and told me the Players' Club was giving a stag dinner for him at eight o'clock that night.

"I know," I said. "You're to make a speech, too. Mr. Munro told me about it."

Mr. James immediately became very much agitated.

"But that's all a mistake," he cried passionately. "I never made a speech in my life. I could not make a speech to *save* my life. I told the worthy Munro so. I made it clear to him. I thought he understood."

"No, they're all expecting a speech," I said unfeelingly. "They know you don't want to make a formal speech, but they're counting on you to stand up and chat with them as a friend and a brother."

Mr. James then looked so miserable that my heart ached for him.

"You have time to prepare a brilliant 'extemporaneous' talk that will lift them out of their chairs," I reminded him.

Mr. James stared thoughtfully into the fire.

"Ah—h—" he murmured. "A-h-h-h. Quite so."

He swallowed a cup of tea and rushed away. David Munro, whose office was next to mine at Harper's, gave me the rest of the story the next morning. Mr. James had made his "extemporaneous" speech and had covered himself with glory. He had been wise and witty and altogether delightful.

"But the new experience and the applause and excitement

went to his head," Mr. Munro ended sadly "He kept getting up all evening to make more speeches."

Three more incidents insist on a place here. The first has to do with the deserved rebuke I overheard Mr. James give a woman who was foolish enough to ask the Master the meaning of a certain passage in *The Wings of the Dove.*

"My dear lady," Mr. James said coldly, "if after the infinite labor I give to my literature I am unable to convey to you my meaning, how can you expect me to do so by mere word of mouth?"

The second incident concerns Mr. James's first article on the American scene, sent back from London after his return there. Colonel Harvey mentioned at a dinner one evening that he had received the manuscript. Immediately there was great interest around the table as to what Mr. James had said.

"Do give us a synopsis of it," one woman begged. The Colonel skidded away from the subject, but at the first pause another guest repeated the request. Colonel Harvey pretended he had not heard it. The next morning he sent the manuscript to my desk. I read it and at once understood the Colonel's unwillingness to contribute a synopsis to his dinner guests. Mr. James had written that chapter from the highest peak of his latest and most involved literary style— the style in which, through his desperate efforts to make his meaning crystal clear, he so often obscured it. I doubt if any one but Mr. James himself could have given a clear synopsis of that contribution to our literature.

The third incident was described to me by Ernest Piexotto, during a Sunday luncheon at the Otis Skinners'. Mr. Piexotto, he told me, had passed a week-end with Henry James the previous summer, at Mr. James' home, Lamb House, in Rye. He mentioned one detail of the visit to illustrate Mr. James's meticulous attention to the comfort of his guests.

The morning after his arrival, Mr. Piexotto said, he was awakened by Mr. James's valet, who stood by the bed-side offering the artist a small golden bowl filled with a clear liquid. Mr. Piexotto, only half awake, stared at the bowl. Was it a finger bowl? Surely not at this hour. Was it something to drink? He put his perplexity to the valet as man to man.

"What the devil is this?"

"The temperature of your bath, sir," the valet intoned. "Will you kindly let me know if it is satisfact'ry?"

Mr. Piexotto thrust a finger into the warm water, and nodded. That was that.

Mr. Duneka's sense of humor found new expression in a story he circulated after Mr. James had returned to England. It swept through the Harper offices and soon was joyously quoted throughout literary circles. Briefly, it recited that just before sailing Mr. James had sent me a written proposal of marriage which, owing to his new and highly involved literary style, I was unable to comprehend. I at once replied, however, asking Mr. James what his letter was about; but owing to my illegible handwriting the Master was unable to read my reply, and received the impression that I had refused him. Mr. Duneka asked the coöperation of the staff in straightening out this tragic tangle. He got it—and so did I.

Mr. Duneka's humor was a hardy perennial that blossomed along the Harper way. He made frequent visits to Mark Twain, which I naturally supposed were due to his desire to bask in that congenial presence. Mr. Duneka assured me that he had a higher and less selfish motive. Colonel Harvey had made a contract securing for Harper and Brothers the exclusive publication of Mark Twain's future work, at forty cents a word. Mr. Duneka loved and vastly admired Mark Twain, but he was anxious to make a good financial showing for the Harpers and he was horrified by these terms.

"Whenever Clemens lets me know he's getting ready to write something for us," Mr. Duneka told me, "I go to see him and encourage him. After I have encouraged him for a day or two he can't write anything for months! I've saved Harpers thousands and thousands of dollars that way," he complacently ended.

I hasten to explain to the literal-minded that this was another of Frederick Atherton Duneka's little jokes.

CHAPTER XIV

CARREL, NOGUCHI, AND SCIENCE

I WAS still making on shipboard some of the most satisfying friendships of my life. Mr. and Mrs. William D. Barbour of New York were among the new friends made on the sea. Harriet and I were again on our way to Spain. Before entering it we were to cross from Gibraltar to Tangiers and Algiers and cast a casual eye over Northern Africa. The Barbours had meant to go straight up through Spain from Gibraltar. They changed their plans and went on the African jaunt with us. After that we four meandered through Spain together—an enchanted and enchanting pilgrimage in congenial company.

When Harriet or Martha or both went abroad with me, as they so often did, I had always been in charge of the expedition—acting as spokesman, interpreter, treasurer, and the like. No doubt I frequently carried out my own wishes with an airy authority. I realized that this would never do in a party that included Mr. Barbour. He, too, was accustomed to planning and managing. At his request Harriet and I put our interests in his hands. I christened him the Czar and retired so far into the background of our party that I could hardly find myself. Nevertheless, as we went on Mr. Barbour christened me the Autocrat and Harriet the Lamb. I retaliated by christening Mrs. Barbour the Patient Sufferer—which she was, the darling! Then I demanded an explanation of my own new title. From the moment we joined forces I had met unquestioningly every plan Mr. Barbour made. It was the Spanish path to peace.

"Have I ever hinted at any little wish of my own on this tour?" I asked him.

"You have not," Mr. Barbour admitted.

"Then why, after a month in which I haven't even intimated that my tooth-brush or the privilege of using it was my own, *why* am I called an autocrat?"

"Because," Mr. Barbour explained serenely, "it was so clear that you *could* have been an autocrat if you had wanted to be!"

For the rest of the summer the Czar, the Autocrat, the Patient Sufferer and the Lamb went their happy way together. We saw our first bull-fight at Linea, just across the neutral strip that divides Gibraltar and Spain. Horses were not used in the fights at Linea, and we saw something like a fair contest, in which the strength and ferocity of the bulls were pitted against the brains and skill of the matadors, with a chance for either side to win. We remained through the entire fight. But later, on a very great occasion in Seville, when the royal family was present at the fight and horses *were* used, I left the scene of diversion with such haste that I must have stepped firmly on the feet of most of the grandees of Spain.

It was during a voyage to Europe that I first met the Marchioness Lagergren, a woman as charming and magnetic in her way as Katherine Barbour, and with whom I corresponded for twenty years afterwards. It was on a ship, too, that I met Mr. and Mrs. Malone.

The Malones were a delightful couple from some small town in Pennsylvania. During the first days of the voyage I observed that they seemed to know everybody on the ship. They occupied steamer chairs in a row that stretched from prow to stern of the big liner. All the passengers in these chairs seemed their intimate friends, and groups of four or more persons were always standing talking to the Malones. When I finally met the popular couple I asked the explanation of this wide acquaintance. Mr. Malone gave it after a careful look around and a long, deep groan.

It appeared that his wife was the most popular woman in their home town—the person every one knew and turned to in joy or sorrow. It appeared also that she had finally broken in health under these demands from loving friends, and had been ordered by her physicians to go abroad for complete rest and quiet. She was to hibernate during the voyage and the weeks abroad. She was to eat and sleep, and talk to no one but her husband. If she failed to follow the prescription the doctors would not be responsible. . . .

The Malones made their preparations and bade their friends affectionate farewells. Their friends had a better idea. The Malones were going abroad? Three rousing cheers! They, too, would go abroad. What could be better than to go with the beloved Malones, who were so experienced and who knew all the ropes? They went—to the number of more than thirty. The Malones found them all on board, with their luggage, when they themselves arrived on the ship just before sailing. It was, their friends asserted with joyful outcries, "a surprise."

"In other words," said Augustus Thomas when I told him this story at the Charles Melville Deweys' dinner table, "their friends wouldn't let 'em Malone!"

I wrote a story around the episode. It came out in *Harper's Monthly* and won me this charming note from Mr. Howells:

65 MT. VERNON STREET, BOSTON
March 21st

DEAR MISS JORDAN,

I have just finished reading *The Crosbys' Rest Cure* to my daughter, and I must tell you of our joy in it, differently expressed:

She: How heavenly!

I: How hellish!

And it is both, and true—cruelly, killingly true, and perfectly done. Do some more—you can't do too many more—like it!

With our joint regards,

Yours sincerely,

W. D. HOWELLS

Subsequently the story was put into moving pictures by Mr. and Mrs. Sidney Drew.

About this time I met Mrs. Abraham Flexner, whose brother-in-law, Dr. Simon Flexner, was then head of the Rockefeller Institute. Mrs. Flexner discovered that I was very much interested in some of the experiments going on at the Institute, and particularly avid to know about Dr. Alexis Carrel's efforts, then in progress, to make an old dog young again. Any experiment at Rockefeller is always its own secret, and quite properly so, up till the time when the Institute authorities are convinced that the results of that experiment are final. This dog experiment was so thrilling in its possibilities that a hint of it had leaked out. I was greatly intrigued. The theory back of the experiment had caught my imagination and was persistently playing with it. When Mrs. Flexner invited me to visit the Institute with her, she must have been surprised by the fervor with which I accepted her invitation.

That day stands out against the background of the past with a special vividness. I think if I were on the witness stand I could account for every minute of it, and could describe in detail every incident and personality in it. Most of all, of course, I was impressed by Dr. Alexis Carrel and Dr. Noguchi, his distinguished Japanese colleague. Both men gave me an amazing amount of their time, and Dr. Noguchi showed me a collection of germs under microscopes that haunted me for months. The one I remember best was the germ of hydrophobia—which looked to me, as I told Dr. Noguchi, exactly like an infernal forget-me-not —small, blue, and in some way hellish. I also hung fascinated over the germ of lockjaw, not quite so picturesque in appearance but quite devilish enough. There were many others. I remember them all so vividly that I think I could make accurate color sketches of them to-day—when more than twenty years separate me from my brief association with them.

I was even more interested in Noguchi himself than in his exhibition of germs. He was a singularly gentle little man, who oddly combined perfection of manner with an extraordinary effect of modesty. He was eager to show his work, because his work was his life: but he succeeded perfectly in making himself merely a background against which that work stood out. I was so deeply impressed by this that years later, when I read of Noguchi's death in Accra, Africa, where he had gone from the Institute to study the yellow fever germ, I could not believe the details of his final hours were accurate. He was represented as having fought death with a furious passion, an outraged passion, in which he beat his breast and cried out again and again, "But I am Noguchi!" as if to frighten death itself by the magic of that name. I could not be convinced that delirium or even death could so transform his gentle, modest soul.

Of course, an instant's reflection gave me the explanation. It was not Noguchi that Noguchi was fighting for, but Noguchi's work—that work of such importance to the whole world. Its interruption filled him with a divine fury. What right had death, he was asking, to stop Noguchi's *work?* But death did stop that work, and when the great Noguchi was only fifty-two. Who can wonder that he died fighting to the last for what was infinitely more to him than his own or any other man's life?

I never saw him "in person," as the moving-picture producers put it, after that day at the Rockefeller Institute. But in memory I have seen him many times, bending over his tubes and slides and microscopes. When I read of his final great battle for science, off in a lonely jungle, I saw that, too.

Dr. Alexis Carrel took me in hand after my visit with Noguchi, and led me to the laboratory where cancer research was going on. He was as different from Dr. Noguchi as one man could be from another—and the difference was not alone one of race. However, they had two points in common—their perfect courtesy, of which the Frenchman's held a fine worldly polish, and their absorption in their work, which made each man seem oblivious to any interest outside of a laboratory. But whereas Noguchi was grave, dignified and persistently self-effacing, Dr. Carrel was smiling, temperamental, serenely self-assured, and alive to his finger-tips.

In the department of cancer research he introduced me to a handsome young blond physician who, I afterwards learned, was then hoped to be on the verge of a discovery that would revolutionize the treatment of cancer and might lead to its cure. His collection of rabbits and guinea pigs, peering up at us from their cages with frightened little eyes, depressed me. I had grave doubts about vivisection and other medical experiments on animals. I was still under the influence of those doubts when I went with Dr. Carrel to the room where his most interesting animal patient lived, the old dog that was being made young.

We entered the room together and a large and very lively dog leaped toward us. He reared up, got both paws on Dr. Carrel's shoulders, and tried to lick his face. The doctor laughed, patted the dog's head, and then pushed him down and put him through his paces.

My heart lightened. I had not realized how seriously I

was taking this animal problem till I felt the wave of relief that rolled over me at sight of that dog. Here was a dog that was being experimented on. Here was the physician who was making the experiment. Yet it was quite clear that dog and man were the best of friends. I, too, patted the dog's head, and he eagerly transferred his attentions to me. He was a mongrel, like Honoria Flannagan's "Patsy," with strains of hound and setter and sheep dog. He had been lonely and was rejoicing in our companionship. He ran back and forth between us, alert and active, teasing us to play, while Dr. Carrel watched him with the eye of a proud parent.

The doctor explained.

The dog chosen for the experiment had to be old but healthy. He must be without ailments other than the inevitable discomforts of age—such as stiffness and other rheumatic symptoms. The dog was, I think, eleven or twelve years old. He had been almost blind when he came, and very stiff and slow of movement; otherwise he was in good condition.

The treatment given him, Dr. Carrel told me, had been of an extreme simplicity. As I recall it, a certain quantity of the old dog's blood had been drawn from his veins and a simple saline solution injected in its place. The dog was then given an interval for care and diet and recuperation. The treatment was repeated and the interval of recuperation lengthened. From the first the animal had steadily improved. His vision had cleared, his stiffness was disappearing. The treatments were only half over—but look at him now!

As if to give us a better opportunity to look at him the dog again reared up on his hind legs and got his paws on the speaker's shoulders. Dr. Carrel glanced at me with a new light in his brilliant eyes.

"You see?" he asked. "But this is *good!* This is very

good indeed. If we have done this to a dog, we can do it to a man!"

I don't know whether they did or not. Probably not, for with the outbreak of the World War soon after that Dr. Carrel went to France and the experiment was interrupted. I took my responsibilities so seriously that though no caution had been given me I did not mention the experiment even to my closest friends. It can do no harm to write of it now.

I have another memory of the Rockefeller Institute group, this time seated around Mrs. Flexner's dinner table that same year. Dr. Simon Flexner was there, tall, thin, austere, but very impressive. So was Mrs. Simon Flexner and Abraham Flexner, my host, then head of the Rockefeller Educational Foundation. Dr. Noguchi was not there. Dr. Carrel was, and also the blond young physician who was interested in cancer. The dinner had begun at eight and we were back in the living-room soon after nine. At the stroke of ten every physician rose as if the sound had been a lever physically lifting him from his chair. This was, it appears, the invariable rule of those Institute workers. They were back in their quarters and in bed by half past ten, and up very early in the morning.

This seems to be as good a time as any to tell the dramatic story of another dog I knew. He was Glenlevit, a magnificent Scotch collie and the noblest dog I have ever met. He belonged to Mrs. Harvey. Both she and the Colonel were very fond of dogs, and Jorjalma was a paradise for the animals. Glenlevit and Ben and a few other special favorites had the run of the house as well as of the big estate. Their presence was never disturbing to their master or mistress, no matter what they did. I had always realized this. I learned it again one Saturday morning, when Colonel

Harvey was suddenly inspired to move several hundred books from one set of shelves in his library to another. Mrs. Harvey and I volunteered to help him.

Glenlevit and Ben and at least two other dogs were in the room, lying asleep directly in the path we were using in our arm-laden journeys back and forth. It would have simplified our work very much if we had not been forced to step over or around them as we came and went, but Colonel and Mrs. Harvey seemed as oblivious to that theory as the dogs were. Warily, holding as many books as we could, we made dozens of detours around them, while the dogs dozed in peace.

It was during this same morning that Mrs. Harvey passed on to the Colonel a discovery she had just made.

"Geordie," she said, "we must change Ben's name."

"Why?" the Colonel asked, stopping to wipe his perspiring brow. It was a very hot day and we were all tired. The selection of a new name in such conditions struck me as a strenuous job.

"Well—because Ben isn't that kind of a dog," Mrs. Harvey laughed. "We've got to think of a new name."

"We might call him Ben Hur," the Colonel suggested, and picked up another load of books with a groan. His suggestion so cheered me that I stepped across Ben Hur uncomplainingly the rest of the morning. But this is a digression.

Mrs. Harvey had discovered Glenlevit during a visit to some famous kennels in Scotland. He was then a most engaging puppy, and he and his future mistress fell in love with each other at first sight. Mrs. Harvey hung over the railed enclosure which separated her from the puppy and gazed down at him with rapture, while Glenlevit almost broke his small heart trying to scale the partition between them. Colonel Harvey watched the little scene with amusement.

"George," Mrs. Harvey finally told him, "I simply can't go back to America without that puppy. I shall have to settle down in Scotland and live near him."

The Colonel bought the dog for her on the spot, and the Harveys brought him to America when they sailed for home a week later. They had many dogs in their Jorjalma kennels, but from that time there was only one dog in the world for Mrs. Harvey. She was wholly devoted to the new puppy and her affection was returned to an extraordinary degree.

It is said that a collie is a "one-man dog," and that he rarely cares for a woman. Glenlevit was a one-woman-dog, and the woman was his mistress. From the beginning to the end of his life he hardly seemed to know there were other human beings on the earth. He was indifferent even to Colonel Harvey, who was greatly loved by all his dogs. Glenlevit was a shadow at Mrs. Harvey's heels—at first a small and frolicking shadow, then, as time passed, a mighty one, as he grew in strength and beauty. He was far and away the most perfect dog I have ever seen—a dog of superb lines and color, with a noble head and eyes of such beauty and intelligence that every one who saw him spoke of them. The elder J. P. Morgan, who had a kennel of wonderful collies, was so much struck by Glenlevit's beauty that he gave Mrs. Harvey a perfect mate for him. Her name was Nancy, and Glenlevit and Nancy became the unquestioned king and queen of the Harvey kennels.

Glenlevit was Mrs. Harvey's constant companion, in the house or out of it; and he liked to lie at her feet when she read or sewed. He always lay in such a position that he could look up at her and meet her eyes, and so close to her that she could touch him with her hand or the toe of her shoe. His obedience to her slightest gesture or murmured command was instantaneous. When others spoke to him he did not seem to hear them.

Glenlevit had four glorious years at Jorjalma before the tragedy came that ended his life. It began in the early hours of an August afternoon. There was a house-party in progress. There was always a house-party at Jorjalma. I was there that particular week-end. So was Frederick Duneka, with Mrs. Duneka and their only child, Harvey Duneka, four years old. There were half a dozen other guests, one of them Thomas Fortune Ryan. It was just after luncheon and very hot. Most of the women had gone to their rooms to read and rest. The men, I think, were with Colonel Harvey in a tower he had built in the garden. It held a second library he often vanished into for work.

Everything was very quiet. The dogs were sleeping, too, all except Glenlevit. He was in the grounds, keeping a careful eye on young Harvey Duneka, who had escaped from his nurse and was taking a solitary promenade on the estate. Glenlevit evidently realized that this was unusual and that the youngster should be kept in sight. He nonchalantly trailed little Harvey, who toddled gaily toward a spot some distance from the house, where death was waiting for him.

No one ever knew by which gate the strange dog that entered the grounds of Jorjalma that afternoon got in. But there he was, far down at the left of the lawn, near the fence that shut out the public highway. As the child approached the dog rose in his path, not thirty feet away.

Little Harvey went toward the stranger with hospitable gurgles. This was just another dog, and Harvey liked dogs, even when they were muddy and disheveled and blood-stained as this animal was. He cooed to the dog, which flattened itself for a spring, hot eyes on him, growling deep in its throat.

Glenlevit did not like strange dogs, and he especially disliked the looks of this one. He had been a little distance behind Harvey. Now he came through the air like a torpedo, almost knocking the child down as he passed, and hurled himself on the unwelcome visitor. The next instant there was a life-and-death battle in progress. Young Harvey, who had never seen a dog-fight before, stood transfixed, lending himself whole-heartedly to this one. Up in the left wing of Jorjalma a housemaid, almost as inexperienced as the child, stood at a window and watched the battle from that safe point. Later, when she described it to me, I asked her whether it had not occurred to her to call a man-servant and send him out for the boy. She shook her head.

"I didn't think he was in any danger," she said. "Glenlevit was there. It was just a dog-fight. Glen was a match for ten dogs. It was terrible exciting, though."

Glenlevit was certainly there; and ordinarily he might have been, as the maid had said, a match for ten dogs. Even Glenlevit had his work cut out for him to conquer a mad dog. The fight lasted a long time. All of ten or fifteen minutes, the maid thought. At the end of it the strange dog crawled away and Glenlevit, exhausted but triumphant, shepherded young Harvey back to the house.

The child went willingly. He wanted to talk now, to tell about the fight. He soon had an interested audience. The maid added her tale. No one was excited or alarmed. The young superintendent of Jorjalma administered first aid to Glenlevit and put him in his kennel, where he seemed content to stay. The men guests and men-servants felt a bit injured because they had missed an exciting fight. It would have been great to see Glenlevit in action.

That night a general alarm was broadcast throughout the region. A mad dog had been at large there. He had bitten several dogs and a cow. Many citizens had fled before him. He had been captured and shot. He had exhibited every sign of hydrophobia, but a special analysis was being made.

Would any residents who had seen the dog or heard of other injuries report to the police?

Within an hour Colonel and Mrs. Harvey had the best veterinarian in the region at Jorjalma. The vet made a careful examination of Glenlevit and was reassuring. In the first place, he reminded them, the supposed "mad dog" might not have been mad at all. This was probably one of the baseless "mad-dog" scares that spread so quickly. If the dog had done any biting it was probably because he was lost, hungry, tired, and in a panic. This also was the theory of Colonel and Mrs. Harvey. Glenlevit, the vet added, though exhausted, was in good condition. He had been terribly mauled. There were marks of bites, but apparently none had cut through his thick fur deeply enough to penetrate the skin. Of course, the saliva of the two dogs had mingled and if, by any chance.... The thing to do now was to isolate Glenlevit for a time and watch him carefully. This must be done at once. It was done. The dog was moved to a wired runway. The vet promised to examine him daily, to give him the best possible treatment.

Glenlevit could not understand this move, nor his isolation, nor the fact that his mistress did not touch him. He looked questioningly at Mrs. Harvey. She explained to him as she would have explained to a child. He was to have rest and care. She would watch over him and see him constantly. He must not worry.

Glenlevit was still very tired. He wagged his tail feebly and went to sleep. She was allowing this to happen—so it must be all right. The next morning he seemed much better, but the news was worse. The analysis of the other dog's brain had shown that he really had been the victim of hydrophobia. Glenlevit must be most carefully watched and, of course, still isolated.

The Harveys built a special runway for him, long and

wide, with high wire sides but open at the top, and with a roomy kennel at one end. Here the dog would have plenty of air and exercise, and every comfort. A special man was told off to watch him closely and carry out the vet's orders. Mrs. Harvey visited him constantly and talked to him through the wire netting. So did the Colonel and their house guests. We were always visiting Glenlevit's runway to have a chat with him.

In many ways Glen seemed his old self as the weeks passed; but he made it clear from the first that he fiercely resented his imprisonment and isolation. He simply could not understand these. He, the king of the kennels, was being treated like an outlaw. He was caged. Humans and his own kind visited him remotely, on the outside of that cage.

"Yes, he feels it," the vet admitted. "But it's got to be this way. I think everything is going to be all right, but we must continue to take every precaution."

"But how much longer?" Mrs. Harvey cried. "We're breaking his heart!"

"We're being sensible," the vet said. "It won't be much longer now."

Glen had ceased to notice any of us except his mistress. Even with her he was remote. He no longer hastened to the wire sides of the runway when she appeared. He looked at her and wagged his tail, but his splendid head drooped and his whole manner had changed.

"He will never forgive me," Mrs. Harvey said with tears in her eyes.

At last the day came when it seemed safe to give the superb dog his freedom. We made a little ceremony of his release. We all went to the kennels and watched the end-door open, and waited for Glenlevit to bound forth. He merely looked at us and walked away.

"Leave him alone," said the vet. "Don't pay any attention

to him. The door is open. He'll come out when he wants to."

The bystanders dispersed. Mrs. Harvey and a few of us went back to the rear veranda of the house, which overlooked the kennels. Mrs. Harvey sewed and the rest of us read and chatted. Each of us kept an unobtrusive but watchful eye on Glenlevit. For half an hour the dog did not leave the runway. At last he walked slowly and majestically out of it and stood for some moments looking over his domain—at the near-by meadows, the orchards, at the lively dogs playing down near the brook.

Then he turned and looked at Mrs. Harvey.

"Come here, Glen," she called in a shaking voice. "Come, old boy."

He started toward her very slowly, and came to within ten feet of the veranda. There he stopped again. She called once more. For the first time in his life he disobeyed her. He stood still. She rose, descended the veranda steps, and went toward him. He retreated hastily, making it impossible for her to reach and touch him.

"He hasn't forgiven me," she said. "He will never forgive me. He saved Harvey Duneka's life, and we have rewarded him by breaking his heart."

She went back to her chair and turned her face away from us. She was not an emotional woman, but she was weeping now. Very slowly Glenlevit came back to the point where he had stood before, ten feet from the veranda. Very slowly he lay down. He lay there through the afternoon, through the tea hour. When Mrs. Harvey went toward him, as she did several times, he rose before she could reach him and edged away, glancing back at her with a strange, side-long, furtive look, utterly unlike his proud, straight gaze.

"He'll never forgive me," Mrs. Harvey repeated.

"But he still loves you, and he's lying where he can watch

you," some one pointed out. "He's not sleeping. He's watching you every minute."

When the dressing gong sounded Mrs. Harvey got up to go into the house. Glen was escorted to his kennel by his special attendant. He went reluctantly, looking back. When Mrs. Harvey again tried to approach him he slunk away with that strange side-long glance that was so unlike him. There is no other word for his retreat. The proud, magnificent dog was slinking like the pariah he thought himself. Just before he entered his kennel he stopped and turned on his beloved mistress a long look. It was his last.

He went mad that night, and was shot in the morning.

Up till the last Mrs. Harvey would not believe that he had hydrophobia. He had, as the post-mortem proved. I think he knew it, and that he must have longed with all his loyal heart for her nearness and for the touch of her hand. But in his final hours he had given his beloved mistress a last proof of his devotion—by keeping at a safe distance from her.

CHAPTER XV

A Play, a Blizzard, and a Message

I HAD written half a dozen books of short stories, and as many novels. Now, of course, I wrote a play. Almost every one does, at one time or another. My play had been standing on the threshold of my consciousness for years, but I did not recognize it when it knocked. I put it into a short story, *Mrs. Dixon's Culture Course,* published in the *Atlantic Monthly.* It was not until I received several requests from playwrights to be allowed to make a play of the story that I knew it was play material.

My response to the playwrights' letters was automatic. If there was a play in the story why not have the fun—and the rewards—of dramatizing it myself? I did this, in a casual, off-hand fashion, passing three two-day week-ends at the task, and giving the play the title *The Lady from Oklahoma.* I was amazed by the ease with which a play could be written. But I subsequently wrote and rewrote that play dozens and dozens of times.

Suggestions were as leaves in Vallombrosa, and I listened to them all. Every one interested in the production, from the producers to the office boys and the scrubwomen in the theaters, felt quite sure they knew more about playwriting than I knew, and most of them did. All this came later. First I had to sell the play in the form in which it left my own hands.

The story was a simple one, of a little far-western woman whose self-educated husband had grown rich and famous while she remained a country mouse. She was losing him and she knew it. She had plenty of money and some brains. She came to New York to make herself over, physically and mentally, and thus recover his waning affections. She engaged a corps of social and educational coaches. One entire act was played in a beauty parlor, where she was put through all the beautifying processes of that period—the permanent wave (just beginning), reduction baths, hair-dressing, facial massage, and the like, while she chatted with the operators and her coach corrected her grammar. She entered the beauty parlor an unpolished product of Oklahoma. The end of the act showed her transformed into a beauty.

All this was "new stuff" at that time, though much of it has been used often enough since then—notably in *The Governor's Lady, Years of Discretion,* and—even as I write —in *The Women.* Years later Alan Dale, speculating in some magazine as to why *The Lady from Oklahoma* did not have the big success he had predicted for it, said he had finally decided that it was because the play ridiculed women. Women, he thought, did not like to be ridiculed. Women must have changed since then, as the success of *The Women* proves in 1937. However this may be, *The Lady from Oklahoma* was one of those maddening theatrical affairs that will neither live nor die. If a play fails immediately one can bury it and remember it sentimentally. If it succeeds one rejoices greatly, for a really successful play may make its author financially independent. A play that will neither succeed nor perish is a thorn in the side of every one who has any interest in it.

Elisabeth Marbury and Roi Cooper Megrue, who were my agents, had faith in *The Lady from Oklahoma* from start to finish and made a splendid fight for it. Lured by the humor of the beauty-parlor act three different firms of producers successively hurled themselves into the production. First, the Shuberts, with Minnie Dupree; next a producer named Delamater, with Kelsey and Shannon as stars; last of all, William A. Brady and Jessie Bonstelle. Inspired by this display of optimism the Shuberts took a second bite of the cherry, and bought a third interest from Mr. Brady and Miss Bonstelle. All of them lost money.

The Lady from Oklahoma had three brilliant opening nights—one in Baltimore, one in Chicago, the last in New York. At each of these an outsider would have received the impression that the play was one of the hits of its day. Undaunted by the constant changes in the theatrical child I was mothering I went to every opening and made a speech—one of the few things my theatrical associates agreed that I could do. In the final version of the play there was, I think, only one paragraph I had not rewritten. This was "The Lady's" curtain line, as her recovered husband kneels before her, his head in her lap.

"Why, Joe, you ain't cryin', are you? Yes, you be! An' I'm so happy I'm forgettin' my grammar!"

I always felt when we reached that solitary landmark in the performance that I, too, had reached home. I remained there. I never wrote another play, though many theatrical optimists urged me to do so. After the tumult and shouting of those first nights had died down public interest also died. In the end the beauty-parlor act was put on separately and ran eighteen months as a "big time" feature of the Keith vaudeville circuit. I received a flat payment of sixty dollars a week during that run, which cheered me a little.

I learned much from the play experience. Going through three productions, with three separate companies, I learned that the first impulse of every one connected with any play in any way is to have most of that play rewritten. I learned to rewrite whole scenes during rehearsals, while the director stood with extended hand waiting for the new copy. I learned to have an undying admiration for the men and women of the American stage—the bravest, most generous, hardest-working and most philosophic group of professionals in the world. I learned that they were the best actors and actresses to be found anywhere. I learned that—in those days—they would cheerfully rehearse all day and all night without payment and without interruption for meals or sleep. I learned more about the extraordinary kindness of my friends Maud and Otis Skinner, who were so helpful and so understanding throughout. And I learned that when the leading lady sank languidly into the arms of the leading man during a few minutes' intermission at rehearsals, and cradled her head on his breast, it did not indicate that the two were living in sin.

In short, I learned so much, especially during the New York production, that I could feel my brain bulge. The lessons of that production were especially valuable. If I had tried again right after them I might possibly have written a real play. But I was fed up. No one was asking me to change my short stories or novels and write them over. Wearily and gratefully I returned to my own last.

The third production was especially educative because William A. Brady directed it, and Mr. Brady is an inspiring director. He even amazed me by occasionally seeing things as I did—a rare experience for a playwright whose first effort is being rehearsed. Jessie Bonstelle was the star. The night before the play opened in New York Mr. Brady kept the company rehearsing till four o'clock in the morning, while I still rewrote scenes down in the dark auditorium or made suggestions no one seemed to hear. When at last we were dismissed Miss Bonstelle and I fell into a taxicab, almost too limp to tell the driver where to go. Like the rest of the company neither of us had lunched or dined.

"We can't go to a restaurant at this hour," Miss Bonstelle said. "Have you anything to eat at home? I haven't."

I had. My ice box was like one of those in stories—always supplied with cold meats and salads and other satisfying left-overs. In my newspaper days I had learned to keep it so for my arrival home at dawn, and I had continued the habit. I took Miss Bonstelle to my apartment and spread forth our banquet. We ate and talked till after five. When the sun's first rays were creeping into the dining-room and touching up the lines in our haggard faces Miss Bonstelle got up to go; but she delivered a few final remarks at the door of the elevator, and I shall always remember her peroration.

"Get all the sleep you can to-day," she advised, "and don't worry about to-night. Of course, the New York critics are simply merciless. They will probably be worse than usual to-night because it's late in the season and they're all tired. I used to be terribly afraid of them. They were actual nightmares to me. But I'm a Christian Scientist and lately I have been trying my Christian Science on them. I don't know what it will do to them, but it has certainly changed my own point of view. I'm not afraid of the critics any more. You may not believe it," she ended impressively, "but now I almost *love* the damned things!"

As I have said, both Maud and Otis Skinner had been wonderfully kind in advising me about the play. But Otis did not help much when he called me on the telephone just before I went to the theater that night and tried to cheer me by describing how each of the critics would act during the progress of the play. I had never followed these phenomena myself, but it became clear that he had.

"They always do these things," he said, "so they won't mean anything to-night; but as you will be burning at the stake you will probably think they do. Wattle will get up at the end of the first act and look wearily around the house and yawn deeply. Blank will stalk down the middle aisle during the second act and will not come back. Blub will turn to his companion and groan and shake his head. They will all get into a huddle in the lobby and discuss the play loudly and severely as the audience files out. Don't pay any attention to any of them."

I didn't—till the next morning when the newspapers were brought to me. The night had been a triumphant one—with a crowded house, plenty of laughter and applause, calls for the author, a speech, and all the other signs of a hit. They deceived even Mr. Brady, who crisply announced that we had a winner. To me, the taxicab horn seemed to be saying "Author, author," all the way home from the theater. But the next morning the critics disagreed. Lawrence Reamer gave the play a solid column of praise in the New York *Sun,* and Alan Dale said, "Nothing more gorgeous than the Jordanian humor has bloomed on Broadway for years." A representative of New York's leading theatrical weekly came to interview me on how it feels to have "arrived" with a first effort. Certain critics damned with faint praise, and several saw nothing in the play at all. In short, the love story of a middle-aged married couple had little more appeal to the general public then than it would have now—and we all know how much it would have now. This fact, if you ask *me,* explains in part at least why *The Lady from Oklahoma* disappointed so many kind friends.

Arthur Brisbane was among the kindest of those friends. I had not asked him to help the play but when he heard that it was going to Chicago he showed his immediate interest, in this letter:

June 10th, 1911

My DEAR MISS JORDAN:

I should be very glad indeed to do anything I can to help your play in Chicago. I go to Chicago next Monday or Tuesday and shall talk to people out there myself. Meanwhile I have written to Foster Coates, who is manager of the Chicago *American*. I have also written to Andrew Lawrence, who runs the *Examiner,* and to the dramatic critic of the *Examiner*. On the *American* we have no dramatic critic as I do not believe in dramatic criticism of the usual kind. Roswell Field is on the Chicago *Examiner* doing book reviews. I think it would be a good idea to write to him. I have control, to some extent, of the Chicago *American,* which like the other Hearst evening newspapers is under my direction. I will be very glad to help you there, without any doubt, and use what influence I may have elsewhere.

I think it might be well for you to write to Mr. Keely, editor of the Chicago *Tribune*. I should also write to John C. Eastman, who is editor of the Chicago *Journal* and who used to be, I think, on the *World*. I should also advise you to write a long and friendly letter to "Amy Leslie" who is the dramatic critic of the Chicago *News,* whether you know her or not. If you do know her so much the better; if you do not know her tell her, if you please, that I advised you to write her.

I wish you all success in your play.

Yours sincerely,

ARTHUR BRISBANE

My old friend Foster Coates was quick to respond to Mr. Brisbane's nudge. He wrote:

CHICAGO, June 15, 1911

MY DEAR MISS JORDAN:

I had a note from Mr. Brisbane the other day asking me to do anything I could do to help your new play that is to open here on July 1, and I wrote him that I would do so. How long I may remain in Chicago I do not know, but so long as I am here I will help you in every way possible. You know I am not located permanently here, but I can arrange to have some good notices published in the *American*.

If there is any preliminary matter that you have on hand, and if you will send it to me, I will publish it in advance of the opening night.

I certainly hope, for your sake, that the play will be a success. I have always had unbounded admiration for your ability, as far

back as when we were both on the New York *World* together.
Your touch should be very steady and your point of view accurate. If your play is not a success I shall be more surprised and
disappointed than you.

With my best wishes,

Very truly yours,

FOSTER COATES

Frederick Duneka had the same friendly little ways. Even
in the last days of his life, when he could no longer come to
the Harper offices, he sent me this characteristic note about
a story of mine he had just read:

SUMMIT, June 15

When it comes to *Saturday Evening Post* stories about
people's hats, Mark Twain has nothing on Little Elizabeth.

"ADMIRING FRIEND"

F.A.D. to E.J.

And here's another kind word from a notable stranger in
California, about *May Iverson's* experience in writing a play,
into which I had put my own experience.

LOS ANGELES, CAL., June 5

DEAR MISS JORDAN:

We—the reading ones and writing ones of the *Times*, the
editors, publishers, literary critics, dramatic critics, musical
critics, reporters and errand boys, all play-writers, of course—
wish to thank you for your delicious, yes, bully story in the
June *Harper's*. It ranks with the very best short stories of the
French masters. That is not saying enough. It is better than
anything any of us ever wrote. We could not let the joy of it
pass without writing to you.

Sincerely yours,

HARRY E. ANDREWS,
Managing Editor the *Times*

That winter Colonel and Mrs. Harvey had their twenty-
fifth wedding anniversary, and some of us at Franklin

Square decided to celebrate it fittingly with a dinner at Delmonico's. I headed the reception committee, and it was important that I should get to Delmonico's well in advance of the dinner hour, which was eight o'clock. Unfortunately New York was also entertaining that night. She had given the freedom of the city to the worst blizzard that had visited her since the historic affair of 1888.

Knowing that traffic would be greatly interfered with I dressed early and impressively in a new cloth-of-gold evening gown, made for the occasion, gold slippers and a rather light-weight velvet evening wrap. I describe this splendor because of what happened to it later. I telephoned for a taxicab and received my first shock. No taxicabs were to be had at any price. They were stalled in snowdrifts all over town and the companies were busy sending out wrecking crews to rescue them. It was useless to send out more cabs. They would only be added to the casualty list. I asked for the general manager and coldly reminded him that for many years I had paid over to his company an impressive part of my income in taxicab fares. He finally and grumpily promised to send a cab. It arrived forty minutes later—at seven o'clock. That was all right. It couldn't take me more than an hour, I decided, to drive from Gramercy Park to Delmonico's, even through the blizzard and snow blockades. But it did.

That taxicab carried me exactly one short cross-town block —from my apartment house to the corner of Lexington Avenue and Twenty-first Street. There it became stalled in a snowdrift the size of a cottage, and after the driver had worked over and sworn at it for fifteen minutes I left it. I had seen a solitary electric car fighting its way up Fourth Avenue. If I could get that all might still be well. I ran— in the storm, in the gold slippers, in the new evening gown —through the drifts. The blizzard was growing fiercer every minute and the wind was so strong that it was almost impossible to keep my feet. I missed the car, which passed the corner of Twenty-first Street before I could reach it. I pursued that car up Fourth Avenue and caught it by the elbow after a chase of half a dozen blocks. It was making slow time, but so was I. My slippers and gown were almost ruined. My evening coat was too thin, and I was almost frozen. I sank into a corner of the car with a gasp of relief.

The car entered the tunnel at Thirty-fourth Street, stopped, jerked, started again, went on another block, stopped, started, reached the middle of the tunnel, and then stopped for good. There was only one other passenger, also a woman. The conductor ordered us both out. We protested, we almost prayed; we tried to bribe; but without success. He was profane and furious. The car was stalled and he was leaving it to telephone for a relief crew. I took the new gown and the slippers and the evening wrap out into the storm again. My fighting blood was up. I would get to Delmonico's if I died doing it.

I made my way along the tunnel, risking possible "live wires," reached an exit, and eventually found myself up on Fourth Avenue, near Thirty-eighth Street. By this time my slippers and gown and my nicely dressed hair were in a condition that made me wonder whether I dared present myself to the guests at that dinner. But I plunged on, breasting the wind and the snowdrifts as apparently neither taxicabs nor electric cars were able to do. Not another human being nor a vehicle of any kind was on the sidewalk or in the road, so far as I could see. I couldn't see far, with pellets of ice striking my eyeballs.

Suddenly something loomed up near me in the middle of the road. It seemed to be in trouble. I investigated and discovered that it was a hansom cab, attached to a horse which had fallen between the shafts and could not get up again.

Crouched in a snowdrift near it the Negro driver sat in utter helplessness and despair. His eyes were closed and he was making no effort whatever to move himself or the horse. I spoke with a robust confidence I did not feel. Judging by the little I could see of the buildings around me we were now near Thirty-ninth Street.

"I'll give you five dollars," I told the driver, "to take me to Delmonico's. It's only about six blocks from here."

He opened his eyes, looked up at me, and closed them again.

"Lady," he groaned, "I ain't gwine take nobody nowhere. This horse has broke his laig."

I looked at the horse. His expression was one of peaceful resignation. He seemed even more willing than the driver to keep quiet and let the blanket of snow cover him. My father was a horse lover and I had driven and ridden horses all my life.

"Get up," I ordered the driver. "If you go to sleep you may never wake. Let's see what's the matter with this horse. I don't believe his leg is broken. Come on now, quick!"

The Negro groaned and got to his feet with almost as much fuss as if his own leg had been broken. Together we knelt in the snow and examined the horse. Nothing was the matter with his legs except that they were half frozen.

"Now we'll get him out of his harness and up on his feet," I said. "Take hold."

We actually did it. The job took a long time. It finished my slippers and gown and evening wrap and hair, and almost finished me. Several times during the process of raising him the horse laid his head restfully on my breast, leaving thin icicles on the front of my gown. We finally got him up and harnessed again and back into the shafts.

"Now take me to Delmonico's," I said. "Five dollars."

I climbed into the cab. The front windows had been left

open and were frozen into place. The cab was full of snow. I cleaned off the seat as well as I could and sat back. Wind and ice pellets blew in on me, snow soon covered me. The driver was still hesitating.

"Lady," he wailed, "it cain't be done nohow!"

I leaned forward and gathered up the dragging reins.

"All right," I said, "if you can't get there, I can."

Groaning and protesting he got up into his high seat and we started off. Refreshed by his rest the horse was plodding along philosophically, but the driver sent me a pathetic bulletin from his perch.

"My hands is froze," he assured me. "I cain't hol' these here reins, nohow."

The experience was becoming a nightmare. My own hands felt frozen. So did my nose and ears. The horse did his best, but the going was terribly slow.

At long last, as the British say, we reached the entrance of Delmonico's. The hansom cab stopped and the horse stood sagging like an image in the snow, his head almost down to his knees. The driver remained on his perch, huddled into a mass of misery. He seemed lost to his surroundings. If I had walked into the restaurant and left him, I'm sure he would not have found voice to protest. I got out and offered him a five dollar bank-note. He made no motion to take it.

"Put down your hand," I said.

He did so. I tried to put the money into his hand but the bank-note slipped out of his stiff fingers. I had just time to step on it as it struck the snow, and keep it from blowing away. I picked it up and this time the driver bent toward me. I was afraid to trust his hand again. I got back into the cab and standing in it reached up and put the bank-note into the side pocket of his coat. He let me do it without help or comment.

"There's a garage just around the corner," I told him, and

added explicit instructions as to how to reach it. "Go to it and get yourself and the horse warm." He and the old horse were still there when I looked back at them from the welcome warmth of the restaurant.

I went up to the private suite we had engaged and was received with touching demonstrations of sympathy. It was almost ten o'clock. Most of my fellow guests had arrived in their private cars and because they had made the journey on Fifth Avenue, where the only snow-plow of the night was operating. They had not been forced to negotiate side streets and side avenues, as I had done. A cup of hot soup was pressed into one of my hands and a glass of champagne into the other. As I drank them I told the story of my experience. When I finished it Colonel Harvey spoke slowly and thoughtfully.

"I will believe the part about the taxicab," he announced. "Duneka will believe the part about the electric car. But I warn you now, Elizabeth, that you will never find *any one* who will believe that yarn about the hansom cab!"

The episode occurred exactly as I have told it. The fact that I was never again able to wear the new evening gown or wrap or those golden slippers is too trivial to mention.

Memory throws its high-lights on many special festivities during those years. The most important of these were Colonel Harvey's literary dinners. He gave at least four that will remain a part of America's literary history. The most discussed of them, though they were all discussed throughout the country, was his famous dinner to Mark Twain, when the great humorist was seventy. Almost every one of distinction in the literary world was invited to this dinner, and attended it if he or she was physically able to come.

Thirty years later I attended a mournful aftermath of that great occasion. Another New York dinner was arranged by Mark Twain's admirers to celebrate the hundredth anni-

versary of his birth. Professor William Lyon Phelps pre-
sided admirably, and toward the close of the banquet he
asked those who had attended the Harvey dinner, thirty
years before, to stand up. Seven persons in that great assemblage rose. Four of them were Mrs. Henry Mills Alden,
Edith Wyatt of Chicago, Josephine Daskam Bacon, and myself. The other three I did not recognize. We all felt like
"survivors," at that banquet, and of course we were. I felt
a hundred years old when a handsome man with becoming
gray hair greeted me and I recognized Henry Hoyns, the
present Chairman of the Board of Harper and Brothers.
In my day at Harper's Henry Hoyns had been just a
promising youth, and we had all patted his head. I'm
quite sure he would not let me do that now—and the realization is depressing.

That hundredth anniversary dinner was well-meant and
as successful as any anti-climax could be; but it was a wraith
in the dawn compared to the brilliant night of thirty years
before, when Mark Twain himself was there to describe the
state he had been in seventy years earlier.

"I had no hair, no teeth, no clothes," he told us—"and in
that disgusting condition I attended my first banquet!"

Colonel Harvey gave an almost equally brilliant dinner to
William Dean Howells on Mr. Howells' seventieth birthday,
and still another for Henry Mills Alden to celebrate Mr.
Alden's fiftieth anniversary as editor of *Harper's Magazine*.
All these dinners were held in the great counting-room of
Harper and Brothers, in Franklin Square, and the room was
made over for the occasions. I attended each of them, and
it would be quite easy to write a book on the guests and
episodes—not forgetting a smaller dinner the Colonel gave
for Henry James at Delmonico's, when Mr. James returned
to America after his long absence.

Another striking social feature of the day was Mrs.

Wightman Walker's musicales. Later she became Mrs. Frederick C. Penfield, and made a splendid record in relief work in Austria during her husband's service there as American Ambassador until America entered the World War. Her New York musicales antedated these. She was supposed to be worth eighty million dollars, and she obviously spent a large part of her income on music. During New York's opera season she frequently engaged half a dozen or more of the world's greatest singers to entertain her friends, and added a famous violinist or pianiste for good measure.

I attended all her musicales, and I remember afternoons when we heard Calvé, Emmy Destinn, Caruso, Geraldine Farrar, Scotti, and Fritz Kreisler.

That is, we were expected to hear them. But Mrs. Walker's guests were constantly coming and going, and the rooms adjoining the music-room were filled with their happy voices. I recall sitting in the front row of chairs in the music-room one day when Mischa Elman began to play. The uproar in the connecting rooms was even louder than usual, and as he raised his bow Mr. Elman favored me with a large and eloquent wink. We had never met, but that was an instant of such understanding between us as comes into few lives.

Mrs. Arthur Murray Dodge's Friday luncheons were also among my favorite diversions and I attended them quite regularly for twenty years. Half a dozen of us had standing invitations to be there as often as we could. This group included Mrs. Edward Ringwood Hewitt, Mrs. Francis Scott, Kate Douglas Wiggin, and Mrs. La Farge. Other guests were invited from week to week and there were always a dozen or more really brilliant women around the table. Some of the best talk in New York was heard there.

I was devoted to Mrs. Dodge. Hers was one of the finest characters I have known—forthright, loyal, absolutely sin-

cere, and perfectly poised. She was a social leader of unquestioned authority, but no dull person, however lofty in
position, got into her circle. Every guest produced the best
that was in her at those luncheons.

One day a woman who had been announced as "Mrs.
Joseph" entered my office. She had telephoned in advance
for an appointment, but no one knew who she was. She
proved to be a very handsome woman in her forties, beautifully dressed, and carrying her fine figure superbly. She
explained at once that she had come for advice—that it had
suddenly become necessary for her to earn a living for herself and her mother, eighty years old. How could she do it?
She said she had considerable executive and administrative
experience.

I watched her as she talked, and then asked the question
which had been in my mind from the moment of her entrance.

"When did you leave your Order?"

She blushed hotly.

"How did you know?" she asked.

"I've lived among nuns too long not to recognize one
when I see her," I explained.

She told her story. She had founded an Order which had
grown large and prosperous. She had built convents in many
cities, had established many successful schools. Then, she
went on to say, a dozen leading Sisters in her Order decided
to depose her. They considered her too venturesome, too ex-
travagant. Her wish was to build more schools and convents.
Theirs was to be conservative now and hold what they had.
Among them they had succeeded in ousting her. What should
she do? Try to find work in New York and support herself
and her mother, or carry out another plan and go to Rome
to put her case before the Pope? A wealthy friend was sup-

porting her for the time, and had given her an outfit; but, of course, such help could not go on indefinitely.

I advised the appeal in Rome, and she and her mother dined with me before they sailed. The mother, Mrs. Fuller, was a dear old lady, obviously well-born, well-bred, and used to comfort. She had occupied a suite of her own in the Mother House of her daughter's Order, she told me, and all the Sisters had been very kind to her. They had offered her a continued haven there when her daughter was deposed; of course she could not accept such an invitation. She must be with her daughter. But notwithstanding the latter's air of sophistication, her high intelligence and obvious ability, she was in a way as inexperienced as her mother, outside of convent walls. In New York the two would have been as helpless as babies.

They went to a Roman convent, where they were accepted as guests. There the daughter died, very suddenly, of influenza. The Italian Sisters offered to keep the gentle old mother with them, even though she was not a Catholic. (The daughter had been a convert.) But the mother wrote me a tragic letter. She was alone. She could not speak or understand the language around her. She was too old to begin a new life. She was coming back to America. Her daughter had left her just enough money to pay her passage. Her steamer reservations had been made. She would be in America almost as soon as her letter. Would I meet her and advise her?

I did, of course. There was only one thing to do for her. That was to get her into a home for aged gentlewomen. Pending her acceptance in such an institution I took her into my own home.

The Miriam Osborne Memorial Home, at Harrison, New York, on which I had set my heart as a refuge for her, was not yet ready to open its third floor. It could not add another

member to its family till it did this, "in a year or two." I
gave Mrs. Fuller my mother's room during the summer,
while Mother was in the country. When she returned in the
autumn I had to engage quarters for Mrs. Fuller next door,
where I could keep an eye on her. She was very forlorn and
lonely, accustomed as she had been to the constant companionship of her daughter.

Incidentally I kept up a ceaseless search for a temporary
home. Mrs. Fuller had no friends to whom she could appeal.
The demands on my own time and income were constantly
increasing. I was supporting my mother and two members
of Mother's family. I could not afford the heavy expense of
separate support for Mrs. Fuller in New York for a year or
two. Neither could I let her down, nor let her suspect what
a problem she was, though she was really almost a stranger
to me. I had met her only once, before she sailed for Rome.
She was a tooth breaking, heartbreaking nut to crack. I
could not find a temporary home where she could be comfortable, though I pulled countless wires and visited dozens
of institutions. During the winter, in her quarters next door
to me in Gramercy Park, she developed pneumonia. That
meant doctors' bills and a trained nurse for many weeks.

The second summer, when my mother again went to the
country, I again brought Mrs. Fuller to our apartment and
gave her Mother's room. I was by this time almost desperate over the problem she presented. I was going abroad
in August and did not know where to leave her. I put in
all my spare time investigating possible places where she
could be happy until the beautiful Miriam Osborne Home
for Gentlewomen opened that third floor. The summer was
the hottest New York had experienced in many years. I was
still putting in my evenings and Saturdays and Sundays investigating so-called "homes" which turned out no "homes"
at all, but merely places where Mrs. Fuller would have been

wretched. Again and again I traveled out of town to look up "leads" which were no leads.

One extremely hot Sunday in August I went up to Westchester full of hope. I had heard of something very promising. The rainbow had arched my heaven just in time. I was sailing for Europe within two weeks. I *must* place Mrs. Fuller somewhere before I left. But that rainbow faded also, and for the first time I was thoroughly discouraged. On my way home I stopped at a favorite Chapel, went down on my knees and definitely put the matter up to God, who seemed for the time to be overlooking it. I also, and even more directly, addressed Mrs. Fuller's daughter.

"You must help me," I reminded her. "I'm at the end of my string. Do something about this. Let me know that you will. *Please!*"

When I got home, exhausted by the heat and, I must admit, not greatly cheered by my petitions, Mrs. Fuller came to meet me as I entered the door. She was quite unlike her usual immaculate self. She looked dusty and disheveled.

"My dear," I cried, "what *have* you been doing?"

She flushed like a guilty child.

"I've been down in the trunk room," she admitted, "going through my trunks."

"But Mrs. Fuller," I pointed out, "it's *Sunday*. And the temperature down there this broiling day must be a hundred and ten!"

"I know," she admitted. "It was very foolish—and it wasn't as if I needed more clothes, either. It was just—well, I can't explain, but I suddenly felt that I *had* to do it."

"Sit down and rest," I suggested. "Then you would better take a bath and get into some fresh clothes. You're all cobwebby."

I ordered cold lemonade for us both, and started for my

own room. Mrs. Fuller held me back with a touch on my arm.

"I unpacked those trunks this afternoon to find something my daughter told me to hand you," she faltered. "When she was dying she made me promise that I would give it to you if I ever came back to America: You wouldn't think I'd forget a thing like that, would you? But I did. It went right out of my mind, there was so much to think of. To-day I remembered it very suddenly. About five o'clock. So I just *had* to go down to those trunks and find it, even if it was Sunday and terribly hot."

She was holding something in her hand, and now she put it into mine. It was a gold ring, like a wedding ring—the ring her daughter had worn as a symbol of her vocation. There was a Latin inscription on it in raised gold lettering. I bent to read it.

Adveniat regnum tuum. (Thy kingdom come.)

There are a dozen possible explanations of the coincidence. The vagaries of age are great. An old lady of eighty-one who wishes to do anything usually does it if she can, regardless of day or temperature. To me there was only one correct interpretation of that episode. My theory was strengthened a few days later when Martha's mother wrote me from Massachusetts offering to take in Mrs. Fuller while I was in Europe. Before I sailed, word was sent me from the Miriam Osborne Home that the third floor was to be opened earlier than had been expected, and that Mrs. Fuller would be welcome there in the autumn.

She passed six very happy years in that haven before she died, coming to New York for frequent week-end visits and jaunts to matinées.

CHAPTER XVI

"THE WHOLE FAMILY"

I NEEDED a chastening experience after the unusual success of *The Masquerader* and *The Awakening of Helena Ritchie*. It came in connection with a *Bazar* serial for which I had cherished the most iridescent hopes. This was a composite novel suggested by Mr. Howells, who continued to have a fatherly feeling for the *Bazar*.

He thought it might be interesting to publish a novel of twelve chapters, to be written by twelve authors, under the title *The Whole Family*. Of these, eleven would write their chapters as supposed members of that family, while a twelfth, the Friend of the Family, would "sum up" in the final chapter. Thus, Mr. Howells said, he himself might start the book with the father's chapter; another author would write the mother's chapter, a third the married son's chapter, and so on—each author in turn taking up and carrying on the tale from the point where the last writer had dropped it.

The suggestion was an exciting one, and I immediately began to carry it out. Just as promptly my troubles developed. Naturally, with Mr. Howells making the first drive from the literary tee, and the coöperation of Henry James and Mark Twain practically assured, my ambition was to bring together what P. T. Barnum would have called the greatest, grandest, most gorgeous group of authors ever collaborating on a literary production. I prepared a preliminary list of possibilities that made me blink, accustomed though I was, by that time, to literary effulgence. This, with

258

a letter designed to lure those authors from any other work they were then considering, I submitted to Mr. Howells. It drew from him this encouraging comment:

"I cannot praise this too highly in matter or manner. May it start the venture right!"

Within a week of my first talk with Mr. Howells I had mailed that letter to every author on the list and was waiting for joyous promises of coöperation. On the *World* I could have started the little enterprise in a day. But we newcomers at Franklin Square had learned our lesson, and our pace had slowed.

Some of the joyous promises came. Henry James at once consented to write the married son's chapter, as I had counted on him to do. Dr. Henry van Dyke was equally prompt in his consent to be the friend of the family. Disappointments, however, rubbed shoulders with these triumphs. Mr. Howells and I had set our hearts on having Mr. Clemens (Mark Twain) write the school-boy's chapter. We used on him all our powers of persuasion, and then drew on reservoirs we had not suspected lay within us. Mr. Clemens would not coöperate with us at any price. Later he confided to me that he had conceived a fairly clear notion of what would happen to that family. The letter I quote here shows how charmingly but how firmly he could refuse a request:

DUBLIN, NEW HAMPSHIRE, August 4, 1906

DEAR MISS JORDAN,

I was hoping, and indeed expecting, that that boy would look in and report for duty. But it has not happened. After this long waiting he has never once rung the bell. This can only mean one thing—that he is not coming; that even if he has a story to tell he is not moved to tell it through me. I could compel him, but the children of the fancy are sensitive, and I do not offend them with compulsion. So I have given him up, and dismissed the thought of him from my mind—permanently.

I would so gladly have allowed him to tell his tale by my

hand, but under no conditions would I tell it *for* him. It gives me a sharp pang to say these things and disappoint you, but there is no alternative. The thought of the boy keeps tagging around after me, and interfering with my affairs. For my own comfort I have to take this course with him.

Sincerely yours,
S. L. CLEMENS

Commenting on this refusal, Mr. James wrote me soothingly:

His chapter would be a clarionet solo only, and wouldn't do much to crown *my* edifice!

Several authors promised chapters and later fell by the literary wayside. One of these was Kate Douglas Wiggin Riggs:

QUILLCOTE-ON-SACO, HOLLIS, MAINE
June 13, 1906

DEAR MISS JORDAN,

I can say with my hand on my heart that Mr. Howells' idea and your proposition unite in making the only interesting scheme ever propounded to me by an editor! This does not mean that editors are uninspired, but that I am exceedingly rocky and sterile to all suggestions from the outside. There is a fiendish riskiness and difficulty and mystery in this scheme that render it most attractive and I think I can lend a hand *if* my part comes somewhere near the *middle*. It is complicated from the editorial standpoint, because I assume that each contributor must have a copy of the chapters preceding his. I am submerged in other things I want to do, but if the typewritten manuscript which I have to carry on and dovetail can reach me by September I shall have a month here still. I can't promise to do anything "inspired" after October first.

If Mr. Bangs is in town tell him it will take him all summer to make, train, and educate a young man half nice enough for the girl I shall get ready for him to marry—unless indeed my predecessors hand over to me a creature who can only be whitened, plated out and furbished up externally.

Yours sincerely,
KATE DOUGLAS WIGGIN RIGGS

Several authors were tied up and could not write a chapter till their contracts had been carried out. Others could not begin the work for two years. My daily mail was made up of large problems. Many authors preferred to write chapters other than those assigned to them—often chapters already assigned to some one else. The mother selected yearned to contribute the chapter of the married daughter; the selected son-in-law passionately preferred to be the friend of the family. Every author except Mr. Howells desired to write a final chapter, and have the benefit of the literary spading done by his predecessors. But most of them saw the possibilities of interest that lay in the plan and several, like Mark Twain, caught a glimpse of the bombs at the bottom of the literary barrel and warned me of their presence. Margaret Deland was quick in her refusal to contribute, though I had earnestly assured her the work would be no more taxing than the writing of a short story. Incidentally, she threw a stimulating dash of cold water on the whole project:

35 NEWBURY STREET, BOSTON
June 5, 1906

DEAR MISS JORDAN,

I think it is very unkind in you to press home upon me the cruel fact of my inefficiency. You know perfectly well that I have to give a whole summer to a story. I am no smart New York author, that can reel off stories and papers every few minutes; I am nothing but a Bostonian, who plods, and plods, and plods; and it would certainly take me a summer and probably a winter, to write a short story for any magazine.

No; you must let me out of your "family," but I will try and send you a paper this summer, so that you may know my heart is true to Pol. I really can't write "The Mother"; but I wonder if you would be very much disgusted with me if I say that if I could, the project does not appeal to me? I am dazzled at the distinguished names that have entered your domestic circle; but it doesn't seem to me that you are, any of you, taking the rank that belongs to you in literature when you make yourselves into this pleasant sandwich. There now! You can throw me down and jump on me if you want to.

Sadly yours,
MARGARET DELAND

In the end, however, I got together this list of authors who were ready to stand by.

```
The Father .............William Dean Howells
The Old Maid ..........Mary E. Wilkins Freeman
The Grandmother .......Mary Heaton Vorse
The Daughter-in-law  ....Mary Stewart Cutting
The School Girl ........Elizabeth Jordan *
The Son-in-law .........John Kendrick Bangs
The Married Son .......Henry James
The Married Daughter ..Elizabeth Stuart Phelps
The Mother ............Edith Wyatt †
The School Boy ........Mary Raymond Shipman Andrews
Peggy (the heroine) .....Alice Brown
Friend of the Family .....Henry van Dyke
```

So far, so good. Every author was now vastly interested. Mr. Howells had suggested that Miss Wyatt, his choice as the mother of the family, should write the second chapter. This proved impossible. In making the schedule I had to consider the convenience and other plans of every author, and give each all possible leeway for the work. The only author who could immediately write the second chapter was Miss Wilkins, the old maid aunt of the family. The schedule for the remaining chapters depended, of course, on the dates on which the various writers could turn in their work. If we had not followed this timing the writing of *The Whole Family* would have spread itself over two or three years, and every contributor would have lost interest in it. Mr.

---

* It was Mr. Howells who—with consummate ease—persuaded that author to join the circle.

† Also Mr. Howells' selection.

Howells and I were equally anxious to have the novel completed within a year.

If I had realized the possibilities of the situation I would not have sent to any one of those twelve authors any part of that novel until the time came for him or her to write a chapter. Then I would have sent all the preceding chapters together, and the waiting author would have had the cumulative effect of them. He would also have had the inevitable literary spasm caused by the collaboration to date—but it would have been only one spasm instead of eleven—and his mind would have been promptly diverted by the need of writing his own chapter at once.

In the exuberance of my optimism and desire to please everybody, I made a serious blunder. I began by sending proofs of Mr. Howells's chapter to every author on the list. This established a precedent. They all read his introduction, however, with the interest and respect due to the work of the Dean of American Literature. When the second chapter came in, written by Mary E. Wilkins Freeman as the Old Maid, I read it and rushed it to the composing-room. As soon as it was put into type I sent proofs of it to the ten authors who were to follow her—and the epoch-making row of *The Whole Family* began!

In his first chapter Mr. Howells had set forth the characters and background of the Family and had mentioned that the young heroine, Peggy, was to be married. Reading this chapter with the seeing eye and mind of the author who is to follow it, Miss Wilkins discovered from Mr. Howells's passing mention of Peggy's aunt, Elizabeth Talbert, that the "old maid" was about thirty-four. Consciously or unconsciously Mr. Howells had relegated Elizabeth to the chimney corner. He was not interested in her. She had no real value in the story as he saw it. Miss Wilkins, however, had a very different idea. She made this old maid of thirty-four an up-and-coming character, attractive, and modern in dress and ideas. She revealed that a year or two before the story opened Harry, the young lover, had experienced for Elizabeth a boyish infatuation that made her a dangerous rival to Peggy.

This wholly unexpected twist of the tale proved to be the explosion of a bomb-shell on our literary hearthstone. Every author on the list dropped all other interests to write me about it. They all knew me well, and many of them were my friends. They wrote intimately and in a state of high excitement. Some of them, especially Mr. Howells and Dr. van Dyke, were crushed by what they considered the destruction of the whole plan. Others, including Mary Raymond Shipman Andrews, Mrs. Vorse, and—to a degree— Henry James, felt that Miss Wilkins had "trumped the trick" and given a slow-starting story the impetus it needed. The gentle and lovable William Dean Howells sent me a letter that almost scorched the paper it was written on. I must not quote it here, for he wouldn't like that. But after more than thirty years, and with all the authors but three now in their graves, it can do no harm to give the gist of his letter in a sentence or two. He told me what he thought of Miss Wilkins's chapter, and he implored me not to publish it. He ended with the prayer, "Don't, *don't* let her ruin our beautiful story!"

His letter planted me firmly on the horns of a very serious dilemma. I had to take full responsibility in all *Bazar* matters. Colonel Harvey's sole instruction when he engaged me as the *Bazar's* editor was: "Run it to suit yourself. You won't be interfered with." In considering this problem I had to remember that, like Mr. Howells, Miss Wilkins was one of Harper's most valued and successful authors. To reject her chapter was impossible. Moreover, I felt as many other members of the Family did, that a plot must be started and

Elizabeth Jordan at Thirty

quickened. In my perplexity I turned to a fellow-editor—
none other than Henry Mills Alden, editor of *Harper's Magazine*. He was a life-long friend of Mr. Howells, and Mary
E. Wilkins was his beloved literary daughter. He could pass
dispassionately on their conflicting viewpoints.

He did. He was as interested and as understanding as I
had known he would be. Miss Wilkins, who had obviously
realized that her chapter would not please Mr. Howells—
or perhaps some one had whispered to her that it did not—
explained her viewpoint in the following letters. Incidentally,
in the second one, she also freely expressed her opinion of
Mr. Howells's chapter. She began with these pregnant comments:

METUCHEN, N. J., July 24, 1906

DEAR MISS JORDAN,

You would have received my chapter before this but it was
more work than I had anticipated. I began to realize that I must
start some action or plot, or rather indicate a plot, and at the
same time not diverge from Mr. Howells's character description. It was quite a task. I hope I have succeeded reasonably
well.... To tell the truth such an innovation in the shape of a
maiden aunt rather frightened me, but the old conception of her
was so hackneyed.... I did think some plot ought to be started
—and I could see no other way....

M.E.W.F.

METUCHEN, N. J., August 1, 1906

DEAR MISS JORDAN,

You are most decidedly right in your conception of the old
maid aunt. Mr. Howells evidently clings to the old conception
of her. You and I know that in these days of voluntary celibacy
on the part of women an old maid only fifteen years older than
a young girl is a sheer impossibility, if she is an educated woman
with a fair amount of brains. Moreover, a young man is really
more apt to fall in love with her.... Why, the whole plot of
the novel must be relegated back to Miss Austen, and *Godey's
Lady's Book,* and all that sort of thing, if the old conception
holds.

At this minute I can think of a score of women who fifty years ago would have carried out Mr. Howells's idea of the old maid aunt. To-day they look as pretty and as up-to-date as their young nieces—and no pretence about it, either. They really *are*. Their single state is deliberate choice on their own part, and men are at their feet. Single women have caught up with, and passed, old bachelors in the last half of the century.

I don't think Mr. Howells realizes this. He is thinking of the time when women of thirty put on caps, and renounced the world. That was because they married at fifteen and sixteen, and at thirty had about a dozen children. Now they simply do not do it.

Peggy was twenty, and her aunt thirty-four. It is obvious nonsense to make it impossible that a man should fall in love with Elizabeth, and that she should still be beautiful. . . . Suppose Peggy was even considerably older; the possibility, even probability, remains that the aunt would still have the advantage. . . .

I do think the whole freshness and novelty of the book depends upon my conception of that part, and I hope it will hold with the other authors. Otherwise it will be just a hackneyed *Way Down East* sort of novel, and the situations will be completely spoiled. In fact, there will be no situation except one of opéra bouffe.

That young man was as much in love with Miss Talbert as Thackeray makes Pendennis in love with the actress, and poor Peggy was confronted with a hard fact. . . .

I am glad you look at the character as I do. Otherwise I should think I had written very stupidly.

Very sincerely yours,
MARY E. WILKINS FREEMAN

The following comment, quoted as a fair sample of the attitude of the extreme left, came from my friend Dr. Henry van Dyke:

SEAL HARBOR, MAINE

DEAR MISS JORDAN,

This is just a line to acknowledge the arrival of "the Hull Family." Heavens! what a catastrophe! Who would have thought that the maiden aunt would go mad in the second chapter? Poor lady. Red hair and a pink hat and boys in beau knots all over the costume. What *will* Mr. Howells say?

For my part I think it distinctly crewel work to put a respectable spinster into such a hattitude before the world. I believe Mark Twain will arraign this outrage on an innocent sex. *My* own hope now lies in further complications, bloodshed, dark chambers, ghosts, and clanking chains coming down the corridor. *Then* I can come in sweetly with the final melody of peace, *fluto obligato*.

Yours,
HENRY VAN DYKE

Mr. Alden read the letters and chapters of Mr. Howells and Miss Wilkins and pronounced himself heartily enthusiastic over the old maid's chapter. From that hour he firmly took his stand beside Miss Wilkins and me, and stood with us four square against the storms that came from every side. But our authors were still having more to say than two mere editors could understand. Their discussion grew so fiery that I also consulted first Colonel Harvey and then Mr. Duneka. To my relief both men were delighted with Miss Wilkins's chapter. They thought it gave the novel the push it needed for cumulative interest. My own feeling was definitely the same, as I had written Miss Wilkins. I also agreed with her that an up-to-date woman of thirty-four was still in the ring. (I myself was in my thirties and convinced that I was going strong.)

Greatly encouraged by the support of the president and the general manager of Harper and Brothers I wrote Mr. Howells a letter—tender, I know, and tactful, I hope—setting the whole situation before him and explaining that "we" felt we must continue the story with Miss Wilkins's chapter. He took the decision like the scholar and gentleman he was; but he let me see that he thought the novel was wrecked and that he himself lay buried among the ruins.

To my further relief Henry James was not at all dismayed by the twist in Miss Wilkins's chapter. He, too, wanted plot and movement. His doubts had to do with the manner of Miss Wilkins's development. His sole question was whether she had made her premises as effective as they might have been.

My troubles continued, and I dropped from one pitfall into another. In my eager desire to please our literary Family I had not realized that its members would accept the proofs of the chapters preceding their own as tacit invitations to comment, praise, blame, suggest, and, in general, to take part in the editorial work on the novel. With only a few exceptions they did all these things, and several of them did more.

I, of course, regarded everything concerning *The Whole Family* as highly confidential, to be confined to that Family and to the heart of the family in Franklin Square. Many of the other authors had no such inhibitions. They not only wrote me what they thought of Miss Wilkins's chapter and subsequent chapters of which they held strongly varying opinions, but some of them confided in their friends as well. Intriguing gossip about the upheaval in *The Whole Family* spread, and all literary New York discussed it.

Notwithstanding our announced decision to print Miss Wilkins's chapter, Mr. Howells made one more desperate effort to send Elizabeth back to her corner. In his second letter about it he wrote me, not knowing that I had already sent off the proofs, "I would not send Mrs. Freeman's chapter to the others. They might take their color from it and lose originality of composition."

I had been afraid that he would refuse to have anything more to do with our unfortunate Family, but to my relief he continued to advise and comment. He was severe about some of the other chapters as they came in. Of one of these he wrote:

Billy will be the better for much combing and brushing. He seems to me not so much like a boy as like what a girl would be if she were a boy.

But after the second big storm broke—this time over the mother's chapter—which deeply agitated Henry James and others—Mr. Howells wrote me:

I think the mother's chapter is charming—delicately true to nature and abounding in fine bits of observation.

Letters from the other authors continued to pour in. I quote a few more examples of the contents of my mail those days, beginning with several letters in which, later in the year, Henry James unburdened his mind:

LAMB HOUSE, RYE, SUSSEX

DEAR MISS JORDAN,

"The Married Son" goes to you by this mail, and I leave him and his proportions, and everything else about him, to your merciful judgment. Obviously, a firm hand is required to take up the rest of the business of the "fugitives." It was impossible to me to adequately *prepare* my interest in C.E. and his wife (for I may murmur ever so softly in your ear that the others hadn't, to my battered imagination, so very overwhelmingly prepared it) and then carry on the "action" all the rest of the way. I should have had to do thus much more than any of the others have done. So I have, of course, but left my conduct of it—of the "action"—where whoever follows me must take it up. I have inanely lost—I find—the sketch-list of contributive hands you originally sent me; but I hope at any rate I'm not indiscreet in saying that, at the point the thing has reached, the Engaged Youth ought to have a showing in it. To wind up, on what I have myself done, I should have taken *him*—reporting on C.E., from his view, on all the rest of it, and above all on the aunt: though I confess I do myself rather break my heart at not having been able to work in (as C.E.) a direct chance at her. She is the person, in the whole thing, to have been *objectively* done—Miss Wilkins making her, to my sense, too subjectively sentimental. My own restricted effort with C.E. was, frankly, to objectify them all as much as possible. But what complications I evoke! I leave them to you, I shamelessly shuffle them off on you, and am yours,

HENRY JAMES

P.S. Let me say that if you prefer to terminate my part at Charles Edward's simple speeding from Mrs. Chataway's door you are quite welcome. Only I do love, I confess, some of the appreciative, interpretative part about Mrs. Chataway that follows!

58 RUE DE VARENNE, PARIS

DEAR MISS JORDAN,

Just a word to say what pleasure I take in your letter of the 1st March, telling me that Mrs. Chataway shall play her little part. Poor thing—it's so brief an apparition. I did feel—in doing my bit—that some further enrichment of the characterization (of everyone indeed, but in particular of Elizabeth) is greatly wanted for her, Elizabeth, not to perish of thinness, of vagueness—and I am duly inconsolable at not having been able to get straight at her myself.

The touch of C.E.'s observation in New York was a step toward that and, therefore, somehow valuable, it seemed to me, for his successors. But they must get at her, and keep at her (through others' spectacles) as I hope they feel. Otherwise I fear she will, as interest, shipwreck at the dock, as it were; for I didn't feel that up to Part VIII she had been sufficiently *launched.*

What I had hoped for myself was to give a good blow of wind into her sail—but there was so much else in space first to do. . . .

HENRY JAMES

LAMB HOUSE, RYE, SUSSEX

DEAR MISS JORDAN,

I have from you 9, 10 and 11 of *The Whole Family* and I don't—frankly—know what to say. For when I have said that I think it well, or at least not bad, that Elizabeth in 11, is finally "referred back" to Mrs. Chataway etc. in N. Y., or that her predicament, such as it was, is not sentimentally patched up for her, I am really afraid I have said all I find sayable!

For one can but view the little course of the flurry (and alas, the flurry was a fundamentally weak and not very promising little flurry from the first of its being started, I thought!) in the light of the turn one had tried to give the thing, for dear life, in one's own Number. And so viewing it, nothing of my own imagined little direction given affects me as having come about.

I think there was a little to be done from the end of VIII (if that was my number) or with the Situation with an effected presence of three of the persons in New York, and with the picture of Charles Edward's action and passion (so to speak) there, his dealings with Elizabeth and the young man, his "line taken" on behalf of or in the interest of his Mother—and with more other things than I can say. I tried to suggest his confidences with the kidnapped and compromised youth in the Park as a Value, his then meeting (his "having it out") with Elizabeth and, as it were, disposal of her, as a value. And I left them, these *values,* fairly dangling there, to my best ability, as it were, for my successors to catch at. But alas they haven't, by my vision, caught much—and my vision, such as it was, of the elements, such as they were, has fallen to the ground.

Of 9 and 10, as they stand, I can't—in a manner—"trust myself to speak"! And I think it is a real misfortune for our series that the small boy's stuff comes in. I think it indeed a pity that the scheme involved from the first the exhibition of *two* children. It should have rested, as to that, with your so-happily-done little girl.

I saw, at any rate at the point where I stopped, an excellent action for the Part of the mother—*the* Part of the whole thing! I—oh, if one could have, impossibly (disguisedly) done it one's self! And what I should have liked to hypnotize my successor into seeing was that there would be with her the chance to give through her recital the (all-vividly) summarized picture *from* (and by) C.E. of the situation in New York. I see a thing of the highest value—for the whole—to have been done, in fine, with the mother in respect now to Elizabeth, to

Maria, to the Father. The mother above all in respect to C.E. himself (which his part was all a preparation for, leading up to an effect of). But the mother treated as she actually stands seems to me—I confess to you brutally—a positive small convulsion of debility—without irony, without fancy, without anything!

Will your public want that so completely lack-lustre domestic sentimentality? But I'm really going into the matter too much —after Part VIII. My excuse is that I saw, as a sequel to that, the ensuing steps of the little action so fully, vividly, and logically, that I must have been thinking of them as if I had really written them out, and been turning to them in fact, as to find them so written. I feel them, all ruefully, anything but. Yet I do justice to Miss Brown!

HENRY JAMES

LAMB HOUSE, RYE, SUSSEX

DEAR MISS JORDAN,

It is an unwilling accident that I haven't thanked you sooner for the gentle terms of your letter in respect to my comments on the subject of *The Whole Family*. I overflowed into judgment (of its erratic course) and then feared I might have "wounded susceptibilities." I am much reassured and comforted to find I haven't, and that you saw the disaster with the calm of despair.

I can't help saying now that I wish I might have been suffered to take upon myself to save the stuff—which would have interested and amused me. I saw a way, and this even though I hadn't ever thought the hare originally started (the aunt's flirtation, or whatever, with the niece's *fiance*—no gleam of light shed by any pen, nor ever shone on what it was!) would at her best run very far, or was indeed much of a hare. Still, I had engaged to play the game and take over the elements as they were; and I hated to see them so helplessly muddled away, when, oh, one could one's self (according to one's fatuous thought) have made them mean something, given them sense, direction, and form.

It was, and still is, I confess, for me, the feeling of a competent cook who sees good vittles messed. I wince at the vision of the dinner being served. Don't think, however, I mean to tactlessly discomfort you as the hostess. You will smile it out, I am sure, all successfully.

I am yours from below, very red in the face, as you see.

HENRY JAMES

I must repeat here, in justice to the author, that Mr. Howells was as enthusiastic over the mother's chapter as Mr. James was critical. On the whole, however, the mother's chapter caused as great a convulsion among the authors as the old maid's did. One of the final chapters temporarily destroyed Mr. Duneka's sense of humor and caused him to break into the discussion with this letter:

December 19, 1906

DEAR MISS JORDAN,

This chapter of *The Whole Family* is simply awful—confused, dull, stupid, vapid, meaningless, halting, lame, holding up the action and movement of the story which has run along so splendidly thus far.

I regard this chapter as simply impossible.

You have got a great book—vigorous, direct, swinging to a well-concealed dénouement—and it would be a calamity to stop it with this cruelly incompetent drivel.

My advice is—don't publish it.

Yours sincerely,
F. A. DUNEKA

The author rewrote that chapter, and I used it, supported by the warm commendation of Mr. Howells and Dr. van Dyke—two allies of whom any author and editor might be proud.

In the interval Alice Brown, like the child in the old story, had "not been idle." These letters convey distinct impressions of *her* reactions:

11 PINCKNEY STREET, BOSTON

DEAR MISS JORDAN,

This is far better than I dared hope. Now let us pray for the small boy. If he doesn't commit us to anything, I can live, but if he lets Peggy *see* Harry or himself sees them in each other's arms, then I shall descend into the water butt with the saintly Jokanaan and the enemies of Mr. F's Aunt, and ask to have the lid put on.

Yours tremulously,
ALICE BROWN

11 PINCKNEY STREET, BOSTON

DEAR MISS JORDAN,

If Mrs. Ward stands for Eliza, then indeed are we in the soup up to our saddle-girths. Verily do I feel upon my ankle bones the laving of the puree.

"The times have been
That when the brains were out the man would die."

Not so Eliza. She springs eternal.

Sincerely yours,
ALICE BROWN

250 WATER STREET, NEWBURYPORT, MASS.

DEAR MISS JORDAN,

"Out of the night that covers me" when I read Billy's revelations I raise a feeble head to ask if Dr. Denbigh is "the friend of the family." Must the confidence be ostensibly addressed to him, or—to the weeds in the river? Must Peggy talk as if she were talking to him personally?

Yours foggily,
ALICE BROWN

11 PINCKNEY STREET, BOSTON

DEAR MISS JORDAN,

A friend who, years ago, was passing through a great emotional crisis, used to preface all her letters by "Burn this." I feel constrained to do likewise, for I am going to tell you what is known euphonistically, as my "whole heart" about *The Whole Family*. So far as the work goes I could sit down to my chapter to-morrow, but I frankly don't dare commit Peggy until I know the votes are all in.

Let me go back a little and present you with my states of mind. I thought we were all to confide in one friend of the family who should turn out to be the friend who draws the threads together at the end, and that his personality should be implied throughout. Again I thought we were to take Mr. Howells's key, being good. He struck it clearly. We had one of his dear entirely natural families of "folks" we should all delight in living with. I understood them at once. I wanted to make them a visit. But in Mrs. Freeman's chapter I had a facer.

Mr. Howells had thrown out a premonitory hint of Aunt Elizabeth. Mrs. Freeman, at one stroke, turned her into an antique and horrible. When I met Aunt Elizabeth, powder-puff to powder-puff, face to face, I was on the point of writing you that I should have to give up the job. I frankly didn't see any un-farcical way out. Either Mr. Howells was mistaken in The Family, or Aunt Elizabeth was mad. She looked at them all through a distorting lens. But at the moment, as I was, of begging to be let off, I reflected that I had promised, and also that it would be a temptingly stiff knot to untie. So I stayed in.

Now, gradually, it seems to me, we have been working out from the impressionist purple shadow of Aunt Elizabeth though we have not yet escaped. One after another has thrown an illuminating ray upon her, and, seen in the light, she is not so formidable. But she is still the knot in the puzzle. If she is mad she can be grappled with. We can pack her off to a symbolic asylum and let the erotic fever which follows her tracks die with the fancy that created it. Or is she sane? And has she lied about her age or has she not? Is she still "eligible"? On that case we've got to regard Harry Goward's neoteric passion as an actual occurrence and see what poppy will do for him.

I begin to think I have been stupid—that Mrs. Freeman didn't mean Aunt Elizabeth seriously at all, but as a delicate and too-convincing satire on the present woman who "getting on in years," continues to play not only as hard but according to the rules of twenty—not the woman who, like Miss Ellen Terry, with the gray in her darkening hair, is bewitching because she can't help it and would wistfully laugh away the hope that "morning's at seven." Not like Mrs. Spofford, who has all the "go" and more than the charm of sweet and twenty, but drapes her darling head. Is Mrs. Freeman kindly but cunningly showing up one of these feminine rocking-horses of modern art who keep on prancing though they do it on castors and don't get anywhere? I believe it is a satire and I've been taken in! But I can only say that my own hair has whitened as Aunt Elizabeth's. She, to paraphrase, "Lies in my bed, walks up and down with me."

I agree with you that the novel ought to end happily, but I certainly am afraid that even if one rise from the dead to testify for him, we can't regard Harry Goward as a very good match. So far, Peggy has been a nice girl. I don't see how we can let her pair off with a cheap kind of wobbly person who has let himself wilt so conspicuously either under circumstances (farcical circumstances) or, on the other hand, Aunt Elizabeth's eldritch spells.

But I have a little plan in my mind which will, I think, ensure Peggy's happiness, even if she sees Goward melting. (He is a kind of snow man, I'm afraid. His nose is gone, as I see him. Can he be saved? Shall we have a big storm and build him up again?) I had, at one time, a faint hope of betrothing her to Dr. van Dyke, but even he seems destined by some of the Family for the insatiable maw of Aunt Elizabeth. Aunt Gargantua, say I! And perhaps he's older than I suspected, though he really has a very young look. So I have tried to find another crevice and I fancy I can squeeze through.

Now here's a bargain. Let me wait, as per agreement, until the votes are all in, and then you see how you like my solution. Meantime, have an understudy up your sleeve, and throw me out if you don't like it. I shall cheerfully acquiesce.

ALICE BROWN

NEWBURYPORT, MASS.

DEAR MISS JORDAN,

"I give thee all! I can no more." If the thing suits I'll go over it carefully in proof and see if my data is all right, reading the other chapters still again. The second chapter I put in for your eye—the Joker you will see I wrote for my own satisfaction in a moment of delirium. You can drop it in the waste basket—or no, let me have it, please. It will do to start archives with.

ALICE BROWN

About this time Elizabeth Stuart Phelps became excited. She wrote among other things:

I shall defend Maria from the aspersions of being "a manager." Such people are often the backbone of family life. But what can happen? I don't know—nor does Mr. James, who refrained from any visible occurrence.

There were, of course, a few gleams of sunshine along my darkening way. All the authors liked Alice Brown's chapter. And all my fellow authors were very nice about my school-girl instalment. (Why wouldn't they be? Wasn't I their friend and editor?) They passed a few peaceful moments patting my head, which would have been aching hard those days if aches could have found a place in it. I was set up for hours over Henry James's approval. He wrote, among other things, "Allow me to congratulate you on your *big* little girl, full of nature and truth." But while this was so pleasantly sinking in a depressing comment on Mr. James's work came from Elizabeth Stuart Phelps. She wrote:

I have read Mr. James' chapter. I think it long and heavy. The flirtatious aunt should not be a vulgar person, except so far as flirtatiousness is always more or less vulgar. And Mr. James's insinuation that she posed as moving in better society than she did seems to me unworthy of *The Whole Family*. I do not see the way out of it, but probably you will.

A little later, Mrs. Ward wrote:

I have pushed the action and the actors all the chapter will bear. I have handled Peggy, the boy, the doctor, Charles Edward, Aunt Elizabeth, and above all, the Letter. I suppose it is not good form to offer suggestions to my successors— but I really wish they would not allow any person but Peggy to read that letter. In fact, the letter is disposed of, to my thinking, and so are a good many difficulties, however poorly done. You are right. It was high time. . . .

E.S.P.W.

An equally somber note was struck by Mary Raymond Shipman Andrews when she turned in her chapter. She wrote:

I could not live up to, or down to, the mincemeat they had made of Harry, so I retrospected a brand new character as hero....

By way of a change from the "kicks and kisses" contributed to the various chapters, and as further chastening of the editorial spirit, this type of letter dropped in on my desk from time to time. The one I quote is from Kate Riggs:

HOLLIS, MAINE

DEAR MISS JORDAN,

A terrible "backwater" has submerged me about *The Whole Family*—partly because my husband wishes me to go away with him for the entire month of September and partly because an unexpected drain upon my time occurred the day before yesterday. A proposition to edit a long series of children's classics has been before my sister and me for several months, growing out of the un-looked-for and unusual success of our *Golden Numbers* and *The Posy Ring* (anthologies of verse). I find if I decline the enterprise cannot go on, as they wish my name and work as well as my sister's, and I must not interfere with her plans and the publishers' by "standing out"....

I tell you what would be a good idea. *The Whole Family* idea is a charming one and ought to be carried forward by persons above all who are steady, skilful writers of good constructive ability, rather than by a casual author like me. Just see, during the next week or two, if you can't find some one who would know *just* how to do it, for whom it has no terrors, and to whom it would be merely a pleasant fortnight's work. I *worry* so over all work suggested by anybody but myself— and I have four *Rebecca* stories to write this summer for Scribners, which must be as good as I can make them. So I really am better out of *The Whole Family* than in it—much better; though it would be a great lark if one's part turned out well.

K.D.W.R.

A little later Kate slipped out of the Family. "You will hate me for this," she wailed; but, of course, I didn't.

At long intervals two authors agreed as to certain developments and characterization. Then such notes as this chimed out above the battle-field like vesper bells:

AVALON, PRINCETON, N. J.

DEAR MISS JORDAN,

Your letter is certainly delightful. Thank you for it and for the friendly telegram from Miss Alice Brown. It was she that gave Garret Wendell his head, and the old gentleman is still young enough to recognize a nice girl when he sees her. I'm glad he behaved well, though I suspect him of being rather headstrong at times, and inclined to dominate if not to interfere. He needs training. . . .

If you will let me I'm coming back Sunday to ask for another cup of tea.

Faithfully yours,
HENRY VAN DYKE

I need hardly add that there were members of *The Whole Family* who did not share Miss Brown's enthusiasm and mine over Dr. van Dyke's chapter.

It should not be hard for the gentle reader to grasp from these exhibits the situation of the editor handling the letters and successive chapters of *The Whole Family*. Those quoted here are merely a few extracts from a correspondence that in itself would fill volumes, and which all but wrecked an excellent nervous system. The mail was as active as our family setter, Freckles, bringing in bones—the bones of authors, dug up, as it were, by other authors. Almost every author seemed to consider the chapters before his merely as material leading up to his own work, and to judge it solely in its relation to his individual plans. Also, any later departures from the values or leads in his chapter grieved him sorely. Henry James was so upset by these that he actually and quite seriously suggested writing all the final chapters himself! When it came to the point of considering the book as a whole, the authors were very much like members of a theatrical cast listening to the reading of a new play. Each judged it from the viewpoint of his own part and each had grave doubts of the abilities of some of his associates. All the editor could do was to keep smiling—but not, as Henry James had suggested, "all successfully."

The whole situation was natural, probably inevitable; and there was a certain editorial ozone in the fact that every author's interest in the collaboration was intense, almost hectic. But it was a difficult atmosphere to work in, and for me it marked the year 1906-7 with a dark tablet. Editorial criticism was impossible, owing to the distinction of the authors. The appalling candor with which editors of to-day discuss the work of their authors was then undreamed of. Occasionally I passed on hints, always tentatively and with many preliminary tributes and apologies.

"It has been suggested that . . ." "What would you think of . . ." "Does it strike you—perhaps . . ."

It rarely struck them. It was really not to be expected that it would.

In the end the book was finished and published. It had cost a great deal of money, time, and nervous wear-and-tear. It has long been out of print; but during its first years it sold well and earned a reasonable profit for Harper and Brothers. They were satisfied; but my own reaction was different.

After the fine candor of those first weeks, I had grown very coy about expressing my opinion of the various instalments when they came in, or later. However, as I have so freely revealed the impression of the others concerned, it is only fair that I should now confess my own. I do so, with accumulated zest.

The Whole Family was a mess!

ASIDE from my frequent sixteen and eighteen hours of work a day on the *World,* the two fullest days of my life were passed in the pursuit of pleasure—one of them in southern Germany, the other in Bermuda.

The first began in Munich with a delightful luncheon given me by Gertrude Atherton, who was then living there. I had passed the morning in toy factories selecting gifts for my eighteen god-children. Mrs. Atherton's luncheon was followed by the opera—*Tristan and Isolde,* which began in Munich's unique fashion at four in the afternoon and was given uncut. We—this time Martha, Harriet and I—had just time to drive back to our hotel and make a change of costume before the opera began. I was deeply thrilled by the performance, which was one of the finest I have ever seen in any part of the world. Nothing dimmed my rapture in it, not even the fact that in the final act Tristan appeared to be clad snugly in a suit of Jaeger underwear.

There was an interval at six o'clock for dinner in the lobby of the opera house, where we foregathered for an hour with friends and acquaintances. The opera then continued until almost midnight, when we were again whirled back to our hotel to change for a night journey to Partenkirchen, high in the Bavarian Alps. There were no berths left in the wagon-lit, and I for one did not need a berth. I was intensely excited by the music. To sleep was impossible. I gazed out at moonlit Bavaria and mentally went over the score and the various scenes, firmly pushing aside the recurring picture of the dying Tristan's nice warm flannels, which kept thrusting themselves into the foreground.

When we reached Partenkirchen at sunrise I was beginning to feel rather let down. The previous day and night had been strenuous. I suggested to my companions that we go directly to bed for a few hours of sleep, and they agreed. But when we reached the hotel we found a party of twelve just ready to start for the Höllenthal climb. The hotel manager suggested that we join the group, as the day was perfect. The members of the party—largely made up of German, English, and Scandinavian climbers—hospitably repeated the invitation, and after some coy hesitation we ended by accepting it. There·was no time to get into such climbing costumes and hob-nailed shoes as our fellow-climbers were wearing. We were just off a train and we wore the short tweed skirts, shirt waists, jackets and high buttoned boots suited to travel at that period. We decided that these would do for mountain climbing. Our fellow travelers agreed, but looked worried. They waited while each of us swallowed a roll and a cup of coffee. Then the hotel manager lent us some strong alpenstocks, and we started off.

I don't know what the Höllenthal climb has developed into in the past thirty years. The Matterhorn ascent has become so simplified and safe-guarded that kindergarten infants should be able to reach the peak with ease. The Höllenthal was then a good stiff climb, and it had some tricky points. There was, I remember—or perhaps we blundered into it—a long natural tunnel through the mountain, at one place very narrow and not high enough in which to stand upright. This had to be traversed by the light of candles which frequently went out. It led to a high rock wall, almost perpendicular, but with some hand and footholds. Up these we had to climb to an opening just large enough for a person of ordinary size to squeeze through. I have never enjoyed the sensation of being alive in a tomb, and I had experienced it vividly only a year or two earlier, when my guide thoughtlessly mislaid me in the Catacombs of Rome. I did not enjoy the little reminder of that experience offered by the Höllenthal's blind alley.

However, there was a nice German University professor in the party—one of the Heidelberg faculty. He had voluntarily taken me under his wing for the day, and he knew the Höllenthal climb as he knew his own pocket. He did not know any English, and though I was born and educated in America's Munich—Milwaukee—my German was a matter of good intention and a willingness to take verbal chances. We were both fair in French, so we compromised on that and got on admirably. One reason for this was that climbing in the Bavarian Alps does not stimulate conversation.

We completed the climb about five o'clock in the afternoon and got back to the Inn at supper time. My stout boots were in ribbons, my tweed suit was badly torn and stained, and I was sure I was exhausted. My plan was to go to bed at once and have supper sent up to me. But the hotel manager—the same indefatigable soul who had cheered us on our way that morning—had other plans. The most famous troop of yodelers and dancers in Bavaria were to perform at the Inn that evening, he assured us, and it would never do to miss them. We had just time for a hot bath and supper before the entertainment began. We found it well worth staying up for, and we ended by dancing the rest of the night. That meant a strenuous whirl of forty-eight hours without five minutes of sleep. It is pleasant to look back and realize that one ever had enough strength and energy to keep up such a pace and survive. We had about four hours' sleep the third morning, before we started off on another climbing expedition.

The Bermuda day was equally strenuous in a different way. Its program might be called a cumulative conversational marathon. I was passing a month with Frances Hodgson Burnett at her home on Bailey's Bay, and she undertook to show me Somerset, one of Bermuda's show places. Mrs. Burnett had the most perfect team of horses on the island, attached to the most elegant victoria there. They were also attached by reins to a superbly uniformed coachman who would have given distinction to any turnout. In this impressive comfort, behind the splendid horses that raced along the coral roads at full speed and as if they loved doing it, we must have covered almost every mile of Bermuda during that month. The expedition to Somerset had its new features.

We started comfortably between ten and eleven in the morning. We were to stop at noon at the Bermuda home of some friends of Fluffy's who were giving a large luncheon for us. Fluffy (Mrs. Burnett) and I had talked steadily during the morning drive. I have had many friends, and dear ones, too, with whom my association was broken by intervals of restful silence. There was never any silence when Fluffy and I were together and neither of us wanted any. Only Mrs. Burnett's intimates knew how fascinating she could be as a talker. Indeed, one woman I knew gave her the sobriquet of "The Scarlet Rambler" because, when she was not interested, Fluffy sometimes prattled on rather vaguely through a sense of social obligation. When she was interested she was also intensely interesting; and, incredibly, she could listen as well as she talked.

On this day we talked steadily till we reached the home of our hostess. There, finding twenty luncheon guests invited to meet us, we both went into conversational action again. The weather was warm and most of the guests were the kind who preferred to listen rather than exert themselves.

We left at three, and continued to talk steadily till we reached Somerset. There a tea and later a dinner was given for us, and we passed lightly from these diversions to a dance on a British warship that was lying in the harbor. We were back in the hotel about one o'clock in the morning and, with a brisk undercurrent of conversation, were ready for bed by two.

We had connecting rooms. Fluffy's windows looked out on a heavenly tropical garden. Mine overlooked the sea. A great moon had laid a wide golden runway across the water, and through the open windows the night song of the waves came in. I was in bed and expecting to be asleep in exactly five minutes when Fluffy, in her nightgown, came to the connecting door to say good night. I thought we had said it, but evidently we had not. She took in the beauty of the picture that lay beyond the windows, the coolness of the room, the soothing murmur of the waves, and saw in all this the perfect setting for a pleasant chat. She sat down on the side of my bed and started one.

I would have made a heavy wager that no conversationalist on earth could have held my attention that night. But Fluffy did it. Fearing the effects on her of the breezes that came through the open windows I finally invited her into bed. She came without interrupting her narrative, which had to do with a country house she had once occupied not far from London. She told me of her week-end parties there, of interesting types among her neighbors, of her various London guests, many of whom I knew. We compared our impressions of Henry James and others. We talked till dawn. I remember seeing it peer in at us with a certain effect of surprise, which I shared. Fluffy was still talking, but I must have gone to sleep almost immediately after that.

I was awakened in five or ten minutes, I thought, by the ringing of a telephone bell. The hour was now seven, however, and Fluffy, after answering the call in her own room, was back at my bedside giving me its message.

The officers of the British warship—probably fascinated by our ability the night before to keep a conversation going with no effort whatever on their part—were inviting us to breakfast with them on board. It appeared that there was to be some kind of special drill after breakfast, followed by divine services, and some music which we might enjoy. If we could reach the warship in forty minutes, Fluffy added, we would be in time for breakfast.

We did it. The ship services were very restful. I closed my eyes once or twice and voices came to me from great distances. We had to get back to the hotel to dress for a luncheon followed by a tea, and that night there was another dinner with more conversation. Our hosts and hostesses were not exacting. Almost any conversation would do. I remember maintaining a resolute silence after dinner, while I encouraged a nice young English girl to talk about her experiences in India. The men were still at the table, lingering over their cigars and brandy. The women were out on a terrace from which marble steps led down to lapping blue water. The view was as dream-like as it can only be in tropic countries. In a group a few feet away, made up of women apparently listening to her in a pleasant trance, Fluffy was still chatting animatedly. I wondered how she could, till I caught a sentence.

"That makes them a nice golden brown," she was saying.

As may be inferred, my friendship with Mrs. Burnett was now ripening very fast. For years we had had a pleasant touch-and-go association, meeting at teas and luncheons and dinners, but never intimate. Then, unexpectedly, we had found ourselves loafing across the sea one summer in the same ship. Neither had known the other was to be on board, but I caught a glimpse of Fluffy on deck as we sailed away,

waving good-by to a handsome young man in white flannels.
Later she told me he was the Washington friend from whom
she had drawn her character of Arbuthnot in *Through One
Administration*. Our ship was one that sailed the southern
route and took twelve days to do it, stopping at interesting
points like Patras, Palermo, Algiers, and Naples, and finally
landing us at Trieste, Austria. It was a restful voyage. We
passed hours talking in our deck chairs, and we made many
of the shore excursions together. This experience had preceded the Bermuda episode and was the real beginning of
our close friendship. We separated at Trieste, Fluffy lingering for a "cure," while Harriet and I went on to Vienna and
Budapest. That was the year before the war, and I shall
always be glad I visited those two cities at the height of their
glory and gaiety.

I remember especially the nights in Vienna, when we dined
under the trees in the parks, listening to famous regimental
bands and looking at hundreds of handsome officers in the
most gorgeous uniforms in the world. "Where are they
now?" I remember, too, that with all the rest of Vienna,
our cab-route back to our hotel at midnight was through
the palace courtyard, over its cobblestones, and under the bedroom windows of poor old Emperor Franz Josef, who was
probably the only person in Vienna trying to sleep.

Before leaving Trieste Harriet and I had a memorable
experience. We were anxious to visit Miramar, the palace
originally built by Maximilian of Mexico for Carlotta, but
at this time owned by the Austrian royal family. We were
told that visitors could go through the palace if none of the
family happened to be there. Our authority added that he
thought the palace now held only the caretakers and servants.

Miramar is two or three miles from Trieste, and one
reaches it by an incredibly lovely drive along the shore of the
Adriatic. The weather was perfect the day we went and the

whole experience so soul-satisfying that it hardly mattered whether we saw the inside of Miramar or did not. We were not really disappointed when we reached the palace to find that our friend had been wrong. It was occupied. The royal flag flew above it and there were signs of activity inside the great iron gates.

We drew up on the shore, quite close to these gates, content to give our cab horse a rest before we jogged back to Trieste. The view around us was in itself enough to satisfy any one. Miramar posed before us, perched on its headland, mellow in the sun, its windows like hundreds of shining eyes gazing out over the sea.

Suddenly, as we looked, the great gates swung open. The waiting cabman and idlers around us stiffened into attention. A couple of handsomely uniformed outriders galloped through the entrance, followed by a victoria drawn by two splendid horses, with liveried coachman and footman on the box.

The carriage came slowly, probably out of consideration for the dozens of persons standing near the entrance, all very stiff and straight now, ready to salute. It passed so close to us that we could almost have touched it by stretching out a hand. We had a perfect view of the young man and young woman who sat in it, side by side. We were, I think, the only foreigners in the group, and the couple glanced at us as they passed. We bowed. The young man raised his hat with something like a flourish, and threw in a brilliant smile. The woman bowed, too, unsmilingly and with the deeply bored expression of one who had done that sort of thing till she was fed up with it. The next instant the coachman had given his horses a touch of the whip, and the victoria was really on its way.

I looked at our driver, who was replacing the cap he had taken off.

"Who are those two?" I asked him.

The driver grimaced toward the palace.

"That," he said almost contemptuously, "was the Archduke Ferdinand and his morganatic wife. They are living there this week."

I was puzzled.

"I've always heard that Ferdinand is a very unpleasant person," I said—"arrogant and dour. That young man was charming!"

The driver shrugged his shoulders.

"He can smile when he likes," he said indifferently, "but he is not loved."

He looked after the victoria, almost out of sight now, and repeated the sentence with sudden emphasis. *"He is not loved!"*

I have often recalled that quiet hour, with its dream-like setting, and the momentary picture of those two, rushing toward the sunset. Already the shadow of their doom lay over them. Possibly the actual date of it was already checked on some Servian calendar. But no premonition had come to that smiling man and that bored woman that their murder at Serajevo less than a year later would set the whole world aflame and threaten civilization itself.

CHAPTER XVIII

PRELUDE IN C SHARP MINOR

HARRIET and I were on the ocean, on our way to Europe, when the World War began. Our final destination was Russia, but we were leaving the ship at Christiansand. Our plan was to linger in Norway a fortnight and then go to Sweden to visit my friend the Marchioness Lagergren, who had a château on the Baltic near Stockholm. After that we were to take our first plunge into Russia.

We went abroad so often in those days that our preparations were usually casual. One Friday, I remember, Martha and I unexpectedly decided to sail the next morning, and did so with no preparation at all except the packing of our steamer trunks. We were rarely gone more than five weeks and we regarded these European jaunts very lightly. Sometimes we did not even take a letter of credit with us, but carried our money in American Express checks and American bank-notes, which were good the world over.

Russia was new to us, however, and Harriet and I took unusual precautions for this voyage—very fortunately, as it turned out. We even had a letter of credit for much more money than we expected to spend. In addition we carried our usual American Express checks and bank-notes, and a hundred dollars in gold. The gold Charles A. Conant had persistently urged me to take. He did not explain why, but I realized later that he had not been optimistic over the gathering war clouds. The gold was an unusual precaution in those days, though I remembered that Mrs. Harvey had carried some when she and I went abroad together. Harriet and I had never even carried passports. This time, still following the odd insistence of Charles, we took passports, too, and a highly impressive letter which Charles secured for me from the State Department at Washington. It warmly commended me to the special attention of all embassy and legation heads, and would ordinarily have won me an audience with any of them in five or ten minutes. Charles had foreseen our troubles before we sailed, and had safeguarded us as much as he could; but he had not put any of his grim forebodings into words.

The first news of the War came when we were in mid-ocean. Within forty-eight hours after that all Europe was aflame. It was rather appalling to be headed toward such an inferno, and the views of the first mate of the Norwegian steamer we were on did not lighten our depression. He had told me the news in confidence as soon as it broke, and he added impressively, "It must not get out. Half these people on board would go crazy. Some of them might even jump overboard!"

It did leak out the next day, through a wireless sent to a prominent passenger who broadcast it throughout the ship within five minutes after he received it. The effect was immediate and paralyzing, but the mate's forebodings had done injustice to his passengers. Most of them were foreigners— Scandinavians, Germans, and Russians, traveling straight into tragedy for themselves and their people. They took the incredible fact of a European war not in a frenzy but in a stunned daze. Gathered into groups on deck, they whispered among themselves, as if now afraid to be overheard; or, sitting silent in their steamer chairs, they stared unseeingly across the water. The knowledge of their misery and of the whole European situation depressed the rest of us. A black pall spread over the ship. Even the young things among us had no wish to dance or play cards in the presence of those stricken men and women. The weather was perfect. We walked miles on deck, and found ourselves talking in low voices as the foreigners did.

The big drama of the voyage, aside from the constant knowledge of the strained nerves and heavy hearts around us, came when our steamer, the *Hellig Olaf,* was held up on the North Sea by an English warship. The British had to make sure the Norwegian liner was not carrying coal or food or other supplies for Germany, and there was a racking afternoon while our ship was searched and the great cruiser bulked gray beside us. The European war was really going on. We had thought we realized that. Now war had suddenly become a fact instead of a rumor.

When we landed in Norway we found its people in a desperate panic. They were so sure they would be drawn into the war within a few days or weeks that on the streets of Christiania men and women were selling their five crown notes for three or even two crowns in silver. We left the ship at Christiansand and went directly to Christiania in a train already filled with Russian refugees. These had been peremptorily ordered out of Germany, and forced by military exigencies to take that round-about return route to their own country.

The great problem Harriet and I had been considering was how and when we could get back to America. Now more pressing problems had to be solved. The proprietors of the Grand Hotel of Christiania, the best hotel in the city, had apparently lost their heads with their fellow townsmen. Politely but firmly they refused to honor American Express checks, American bank-notes, or letters of credit on any banks. Our letter of credit was on the Crédit Lyonnais of Paris—one of the strongest financial institutions in Europe. The manager of the Grand Hotel would have none of it. Nothing but gold would he accept, we were told, and meals and rooms must be paid for not only with gold but in advance.

This imbecility, of course, lasted only a few days—but they would have been very difficult days if Charles Conant had not suggested that little gold hoard. One hundred dollars, however, would not have lasted long, especially with the rates for food and rooms pushed to the highest limit. One could understand the management's point of view. Without these precautions the hotel might find itself holding paper money of many nations, much of it almost worthless. In the meantime the general idea, enthusiastically followed out, was to get from those who had gold as much of it as those exacting it could extract.

All this, as the French would say, "gave me furiously to think." By this time I had friends in most European cities and countries, or at least pleasant acquaintances. I must have some in Norway—but who and where were they? Suddenly I remembered that ten years before the war Miss Anna Hvoeslef, editor of the *Aftenposten,* the leading newspaper of Christiania, had visited New York. Before sailing she had written me. We were strangers but fellow editors. She mentioned writers she would like to meet in America—Gertrude Atherton, Mrs. Burnett, Fannie Hurst, and others. When she arrived I gave a tea for her, to which I invited the writers she had selected. She came and so did they. That was the last I heard of Anna Hvoeslef except that she wrote me a charming note of thanks when she got back to her own country.

I thought of her now. She had said all the things one says during such touch-and-go encounters. "If you come to my country—" Here I was. But was she here? That American visit of hers dated back ten years. She might have changed her position or married or even died. . . . However, I optimistically called up the office of the *Aftenposten* and asked for her. The next minute her voice was in my ears—and no music has ever seemed more beautiful. I explained, and she remembered me at once. Half an hour later we were shaking hands in the Grand Hotel while tears ran down Miss Hvoeslef's cheeks.

"Oh," she gulped, "why have you come to us at this terrible time?"

I reminded her that the terrible time had not begun when we sailed. Then I took her up to our rooms, spread our letters of credit, our express checks, our bank-notes and gold before her, and asked what we could do.

"All this seems to be regarded as worthless by the hotel people," I told her, "and our gold won't last more than a few days at the rates this hotel is charging us."

I have always been a believer in the efficacy of bread cast on the waters. The little bun I had so lightly tossed toward Miss Hvoeslef ten years before now came back to me an entire bakery. She dined with us that night and gave us the war news in detail. The next morning she took me to Christiania's leading bank and introduced me to its president —a fine old Norwegian who looked like a haggard Ibsen. Again I spread out our exhibit, this time on his desk. For good measure I added the letter from America's Secretary of State.

Like all his countrymen and countrywomen, the banker was very nervous. He didn't know what this war might do to his country and its banks. But the exhibit was an impressive one and the letter interested him. He consented to cash for each of us every morning, in Norwegian money, an American Express check for ten dollars, and to start at once. That morning, and for two weeks thereafter, each of us had to write most of the story of her life on the back of her express check. Also, after that first morning of prideful association with the president we had to stand humbly in line for hours to get the money. The line was a long one, extending the length of the counting-room and out into the street. We had become "refugees," and there were other "refugees" all around us.

They were a tragic band—men and women representing most of the countries of Europe. One morning, immediately in front of me in the line, stood a woman I discovered to be a man in disguise. I had an hour to study "her" in detail, while we both made our slow progress to the cashier's window. The figure was made up very cleverly as an English woman tourist wearing a gray tailor-made suit, heavy shoes and gloves, a blonde wig, a wide-rimmed hat, and a veil. The blonde wig was twisted very slightly awry. Below the back of the neck I saw a line of short, coarse black hair.

"She" was extremely nervous and once pushed back a glove to reach for something in a handbag. The back of the hand, visible only for a few seconds, showed another crop of that short black hair. As if the owner felt me staring at it "she" turned and gave me the strangest look I have ever received—at once frightened, desperate and menacing. At the same time "she" quickly drew back the concealing fold of the glove. I gave no sign that I had seen anything unusual, and I did not speak of the little encounter to any one but Harriet. It was not a time to show or voice suspicion of any one or anything.

We were prisoners in Christiania, in the sense that we could not get away. All the fiords had been mined. The few trains still running were operating without lights. Russian and German war planes passed above Norway in flocks. In the hotel room next to ours some impassioned amateur pianist, oblivious of all but Art, day after day pounded out the Rachmaninoff Prelude in C sharp minor. It was rather beyond her, but she was an earnest soul and kept at it. It was a fitting undertone of the general atmosphere around us.

Every time I have heard it since, it has brought back the terror and hysteria in Norway during that first fortnight of war.

Not knowing how long we were to be marooned in Norway I tried to rent a piano myself—with the amiable idea of showing the lady next door how the Prelude should be played, as well as of lifting some of the weight of our heavy hours. But when I mentioned the plan the hotel manager threw up his hands as if I were a babbling child, and the idea perished.

At nine o'clock every morning we went to the bank to cash our Express checks. That used up most of our time till noon; but the line of our fellow refugees was always interesting to watch. Every afternoon we walked in and around Christiania, or studied Miss Hvoeslef's great war map, on which the changing positions of the lined-up opposing armies were indicated with red-headed and blue-headed pins. One of Harriet's intimate friends, Ethel Buddington, was barricaded behind the long German lines. She had got a frantic message through to Harriet asking her to cable Miss Buddington's mother that she was "safe and comfortable."

We ourselves were sending home reassuring cables that were never received. We sent Miss Buddington's, with doubts of the result which time justified. We were making ceaseless efforts to get home—efforts equally desperate and futile. Charles Conant, Mrs. McKee, and other influential friends were bestirring themselves in our behalf at the State Department in Washington. It was when these efforts were most intense and hopeless that the only cable of all those sent to me from family and friends in America finally arrived. It was from Harper and Brothers and its simple message cheered me for several days. It read:

"Return at once."

During our first morning in Christiania I had visited the American Legation to deliver my letter from the State Department. I found the building surrounded by a mob which I got through after a struggle that tore my blouse and broke the chain of my lorgnette. Once inside the building, however, the letter did its benign work. I had an immediate interview with an official whose eyes were wild and whose ears seemed to be listening to the roar of distant cannon. He did not seem to be hearing me but he must have been, for he assured me that all steamer transportation from Norway was blocked for the time. If and when it was resumed my friend and I should have passage in the first boat. He had no idea when that boat would sail. Neither had any one else. He sighed deeply and his eyes grew desperate.

"This is appalling," he groaned. "What's going to happen?" He shook his head, and we both exhaled deep sighs as we parted.

In the evenings following those pregnant days we went to a cinema theater to see the first war films—already released by the Germans and picturing their victorious march through Belgium. The pictures were uncensored and were terrible. I have seen nothing like them since, and their showing then was an amazing illustration of Germany's strange psychology. Before the pictures were shown notices in half a dozen languages were flashed on the screen, warning the audience to watch them in absolute silence. Any one who showed any feeling for or against them, the notices warned us, would be instantly put out of the theater.

We were a strange, heart-sick, utterly silent audience. Once or twice an evening, when the scenes before us were almost too tragic for endurance, a long sigh swept the theater like a wind among tree-tops. Then the watchful master of the program, always in sight near the stage, raised a warning hand, or ushers stepped forward, and silence again smothered us. The enlightened Germans at the hotel deplored the showing of those pictures, and very soon some edict must have been issued against them by Germany itself. After the first week we saw much less of human horror and the slaughter of old and young civilians than those first scenes in Belgium revealed. It was during this initial week of the war that I first heard the question of one Belgian child, so often quoted afterwards:

"When will they pick up my mother's head, and put it on again?"

We usually returned to our hotel before eleven o'clock, and joined the assembly in the big lounge in time to see the nightly arrival of Russian refugees, driven out of Germany and still getting back to their own land in roundabout ways. Most of those who came to the Grand Hotel had enough money to pay their way, or they would not have chosen that refuge. A few of them were penniless, and all were deeply tragic. There were old men and old women, swept out of their homes almost without warning and certainly without time to pack their possessions. There were frightened little children, clutching their pet toys in their arms—dolls, woolly lambs, and Teddy bears. One small boy had heroically carried his rocking horse all the way from Berlin. There were sick babies moaning in restless sleep, and there were healthy babies, very wideawake and intensely interested in their new surroundings. For those in need we other refugees in the hotel raised funds to speed them on their way. The effort eased our hearts and made us feel that we were helping a bit.

Those eleventh-hour sights and encounters were not good preparation for restful nights. Neither Harriet nor I had ever indulged in unpleasant dreams, and we were very capable sleepers. Now we had nightmares, both when we were awake and when we slept; and our fellow refugees helped these along by predicting that none of us would be able to get away from Norway for months. It looked that way. Scandinavia still expected to be drawn into the war almost any day, and to be divided against herself. Norway and Denmark were pro-ally. Sweden was strongly pro-German.

Miss Hvoeslef was to us an army with banners. She dined with us several nights a week and told us not only the news that her newspaper was publishing but also the news it was carefully suppressing. We were the best informed refugees in the hotel, but by her wish we kept our information to ourselves. One day Judge Francis M. Scott and Mrs. Scott of New York arrived at the hotel with other refugees. Mrs. Scott and I were old friends, and fellow guests at Mrs. Arthur Dodge's Friday luncheons, and we met with the emotion such a meeting in such conditions made inevitable. But when, for the first and only time and with Miss Hvoeslef's consent, I broke our rule of reserve to tell Judge Scott that the Germans had just taken Brussels, he assured me that this was utterly incredible. He did not accept the news till the next day, when the whole world knew it.

We ourselves would have known very little world news but for Miss Hvoeslef. None of the Americans and English in the hotel knew Norwegian, and the Norwegians either could not or would not translate for us. In desperation we experimented with the servants. We always had our breakfasts in our rooms, and our waiter's few phrases of English were so perfectly pronounced that they misled us. We optimistically had the morning newspaper delivered with the morning meal, though it could mean nothing to us without translation. We knew exactly one word of Norwegian— Tyck, which means Germany. That word was always set forth in the first head-line of the first page—but what its companions meant we had no idea. In the war crisis the Norwegian editors were imitating America's newspapers, in the matter of flaring head-lines, very big and black and stretching across the entire front page.

Every morning I directed the waiter's eye to the shrieking

first line and asked: "Will you tell us what this means?"

He invariably seized the newspaper with enthusiasm and began in a loud clear voice:

"Germany is—is—is—is—"

There was a long pause while he reached mentally and vainly for the English word. I offered friendly assistance.

"Advancing?"

"Yes." The yes was almost a triumphant shout. But if instead I suggested "Retreating?" the "yes" was equally prompt and sonorous. No waiter we had got beyond "Tyck" in his translation, though there was always an extra silver crown on the tray for the one who could tell us what those head-lines meant. In pity over the mental strain the waiters seemed to be giving to their efforts we usually added the crown to the breakfast tip, but it brought us no news. We would have been lost indeed without Miss Hvoeslef.

After ten days of panic and extreme nerve tension Norway quieted down a bit. It was time. The strain had been too intense. Miss Hvoeslef gave a tea for me—a very simple tea, she explained, "on 'count the war." (I should have explained sooner that she spoke English very well. Otherwise where should we have been?) Her guests were fine looking men and women—distinguished leaders in Norwegian life and letters. Their names meant little to us, and very few of them spoke English. My French is effective and fluent with French waiters, cabmen, chambermaids, shop clerks and the like; but when I am talking war or politics with my mental peers I become conscious of the limitations of my French vocabulary. There were all sorts of questions, most of them highly indiscreet, which I longed to ask those interesting looking men and women. It was their good fortune that, like the waiters at the hotel, I could not find the words.

At the end of our second week in Christiania Harriet and I began to feel very restless. We were fed up with human tragedies and our own impotence to alleviate them. We wanted to get away to quiet places. As soon as we arrived I had written to my friend Caroline Lagergren that we would not come to Tyreso. We had no wish to exchange Norwegian panic for Swedish panic, and I was sure my friends in Sweden had no desire for guests at that crisis. Our souls, like those of our Norwegian acquaintances, were a little calmer. There were, in us at least, definite limits to the possibilities of soul tension. I was assured in the Legation that in some way, and without too long a delay, Harriet and I would get back home. It might be a hazardous way—by fishing boat to England perhaps, then home on some craft which I gathered must be miraculously stretched to take us on. But as yet we had seen nothing of Norway except Christiania and its suburbs.

One afternoon I sought out the bank president to whom Miss Hvoeslef had commended us, and whose bank was still cashing every day two of our ten dollar express checks. He, too, had grown calmer. It may have been the calm of despair, for he was very serious. His manner changed from gloom to incredulity when I explained that my friend and I desired to see more of his beautiful country and that we should need more money to do it.

"You desire to *travel*—in these conditions?" he gasped.

I said we did, and that we desired to do it in the only way then possible—by automobile. That, no doubt, would cost us each at least twenty dollars a day. He should allow us twenty-five dollars a day each—and, of course, each wanted a week's allowance in a lump sum, that we might be prepared for emergencies. I pointed out the obvious advantage of leaving this amount among his countrymen at this time. Our plan was to go first to Trondheim and back, then west to Bergen, taking in Stalheim, Finse and other points on the way. One or two boats on the Sogne fiord still operated, notwithstanding the mines, taking a day to the journey that ordinarily covered a few hours. We might even get in such a journey.

The bank president looked at me much as the hotel manager had looked when I suggested a piano in my room the day after our arrival. On the other hand, he plainly saw the advantage of a little money being spent in Norway at this crisis. (I can testify that it was the only money being spent in the regions we visited.) We went to Bennett's travel bureau. The manager there also considered us mildly insane, but was relieved by the form our mania was taking. He arranged our "tour," made up a nice little packet of hotel tickets for us, and warned us that most of the hotels would be closed, and that if they were not we would certainly be the only travelers in them. He was right in both predictions. He passed the word around the bureau that two Americans were planning a Norwegian tour, and his clerks came out of their burrows to look at us. We left the bureau feeling rather depressed.

Miss Hvoeslef, consulted when the plan first struck us, was, as always, most helpful and advisory. She had our itinerary. I was to telephone her for war bulletins every day. We devised a little code. If Norway entered the war she was to notify us and we were to return at once to Christiania. We started off in good spirits, notwithstanding the gloomy forebodings of new friends in the hotel, and we put in ten days of rapid and very exhausting sight-seeing. I have always liked swift motion, but I had all I wanted of it during that brisk inspection. We were without question the only moving objects in the country, and we moved so rapidly that the few Norwegian eyes which rested on us must have been strained as we passed. The first day we sought vainly in our phrase books for the Norwegian word meaning *slower*. We could not find it, and I am convinced that it is not in the Norwegian language. If our chauffeur understood the meaning of our frantic gestures he concealed the knowledge. We made the most fearsome passes over Norway's mighty mountains at forty miles an hour or more, which was high speed at that time.

Late in the afternoon of the first day we discovered a word which might have moderated our pace if we had found it in time: but by then all balance had left us.

"Shall we use it?" Harriet asked doubtfully.

I said "No," with a large and care-free gesture; and the driver, seeing this from the corner of an eye that seemed always watching us instead of the road, promptly increased his speed.

Motoring was still new in Norway and the peasants and horses did not like it. Almost every horse we passed promptly rose on his hind legs, and with starting eyes and intense disapproval surveyed us from that altitude. Many of the ravines we were skirting were thousands of feet deep. If they were on our left we could flatten the car nicely against the mountain side on the right when horses and flocks of goats and sheep were using the middle of the road, as they usually were. When the ravines were on our right, the driver lightly swung the side wheels of the car out over the abyss and turned to give us a care-free grin.

Incidentally, one day, I was moved to enjoy the new experience of driving a *stolkjaerre* (high dog-cart) over a mountain. The Norwegian method is to walk the horse very carefully down hill, and then lash him all the way up hill. Knowing nothing of this tradition, which, of course, I would not have followed if I knew it, I chose my own technique. I let my horse crawl up the hill, in our humane American fashion; then I made time going down the mountain. It was very exciting, but I don't recommend it; for when the horse got well started he couldn't stop. Even Harriet, who will stand almost anything, was critical about that experiment.

Other little incidents stand out. The hotel at Stalheim is one of the most beautiful in Norway. It houses hundreds of guests during the season, and its scores of waiters and waitresses are dressed in the colorful costumes of their provinces. The nights we were there they lent superb high-lights to the vast dining-room, in which Harriet's foot-steps and mine echoed mournfully as we made our way to our table. We were, as Bennett had predicted, the only guests in that vast hotel. We also had a rather sinister experience on the Sogne fiord, leaving our boat at three o'clock in the morning at some unknown village and literally walking the plank—an unrailed plank at that—in utter darkness, over the fiord from the boat deck to the shore. As we felt our way, moving our feet an inch or two at a time, we pleasantly remembered that the fiord below us is supposed to be bottomless. I also recall some somber nights at Drievsteuen, a settlement like a small nutmeg in the bottom of a tall tea-cup. There were only a few hours a day when the sun's rays could reach the nutmeg over the towering mountains that ringed it in, and the place lingers in my memory as an outpost of desolation.

In addition to the *stolkjaerre* experience we varied the monotony of motoring by a little promenade on the Finse glacier, where I succeeded in spraining my ankle. Our ten days were exhausted by that time, and so were we. We were also rather tired of being regarded as amiable maniacs by rural Norwegians. The Grand Hotel of Christiania seemed a bit of home when we returned to it.

Conditions were still improving. Scandinavia had not been drawn into the war, and there was growing hope that she would not be. The Norwegian-American Line would resume sailings in another fortnight or so. We could get passage on the *Frederick the Eighth*—terribly overcrowded, of course, but what would you have? These were war days. We had been in Norway just five weeks when we sailed for home. Miss Hvoeslef, staunch to the end, saw us off. During the return voyage we slept in much of our clothing in deference to the mines in the North Sea and the Atlantic, and we kept coats and sweaters on chairs at the head of our beds. During the day eyes were alert for enemy submarines. But all this was high adventure—and we were refugees on our way home!

My most vivid memory of the voyage, I think, is its end. The vast throng that waited for the ship at her pier; the broken cheers as the steamer swung in to her dock; the tears of recognition and greeting across the narrowing line of water; and finally my mother's face in the crowd, as she alternately waved her handkerchief and wiped her eyes.

CHAPTER XIX

MRS. BURNETT, "ROMANTICK LADY"

THE fate of *Harper's Bazar* was what the far-seeing Edward Bok had predicted in our memorable talk in my office during my first years as editor. The *Bazar* could have carried all its manufacturing and editorial expenses and rental and shown a reasonable profit. It could not carry in addition, without going into the red, a full quarter of the great Harper overhead. I knew to a penny what the manufacturing and editorial costs were and I could prune them judicially. But the overhead, a huge lump sum, was presented to me monthly without explanation or analysis, and there was nothing whatever I could do about it. The preference in the advertising was naturally given, as Mr. Bok had also predicted, to *Harper's Magazine*. All this, of course, was entirely fair, looking at Harper and Brothers' problems as a whole. But when the *Bazar* reached the point where the more circulation it had the more money it lost, the situation seemed hopeless. Colonel Harvey sold it to William Randolph Hearst.

After the *Bazar's* sale to Mr. Hearst I went to Harper's literary department as literary adviser. It was a natural transition. I had always been interested in the Harper books, and the *Bazar's* serials had been good feeders to the book presses. I had proudly presented the first works of such writers as Zona Gale, Dorothy Canfield, Katherine Cecil Thurston, Eleanor Porter ("Pollyanna," who died so many years too soon), and numerous others. I entered now a field in which my job was to pass on the new book manuscripts submitted to us, and to lure books from other authors already established.

In my new contract I made a radical readjustment. In recent years I had discovered that by my short-story writing and syndicate work evenings and holidays I was earning many times as much as I received from Harper's for a working week of six days. I therefore made a contract to put in the first three days of every week at my Harper desk, leaving myself four days a week to work at home—if I chose to work on Sunday, as I often did.

Naturally I began my proselyting on my friend Frances Hodgson Burnett. For years she had been reading aloud to me those novels of hers which were making fortunes for other publishers. I saw no reason why she should not give Harper's a chance to show what they could do for her. As a result she gave us two of her books—*The Way to the House of Santa Claus,* a story for children, and her beautiful and mysterious novel, *The White People.*

By that time she and I had been very close for many years. Most of the week-ends I did not pass at Jorjalma I put in with Fluffy, in her home at Plandome, Long Island It was a beautiful estate, built and furnished along English lines and filled with the treasures she had brought back from Europe. It included an enchanting Japanese writing-room, whose inspiration no author could have resisted and whose threshold no one was supposed to cross when Fluffy was working. Few authors with loved ones around them can count on uninterrupted hours of work, and Fluffy's time was no more sacred than that of her fellow authors. The members of her family, like those of most writers, trotted in and out of her study whenever the spirit moved them.

At this time the family consisted of her widowed sister, Mrs. Jordan—no kin to me, alas, but always a dear friend— Fluffy's son Vivian, and Mrs. Jordan's two sons by a first marriage, Archer and Ernest Fahnstock, who came and went till both married. Later, after Vivian's marriage and when he was settled in the charming house his mother built for him on the grounds of her estate, his wife and children dropped in and out, to Fluffy's rapture. The children were not allowed to interrupt her writing, but she would have dropped any work at any time to play with them. They were enchanting baby girls—Verity and Dorinda. Fluffy's bed was a Matterhorn they climbed every morning, rolling over and around her like ecstatic puppies and taking very small and supposedly prohibited bites of her toast and bacon. The first of the following letters from Fluffy describes her experiences with the children as she alone could do it. She sent it to cheer me when I was recovering from an illness. I lent it to Vivian to include in *The Romantick Lady,* his beautiful biography of his mother—but it cannot be printed too often. She did not like her first name and often signed her letters to me *Querida*—the Spanish "dearest" we had chosen as a substitute. Until I got used to it, I had not liked "Fluffy"—her family's name for her—though this had an amusing history. Her pet question was "Is my hair fluffy?" The family finally adopted the word as both endearment and reassurance.

PLANDOME PARK, PLANDOME, LONG ISLAND
Sunday

DEAREST ELIZABETH,

How have you spent Sunday? I hope you have been quiet and cosy and that some one has been reading something delightful to you so that you have not minded the stormy grayness. I think one sees it more in the country than in town. Twice to-day the sky has darkened in the most extraordinary Day of Judgment way. One felt that some appalling storm was brewing, and each time a mere rush of wind and rain dispelled the whole thing and the end was only grayness and wetness.

Mrs. Gertrude Atherton
Drawing by Dorothy Donnelly

Mrs. Otis Skinner
From a 1920 photograph

From a snapshot

Aimé Dupont

Mrs. Frances Hodgson Burnett

Dr. Anna Howard Shaw

Vivian and Constance came to our midday dinner and in the afternoon Vivian brought the children up in the car and they rushed in out of the rain, dancing and shrieking with joy because Nanda was going to play with them. I am Nanda, you know, and I am considered desperately fascinating.

You see, *le bon Dieu* so made me that I can "be" any number of persons at a moment's notice. I am now "Mrs. Desmond." Verity is my daughter, Lily Desmond, and Dorinda is Mrs. Clarence, our neighbor, who lives in Archie's room and goes to market in the bathroom. Mrs. Desmond's cook has left her, but Lily cooks perfectly and we telephone Mrs. Clarence to come to tea, and have magnificent collations on the top of a box turned upside down, covered with scraps of silk and set with dolls' tea things. A great deal of telephoning is done and the "market man" constantly makes mistakes and hasn't got what we want. My arm chair is a car and gets out of order, and the garage man can't mend it because he's "so busy." Once he was painting his house.

The animated telephoning of these two small things—one four, the other three—forms a résumé of modern housekeeping. They are always without cooks and cannot get things done. They do all the telephoning. "Out of the mouths of babes and sucklings."

Verity is growing prettier and prettier. She has a flower-petal face and a halo of curling corn-silk hair, and dimples, and roguish eyes, *and* darkening lashes, *and* a quaint, elfish little sideways smile.

Dorin is thin and fantastic and elfin, but not pretty yet.

My Den is a nursery. The closet in the corner contains a box full of scraps of silk (it is the tea table when it is emptied and turned upside down) a double set of wicker doll furniture, a box of tea things, and a family of dolls of assorted sizes—half of them dressed in brilliant blue, half in brilliant scarlet. I invented and dressed them. They are the Poppies and Larkspurs. There is Mr. Poppy in scarlet velvet knickerbockers and silk hat and coat; Miss Poppy and little sister Poppy and little brother Poppy—Mrs. Larkspur and an equal set of Larkspurs. Perhaps Mrs. Poppy gave birth to all the poppies, and Mrs. Larkspur to all the Larkspurs—otherwise, how account for the

distinct coloring? They make quite showy parties sitting in the
wicker chairs around the tea table. And Mrs. Desmond and
Lily are most superior in their manners.

Darling Elizabeth, I wish I were quite as gay as this sounds.
But I can pretend I am—and the children adore it. How well
are you, my precious dear? I want you so. You will connect me
again with life. I have been so long climbing slowly up a steep
hill and now and then slipping back. But the slips are fewer
and farther between, and to-day is much better than two weeks
ago and so much, much better than a month before that.

All my love goes to you, Queen Elizabeth.

Your affectionate,

Mrs. Desmond

Plandome Park, Long Island

Beloved Elizabeth,

I have made one of my "corners" under a tree in my garden.
It is made of rustic seats and a table and a cushioned steamer
chair and Me. I am writing on the red-cushioned steamer chair
with a lap-table across the arms, and if mosquitos and gnats
do not arrive in July I shall write many things here.

To-day is bright and heavenly cool after many rains and
thunderstorms. Long may it last. The rose arches are a lovely
riot of bloom. How I wish they would last forever! But they
won't. Thousands and thousands of young plants are thriving
in their beds. Thompson—my new gardener—and I have
planted them, working steadily at it since early in May. Thompson planted and I sat close to him and said "We will fill this
bed with delphinium and border it with Ageratum Fraseria."
"We will fill this with pink and white Antirrhinums and border
it with rose and white petunias"; and then I cheered him on
with sparkling conversation and the recounting of incidents
from a long and virtuous life. He has worked like ten gardeners.
Samuel Thompson is his name and may his seed cover the
earth. But it won't. I never saw one like him before. He is a
gardener. I have never had one in America. I have had plumbers
and bricklayers, disguised as gardeners, but never a gardener.
He is as passionate as I am. He wants as many flowers as I do
—and, of course, I know that I am flower-drunk. I want
millions and I want them always—Spring, Summer, Autumn

and Winter—particularly Winter. Thompson and the garden have kept me from dying so far.

Oh, do tell your mother that I, too, once lived in the top of a tree and shared the domestic life of bird families, and I know how thrilling it is. A certain house I lived in during my earlier Washington days (when Lionel and Vivian were babies and I was a girl) had two large maple trees before it and my Den windows were on the third floor, and the branches touched my window sills. It was lovely—lovely—lovely. . . .

QUERIDA

PLANDOME PARK, PLANDOME, LONG ISLAND

DEAREST ELIZABETH,

I have a passionate desire to see you and I have been thinking each day I should surely send you a few lines if no more. Why cannot the people who need each other live in a little heavenly group of perfect houses in a heavenly place—which would be like the fairy-story I made for my place. . . . I have told you about it, haven't I? Mountains and low hills would enclose us, and gardens and woods and green spaces would surround us—and each pretty house would hide itself in its very own corner. And the beloved and understanding people would stroll in and out when they chose and read to each other under trees on lawns and tell stories on broad porches, while the mountains and the clouds and the birds and the flowers would look on and listen and delight and always understand what everybody meant because they would all *belong*.

I love that fairy-story more than any I have ever made. There are certain people who need certain others very much—and I am one. I do not wonder at your working steadily in that atmosphere of restfulness. I hope you will stock up so much work that you may have more leisure when winter comes. I have given up my dream of Canada. . . .

I am doing something each day, but am not leaping and glowing—except at moments. Perhaps if you lived next door to me and I read to you every evening I should awake. It is so strange how the Fates have tried to drag me from this story.*
We have had a sort of rainy English summer, and I was almost afraid to ask your sister and her husband to come for the week-

* *The Head of the House of Coombe.*

end. But to-day (Friday) it is radiant and the wind is in the
right direction and we have ratified our vows for to-morrow
afternoon. I am so looking forward to having them. . . . My
dearest love to you, my Elizabeth,

                                                    QUERIDA

Sometimes Fluffy and I exchanged confidences about the
daily interruptions to our work. I suppose the earth may
hold authors whose working hours are sacred from family
and friends, but I have never met any of them. I myself
have been called away from what I fatuously believed was
"a big scene" to minister to an ailing goldfish. In the early
days of the radio I was often summoned from the supposed
fortress of my study to my mother's room half a dozen
times in a morning, to get better connections or eliminate
"static."

The "static" was appalling in those days; but it was
warmly supported by my friend Edith Thomas, the poet. I
tried to convince Mother also that it was interesting. Edith
loved it, and soothingly and sincerely assured Mother that
it was beautiful. Edith would never listen to a radio program of any kind, but when "static" developed—as it
usually did—she remained entranced beside the instrument
till the "static" cleared away. I used to remind Mother of
this, and try to persuade her to find the charm in "static"
that Edith Thomas did; but Mother was not to be "drawn."
When she had come to me in New York, after my father's
death, I had made a vow to myself that I would never be
too busy to respond to any call of hers. It was a rash vow
and hard to live up to during writing hours, but I usually
kept it.

As to Edith Thomas, I should like to write a book about
her. All I can do here is to republish my tribute to her in
the syndicated newspaper column I was writing at the time
of her death:

The recent death of Edith M. Thomas, one of America's greatest poets, was followed by long editorial tributes to her in leading newspapers. I am glad to remember, too, that on her seventieth birthday, less than a year before her death, a public banquet was given her by leading men and women, at which she belatedly received the acclaim and recognition she deserved.

Aside from these tributes, the life and death of Edith Thomas were tragedies—if it is tragedy for a genius to live for seventy years almost without recognition and to die poor and alone. Possibly it is not. Probably the pure flame that lights the life of genius makes geniuses oblivious to trials and discomforts that harass the rest of us. Certainly Edith Thomas never seemed sorry for herself, or conscious that any one else could be sorry for her.

She was alone and she must have been intensely lonely, but she never knew it. She was poor, but she never realized her poverty until it became impossible for her to help some one else. That rarely happened. However little she had, and she had very little, she was always giving.

She was intensely shy, and thus made few friends—and this must really have troubled her; for the fine passion and loyalty of her nature would have lent themselves magnificently to many friendships, as they lent themselves to the small group of friends she knew and loved.

Her work, beautiful and deathless as it is, held its strongest appeal for the cultured few. This limitation of her "public" never disturbed Edith Thomas. She poured forth her song as the hermit thrush pours forth his, as naturally and seemingly with as little thought of the hearers. In practical affairs she was as unworldly as the bird. She accepted any price offered her for any poem by any editor; and if, among the smaller publications, the sole recompense for a poem took the form of an editorial letter of thanks, she accepted the thanks as casually as she accepted the checks.

In one respect she was strikingly unlike the typical genius. Though she was visionary and vague and dreamy, she had an almost overdeveloped sense of obligation to life and to her fellow men and women. While she had no regard for money, she was never in debt. Debt would have been a nightmare to her. Intensely as she loved her few close friends she took from them no bounty save that of affection. She was as exacting with herself in the matter of her small obligations—she had no large ones—as in that of her financial responsibilities. When she was entertained she made immediate return in her way—with a book or a flower, or with one of her own songs.

All these may seem small things. If they are, they were the only small things about Edith Thomas. Everything she did was done with the full ardor of her flaming soul.

Her letters to me were few, as we met constantly at Harper's. But if at any time in later years, she heard of any trouble or injury of mine, I received a letter like this:

> 509 WEST 124TH STREET, NEW YORK
> August 7th, 1924

DEAR ELIZABETH,

Shocked tonight to read, for the first time, of the serious automobile accident that overtook you, your mother, and your sister. The account in the *Sun* is optimistic as to your complete restoration, but I shall look anxiously for confirmation.

It is long, long since my eyes have had sight of yours and your dear face; and yet it will be possible for you—from your own constancy to friends—to believe in mine to the thought of you, who gave me so much happiness and reassurance in various situations while we were associated under the old Harper roof. . . .

Many helpful thoughts fly to you, and to those dear ones who suffered hurt and shock with you.

> Affectionately your old
> EDITH M. THOMAS

On the next page is a facsimile of the poem she wrote to me on one of the anniversaries of our first meeting.

Fluffy was writing a great deal in those days—*T. Tembaron, The Lost Prince, The Head of the House of Coombe, Robin,* and other books. She read every book to me as she wrote it, and we followed an interesting schedule during my week-ends with her. The night of my arrival, usually a

For February 9th – 1909

To E. J. –

Oh Perfect Day – – –
Yet, overhead, so grey,
And underfoot, the way
Hard and rough – frozen lay. –
Grimly, I would but say,
   "Fate I obey,
And tread out the road to the sullen end."

   Then Fate laughed, "Nay! –"
And, suddenly, into the Day
Shot a golden, fire-tipped ray;
Gave it the heart of May –
Shrine-light, and Joy-to-stay – –
– – – Oh Perfect Day –
Day when I met and knew my Friend!
            E. M. J. –

Friday night, was given up to the family—and to any other house-guests or neighbors Fluffy had invited.

The party usually broke up about midnight. As a rule Fluffy and I were then ready to go to our rooms and to sleep. But Saturday morning was always sacred to literature.

We breakfasted together in Fluffy's room, she in bed, I stretched out on a chaise-longue beside the bed, very comfortable in pajamas and with a light robe over me. Her room was a lovely background, bright with English chintz, its windows opening on vistas of Manhasset Bay. In the winter there was always a log fire roaring up the big chimney. I would settle myself among my cushions with a deep breath of content. Fluffy, as eager as I, would take up her manuscript with a flamboyant gesture and read aloud what she had written of her novel since my visit a week or a fortnight earlier. Sometimes, if she had been industrious, the reading lasted up till luncheon. At long intervals, it began late Friday night, as soon as we came upstairs. This was when Fluffy had written something she considered unusually good, and couldn't wait till morning to read to me.

We loved those hours equally well. I was like a happy child listening to bed-time stories, and Fluffy was like an equally happy child weaving tales for an engrossed and appreciative playmate. An undercurrent of those hours, during all those years, was a recurrence of my early hero-worship, and of the dreamlike sensation I often had in my early Harper days. I had read and reread in my girlhood every novel Mrs. Burnett had written up till then. Now she was my friend and was reading her stories aloud to the awestruck and fascinated school-girl who had poured over *That Lass of Lowrie's, Through One Administration, Little Lord Fauntleroy,* and the rest. I had dreamed much as a girl, but rarely such dreams as this!

If I had been away for several weeks the reading often went on again Saturday night, and after breakfast Sunday morning. However long or short it was, it held me every moment. At intervals, Fluffy would stop to discuss the story.

"I haven't the faintest idea what I'm going to do about that," she would say of a situation; and add happily in the next breath, "but it will come!"

She was very amusing about her work—tremendously interested by it, often thrilled by it, when it was going well, discussing it with the rapture of an ecstatic child and quite as if it had been written by some one else. She sincerely felt that she could discuss and admire it as freely as if it wore the work of another.

"What credit do I deserve for this power of weaving tales?" she once asked me. "That I have it is purely a matter of chance. Why should one squalling baby in a family be given a fairy gift like this, and the other squalling babies be passed by? It isn't fair. I simply can't understand authors who think they deserve credit for their writing."

Naturally, I learned a great deal in those hours with her, though she had few theories of technique or style. But it was always interesting to see how and where she got her best effects. Once I asked her how much of her story she had in mind when she began a novel.

"Only a strong ghost," she told me. "The rest *comes.*"

She rarely made notes and she never wrote out a synopsis of a plot. Quite literally she took her pen in hand, and her story flowed forth without effort. She revised very little. Her copy was quite amazing. She wrote entirely by hand, scorning a typewriter, and she seemed to make no important changes whatever. Page after page of her large clear script was without the alteration of a single word. Occasionally, she would transpose a phrase. At very long intervals she changed an entire sentence. I have looked over the original copy of dozens of her books. It was always so clear, so legible, so free from alteration, that it could be sent to the printer directly from her hand.

In this she was unique. Most authors write the first outlines of their stories in a fine literary frenzy of achievement, and then rewrite and revise with much care and labor. Margaret Deland was the most painstaking author I knew in this class. She revised up till the last minute before a book went to press, and drove our Franklin Square printers to rebellion by rewriting some of her novels on the galley proofs. But the results were always worth the labor.

Mrs. Burnett's initial "attack" on a book is shown in this letter written in 1916:

PLANDOME PARK, PLANDOME, L. I.

I am so disappointed, dearest Elizabeth, but when I found the performance was for the afternoon I was afraid some work or other would be grappling you with hooks of steel. Both Edith and I, however, accept your noble offer for Wednesday the 22nd with shouts of joy—the louder because you will come back home with us.

It will be fun to hear about the baby Christmas book. Being a baby myself I quite revel in that sort of thing. I think I must write a little "Explanation" as a sort of Foreword. We will talk it over.

I began *The White People* yesterday. I am drawn into it. I am now—the Other part of me—looking out of a deep window in a turret of a dark frowning feudal castle facing a great climbing moor. The moor is haunted by heavy white mists, which writhe and crawl as if they moved with some unearthly life—to cover or uncover things which are not always seen. That moor will not leave me until I have told its story—which is the story of the child who felt as if she had been born looking at it. . . .

QUERIDA

And here is her exuberant finish:

CLIFTON HEIGHTS, BAILEY'S BAY, BERMUDA
May, 1916

Why you are not here this brilliant and entrancing morning, my dearest, I cannot explain at all satisfactorily to myself. You so obviously ought to be here.

In the first place I finished *The White People* yesterday, and the exquisite quiet of this cool room, sweetly full of flowers and sweetly fresh with little breezes from the incredibly blue sea, provides exactly the atmosphere in which I could read to you. It would be very lovely. There is a white wicker chaise-longue, chintz-covered and comfortable, by the wide window—and you could lie there and listen. It is a strange, strange story with new things in it. I shall have it typed here and bring it home—leaving a copy behind in case of accidents. I am sure you are relieved to know it is really completed. I was not able to get at it at all during the first weeks. There was too much to do. Oh, *why* are you not here! It is the thrilling part of the year, though the winter has been windy and chilly and the season is late.

The oleanders are not half in bloom, because a hurricane whipped their leaves off them about six weeks ago. This late-ness of the spring makes the weather deliciously cool, however, and the air as April. May and June are actually brilliant in Bermuda.

There is a peace here I have never found anywhere else. The island seems a being set apart from the world. The steamers only come here once a week and each time we see the *Bermuda* from our hillside, rounding the point at St. George, it is a new sensation. Figure to yourself white coral roads and white coral sands by the incredible sea—and palms and tamaracks and oleanders and hibiscus hedges, and *no* motors and *no* trains and only a few ancient carriages. And the many Negroes with soft voices, and all the people quite calm and sweet. Let us live here forever, Elizabeth, except for a few months a year in less rest-ful places, just to keep up the fine flavor of contrast.

The war has made no outward difference, I am most happy to say. Before we came both Edith and I felt that as letters were censored no one could write to tell us what was happen-ing even if the Islands were in flames. But there was nothing to tell. Bermuda is the drowsy lovely island of dreams we left behind, except that one occasionally meets a hero—who perhaps looks like a boy and has faced Hades and does not know that he is a hero at all.

Did you receive the letter I sent you when we landed? It ought to have gone back with the ship. Really, Elizabeth, I shall drag you to Bermuda with hooks of steel, if you will not come without more resistance. What are you doing, my dearest? Give my love to your mother and tell her that she would adore this place.

All love to yourself,

QUERIDA

Though Frances Hodgson Burnett was so childlike in so many ways, she had a strong sense of her literary dignity. She told me with amazement of a certain young man to whom she had once read a story, and who had actually proceeded to criticize it! I had never felt any impulse to criticize her work, for she was a born story teller. If I had been brash enough to think of criticism, that comment about the indiscreet young man would have checked me. Probably one explanation of her enjoyment in reading to me was the respect as well as the interest with which I listened.

When she was sure she could trust to this she began to put a few of her problems up to me for discussion. They were very few, for her instinct as to her situations was almost unerring. But I remember telling her I thought Lord Coombe and the Duchess talked too much about politics. She sighed and cut out some of their talk—very regretfully and much like a mother thinning her child's golden curls. She had loved those talks.

By the time she wrote *The White People* she had considerable faith in me:

PLANDOME PARK, PLANDOME, L. I.

DEAREST,

I had not thought of a dedication and return mail gives little time. Shall I say "To Lionel"?

And shall I add that verse which I am not *quite* correct in quoting, perhaps, but which you will be sure to know. Is it—or isn't it, Burroughs?

> The stars come nightly to the sky,
> The tidal wave unto the sea;
> Nor time, nor space, nor deep nor high
> Can keep my own from me.
>   JOHN BURROUGHS

I see the human link of connection between it and things Outside. Do you? Will others? Decide for me. I leave it in your hands. The verse, I think, ought to be in different type from the "To Lionel" above it. Or would this mean more to the casual reader?

"To those who would draw near"

If neither really seems to say the thing I mean let us have no dedication. . . .

QUERIDA

She put one scene in *The White People* squarely up to me—the final love scene, in which her hero and heroine faced both love and death.

"It has to be like this, hasn't it?" she asked almost anxiously. "It has to be reserved—and subtle. It couldn't be different—or could it? What do you really think?"

It couldn't. The scene was perfect. I told her so and Fluffy relaxed contentedly. She was sentimental, and that love scene was not. It couldn't be. In her heart she had longed to warm it up, but her sure instinct had saved her. What she wanted now was what we all want all the time and which most of us never get—the assurance that to try to improve our work is to paint the lily.

I have mentioned Vivian Burnett's deeply understanding biography of his mother—*The Romantick Lady*, published, of course, after her death. Before he began it he wrote me this letter:

ESTATE OF FRANCES HODGSON BURNETT
4839 GRAND CENTRAL TERMINAL, NEW YORK
December 19th, 1924

DEAR ELIZABETH:

You will probably not be surprised to know that I am starting out to collect material for a biography of my mother. Realizing what a deep affection she had for you, and what an inspiration you were to her during the latter years of her life, I am naturally turning to you for help. I know that the letters she wrote you must have been among the best from her busy pen; and I am wondering if there are some which you will let me have to help out in the biography. I am going at this work at once to get the book out as soon as possible.

I have established myself in a little office where I can quietly work and also take care of other important things that are coming up in connection with Mammy's literary estate. You may be sure I will take care of any letters you have, and will use the contents according to your wishes.

I want to tell you how much I appreciate all you have been to my mother. I know that her love for you was deep and real, and that the intellectual companionship you gave her was a very important factor in her life and work. Your letters to her in her last days were a great tribute of love, and they meant a great deal to her. And you know that for all of this I have a gratitude that can not be properly expressed in a letter. It was my mother's passion to give joy to others. . . . So few stopped to think of giving joy to her! The few who did stand out in my mind as something akin to angels; and the words of recognition that I can put on paper seem very poor indeed.

I would like, when you can make it convenient, to have a long talk with you over her work and her friendships. With the greatest gratitude, and best wishes for a happy Christmas and a successful New Year.

Very sincerely yours,
VIVIAN BURNETT

During the writing he came to my apartment to read various chapters aloud to me, and the reading was a poignant experience to us both.

When the book appeared he sent me a copy with this inscription and another letter:

> To Elizabeth Jordan
> With the sincere gratitude and affection of one who well knows how much her inspiring friendship contributed to the latter years of *The Romantick Lady*.
>   Vivian Burnett
> March 26, 1928

My Dear Elizabeth:

I am taking the liberty of not writing in your own copy of *The Romantick Lady*, but in a specially bound one which I want to send you. Mammy would want a solid gold, diamond-encrusted volume to be sent to you, with "three rousing cheers." Consider this a gift from both of us. While not so terribly "splendiferous," it goes encrusted with affection.

You will be glad to know that *The Romantick Lady* has been nicely treated by reviewers all over the world, and is selling well.

I wish we might see something of each other. I am just off with the children for an Easter holiday trip to Florida, but will be back after the middle of April. The infant spring will be with us then, with all its daffodils, primroses, and lilacs. Perhaps you would be willing to come down for a week-end with us then, to take in the vernal smells. Could you do it?

                                         Very sincerely yours,
                                         Vivian Burnett

Vivian ("Little Lord Fauntleroy") died in 1937, of a heart attack, after gallantly rescuing four persons from drowning. After the rescue they saw him die on the deck of his yacht. They were taken to shore, and they borrowed money and clothes and hurried away. They have never been seen nor heard from by the Burnett family since that hour!

Mrs. Burnett once strikingly underlined her sense of literary dignity in connection with the publication of one of her novels. When it was published the book made a new record among best sellers; but when she turned in the copy for serial publication to the magazine that had bought it the editor was away. An intrepid young college lad, just at the beginning of a literary career which I think ended soon after this incident, took charge of the manuscript. He graciously approved it, on the whole, but he thought of a great many changes and improvements which could be made in it. Quite off his own bat he wrote them all down and submitted the list to the assistant editor who was in charge of the magazine during the editor's absence. Incredibly, the unfortunate assistant, with no more brains or judgment than his new recruit, sent that list of unbaked criticisms and suggestions to Frances Hodgson Burnett! He added kindly that she "might care to consider some if not all of these points."

The result was an explosion that shook the building which held the magazine and its employees. Mrs. Burnett gave a magnificent illustration of the tempest that can be aroused in gentle souls. She immediately withdrew her manuscript and refused to see the frantic officers of the company—who had known nothing of the editorial criticisms till the storm broke. She would not talk to them by telephone or receive them in her own house. She was equally indifferent to the imploring messages sent her from Europe by the absent editor, who had been cabled the details of the tragedy.

It was many months before the matter was adjusted. Then Mrs. Burnett returned the manuscript on the firm's written agreement that, like all her other material, the novel should be published without the change of even a word; and that neither it nor any subsequent manuscript of hers should ever be touched by the two sub-editors who had caused the debacle.

I was Fluffy's confidant throughout the negotiations, and I was wise enough to confine myself to the rôle of sympathetic listener. When all the excitement had died down, however, and it was safe to ask Fluffy the question that had burned on my lips so long, I put it to her. Why, I inquired, since she so detached herself from credit or praise for her work, did she so fiercely resent criticism of it? She answered from a great height, her words drifting down to me like snow-flakes from a Himalayan range.

"I am the custodian of a gift," she told me. "It is for me to protect its dignity from the driveling of imbeciles!"

A year later she revealed another of the inconsistencies of her fascinating character. She told me with her incomparable gush of laughter that she was now "among the rejected." A certain magazine for women had returned to her a short story she had submitted after a year of editorial urging. She had not had anything rejected for fifty years, so this struck her as an immense joke on the editors—as, of course, it was. She immediately sold the story elsewhere and continued to regard the episode as a high literary adventure.

She had a marvelous sense of humor which could almost always be relied upon. At long intervals it failed her. One of these exceptions occurred when the English film version of *Little Lord Fauntleroy* was produced in this country. The British producer had sent siren songs about the production across the narrowing ocean and Fluffy had listened to those with a touching faith. When the New York showing was imminent he sent her a hundred seats for the first performance, and asked her to distribute them among her friends.

Characteristically, Fluffy arranged a children's party for the event, with herself as hostess. At a casual glance, most of the youngsters on Long Island seemed to be her guests. She and the children were equally enchanted by the prospect of the play. In their zeal they arrived at the theater half an hour before the picture began, making a lovely exhibit for later comers as they composed themselves like a great flower bed in the center of the house.

There were, as the producer had promised, a great many novelties in the British production of *Little Lord Fauntleroy,* but the author and her guests saw only the first of these. Following some strange aberration of his own the director had chosen to begin the film by showing in detail those tragic occurrences which, by killing off his uncles, gave Lord Fauntleroy his title. The first of these was a tragic death on the hunting field. The children bore this with more than fortitude, and the little boys probably enjoyed it. But as the calamities went on the infants became restless. When the last of the old earl's sons died hideously in an attack of delirium tremens, a small boy of eight lost control of his emotions. In piercing accents he addressed space.

"I don't like this play," he announced between loud gulps. "If I knew this play was going to be this kind of a play I wouldn't have come to this play. I want to go home!"

He started down the aisle, wailing loudly. Many of his companions, enchanted by this concise expression of their own views, followed him. There was nothing for the hostess to do but keep her guests in a compact band and shepherd them out of the theater. The small leader's hysteria was contagious, and most of them wept as they went.

I am sorry to confess that all this struck me as extremely funny, and the memory of it has cheered me at intervals throughout the years. To Fluffy it was a tragedy, and I am sure our differing reactions to it were a heavy strain on her affection for me.

As all the readers of her books know—and that means all the world—Mrs. Burnett had her individual creed, of which she wrote and which she personally followed. It was

neither Christian Science nor New Thought, though it had
certain features of both. It was something she evolved herself and which, when she tried to put it into words, was as
nebulous as her theories about writing as an art. She carried out the latter theories by the simple process of writing,
and words flowed from her pen as easily and naturally as
water flows when a faucet is turned on. She rarely stopped
to consider a situation in her stories. She barely hesitated.
"It came." That was all there was to it. She believed that,
just as simply and naturally as "it" came, so this other
force also came to her, out of the universe. All she had to
do was to accept it.

Only once in our twenty-five years of friendship did I
see her faith shaken. That was after the death of her
nephew, Ernest Fahnstock. Fluffy had expected her creed
to save Ernest. She had told me triumphantly only the day
before his death that she was sure it *would* save him. As
gallantly as a soldier going over the top she had gone into
Ernest's room the last day of his life, controlling her abnormal shrinking from death and suffering. She had sat by
his side to help him. She could always be counted on to rise
to crises, though no woman ever lived who had a deeper
and more instinctive dread of suffering, sorrow, and tragedy.
She had been like that all her life. She never went to depressing plays, or read depressing books, or talked of
depressing subjects if she could avoid doing these things.
As soon as her success made it possible she transformed
her life into a sort of fairy-tale, deliberately shutting out
the sordid, the sad, and the unlovely.

Nevertheless, when life called on her to face tragic reali-
ties she always did it with high courage. For two years she
had walked an Appian Way with her beloved son Lionel
when, between fourteen and sixteen, he died lingeringly of
tuberculosis. She was constantly with him. She took him

to a dozen "cures" here and abroad. In his last hours she was close beside him, holding his hand in hers, till the boy's clinging fingers grew cold. Just so she sat, that final day of Ernest's life, beside her sister's son, who was almost like her own son. What she went through in those hours one can only imagine, for death and Ernest Fahnstock waged a mighty battle. But she thought she was helping him, and quite possibly she was. His death and the strain and grief of it shattered her. For the time she had lost not only Ernest but the faith by which she lived. She was at sea and helplessly drifting. Those of us who loved her and watched her were afraid she would have a serious nervous collapse.

I have several unfading memories of her that year. One is of a visit I made her one night at a New York sanitarium where she was taking a rest cure. It was Christmas Eve. Vivian and his wife and children had come to see her and had just left. She was alone, and Christmas bells were ringing outside, and her room was bright with holly and red ribbons. But she must have been feeling lonely. Her nurse was having supper downstairs and I—a frequent visitor—had been told to go up to her room unaccompanied.

I tapped on the door and went in. Fluffy was lying on her back, staring moodily at the ceiling. When she turned her head and recognized me she uttered the crow of a happy child and bounced ecstatically up and down in bed, exactly as the child might have done. For the moment she was five years old.

Another picture of her, registered later, shows her sitting at the desk in my study to autograph one of her books for a friend of mine. She opened the book, took up the pen, and then abruptly leaned back and looked up at me as I stood beside her.

"Oh, Elizabeth," she said with a sudden vitality in her voice, "I haven't held a pen for months. It's a wonderful sensation. It makes me feel natural again. It—why, it makes me feel *well!*"

I shall always remember, too, and with deep emotion, that, as it happened, the last time she ever took up her pen was to write me, a few days before her death, the note which is quoted below. Knowing the end was very near I had motored to New York from my Massachusetts country home to see her, and we had an hour together. I had devoted myself to cheering her up by assuming that she was getting well, and by talking of future plans. I must have succeeded. She had a restful night, and slept without opiates, her nurse told me. Early the next morning she asked for pen and paper, and wrote me the two lines I so cherish:

> DEAREST,
> I love you. You are
> my valentine!!
> FLUFFY

"She wasn't able to address the envelop," the nurse added. "She asked me to do that. But you *had* braced her!"

I love to think I had. I know that our last hour together was affectionately cheerful. I predicted all sorts of future interests and activities and she responded. It was of these Fluffy was thinking as we parted when she said, with a slight catch of her breath on the last words, "This is not good-by, dearest. Three-rousing-cheers!"

CHAPTER XX

DOCTOR ANNA HOWARD SHAW

I WAS writing a novel a year, a syndicated editorial column, and a large number of short stories which appeared with satisfying regularity in *Harper's, Century, Scribner's,* and the *Saturday Evening Post.* I was also doing a good deal of public speaking in connection with women's suffrage campaigns. I knew all the leaders, and had a special affection for Anna Howard Shaw, then President of the National Women's Suffrage Association.

Of all the public women I have known—and I seem to have known most of them more or less intimately—there are not more than half a dozen I myself consider great. Dr. Shaw was one of these. She was a brilliant and an amazingly magnetic leader, and her sense of humor was a lasting delight.

True to my hunting instinct for good books for Harper and Brothers, I tried to persuade Dr. Shaw to write her autobiography. The idea fascinated her, but she could never get around to the work. When she broke her leg one winter day getting off a train in the Grand Central Station, it was clear that she would be a prisoner in her hotel room for weeks. I hardly gave her time to have the bones of her ankle set before I hurried up to the McAlpin Hotel, where she was stopping, to take up again the matter of that book. Now was the time to write it. Dr. Shaw was still evasive. She pointed out that the accident had upset all her plans and work. She said she couldn't think clearly.

In this dilemma Providence came to my aid, in the person

of Sonya Levien, the young assistant editor of the *Metropolitan Magazine*. Miss Levien had the same idea I had. Dr. Shaw ought to write her reminiscences. Miss Levien wanted them for the *Metropolitan*. She went to Dr. Shaw with the proposition and Dr. Shaw, one of the straightest players at the card-table of life, immediately referred her to me. Miss Levien had an inspiration, and brought it with her when she came to see me. Why didn't Dr. Shaw give me the facts of her life? Why didn't I then write her life for the *Metropolitan?*

The suggestion was inspiring as far as it went. I added the little detail Miss Levien had overlooked. Why didn't Harper and Brothers publish the serial in book form—after its publication in the *Metropolitan* was completed? Everybody agreed and everybody was happy. Carl Hovey, then editor of the *Metropolitan,* immediately paid Dr. Shaw a very generous lump sum, for her share of the serial rights. He offered me a good price for the serial as a whole, to be paid by instalments, as fast as I handed in the chapters. I voluntarily and unnecessarily made over to Dr. Shaw all royalties from the sale of the book. She would have been perfectly willing to share these with me. Again everybody was happy, especially Harper and Brothers who were getting the best of the whole transaction.

That was the beginning of one of the most interesting episodes of my life. Obviously, the time to extract Dr. Shaw's reminiscences from her was while she was helpless on a chaise-longue in her room at the McAlpin. The moment she was able to stand unaided she would be off again and on the wing. I concentrated for weeks on Dr. Shaw's book. Every morning at nine o'clock I arrived in her hotel room with my secretary, Charlotte Lambrecht. From then until lunch time I drew from Dr. Shaw the story of her life, while Miss Lambrecht took it down in shorthand.

It was an enchanting experience. Dr. Shaw was a born talker and probably the best woman speaker America ever had. But both she and I had realized from the beginning that she could never have written her reminiscences herself. The moment she picked up a pen she became self-conscious and heavy-handed. We had both known I would have to do an immense amount of careful rewriting on her book, if she ever turned out a book; but I had not dared to dream of the joy of writing it myself. That, however, was what I was to have. Mr. Hovey's contracts with Dr. Shaw and me called for that and for nothing else: and Dr. Shaw was immensely relieved to escape the burden of trying to learn a new art.

The writing, however, was in the future. What I had to do now was to draw out Dr. Shaw's story, as consecutively and fully as possible, and judge of the relative value of its different parts, developing some and limiting others. Naturally, to Dr. Shaw, the important subject was the suffrage work, and this was given full value in the book. However, as every reader of that book will remember, it was the story of Dr. Shaw's early days and struggles—her pioneering experiences as a child in a Michigan wilderness, as a country school-teacher at two dollars a week, as a divinity student in Boston and, later, as minister of two Cape Cod parishes, that furnished the most fascinating reading in *The Story of a Pioneer*. (I had that title in mind even before I wrote the first page.)

Dr. Shaw proved the most inspiring collaborator I have ever worked with. Night after night, unable to sleep because of the pain of her broken ankle, she recalled memories and made notes. In the morning she was all ready for Miss Lambrecht and me, and her memories gushed forth almost without hesitation. Naturally, they were not consecutive. Something that had happened in 1872 would remind her of something else that occurred in 1901 and that in turn would evoke a memory of 1894. She was always "going strong" and I rarely interrupted her.

I think she must have found Miss Lambrecht and me a satisfactory audience. We laughed and cried with her; we were tense with interest during every hour of those three weeks of steady talk. From the first I had been conscious of the one danger in the situation. I was to write the story in the first person—but the spirit of the telling, the big soul back of those reminiscences, must be Anna Howard Shaw's. It would be all too easy to get my soul into it. Dr. Shaw was making me feel as if I had lived her life with her. I must be incessantly on guard against that peril. The day she was describing the death of Susan B. Anthony I found myself inwardly calling for help. "Oh, if it's the last thing I ever do," I reflected, "let me put into this thing the spirit *she* is putting into it—the spirit that has made her what she is!"

Our sessions were amazingly businesslike and orderly. Dr. Shaw could have timed her watch by the promptness of our arrival, and we buckled down to work as soon as hats and coats and gloves were off. In the beginning the telephone rang quite steadily and Dr. Shaw received and sent many messages. She was used to interruptions. They inevitably put her a bit off her stride, however, and I persuaded her to stop them. This was *work* we were doing, I pointed out, and serious work. Nothing should be allowed to interrupt it. I also succeeded in stopping the pageant of friends that appeared. They said they asked nothing but to sit and listen, but, of course, they couldn't do it. They were a hopelessly distracting influence. I got rid of them after the first twenty-four hours.

At the end of three weeks the story was told. Miss Lambrecht, the type of secretary who keeps the ideal of perfection alive in a shaken world, cut her typewritten copy into bits and arranged it with such consecutiveness as she could. Then my job began. As I may have boasted before, I have a rather phenomenal memory—a tricky one, however, which is as inclined to fasten on unessentials as on important matters. However, when I am interested I remember things in quite surprising detail. I could have reeled off Dr. Shaw's whole story without much effort and very accurately. I went all over it again, nevertheless, and made notes and a general outline. After that I wrote the book, chapter by chapter.

As each chapter was written Dr. Shaw came to my apartment to dine, and after dinner we shut ourselves away in my study while I read the chapter aloud to her. She had been wonderful during her own telling of the tale—extraordinarily open-minded, always willing to follow leads and suggestions. She was even more wonderful now. From start to finish of the reading she never interrupted it; and at the end she never suggested a change except a correction of some name or date. This seems too good to be true; but it is true, and it forms a unique record in collaboration.

Some of her spirit of acquiescence may have been due to the welcome Mr. Hovey and Miss Levien were giving the chapters as they appeared. They were both very enthusiastic over them, and Mr. Hovey sent me some letters which I hope I can find and quote here. This is a fair sample of them.

Dear Miss Jordan,

I have just read the first chapter of *The Story of a Pioneer,* and though it is after office hours I cannot go home without telling you how delighted I am with it. It is beautifully told, deeply moving, and full of the strong human interest I have been sure Dr. Shaw's life must contain.

If the other chapters come up to it—and I know they will—we shall all have something to be very proud of.

Very sincerely yours,

Carl Hovey

Mr. Hovey began the serial publication as soon as I had finished this first chapter. From then on he published the Life month by month, as fast as I wrote it; and he continued to be one of the most appreciative and inspiring editors I ever worked with.

Naturally, under all these satisfactory conditions, Dr. Shaw and I became fast friends. I discovered that she never seemed to take any diversion, and I made myself a committee of one to open new joys to her. I took her (as often as she would go) to theaters and concerts. I lured her to occasional luncheons and dinners, where she met literary and stage celebrities. I even enticed her to occasional vaudeville performances, for which Mrs. Burnett and I had a weakness and which we attended about once a month. Dr. Shaw went with us several times. All these new experiences must have formed a pleasant interlude in her life, and she made it plain that she enjoyed them. We went about together a great deal when she was in New York. . . .

One evening when we had seen a good play, and were sailing airily into the dressing-room of its distinguished woman star, Dr. Shaw said to me smilingly but almost enviously, "What an independent cuss you are!" That I could, in a way, control my time seemed amazing to a woman who was constantly scheduled for speeches, rallies, conferences, and conventions all over the country.

Our close friendship continued till her death. I saw her last at New Haven, when she was on a speaking tour for the League to Enforce Peace. She was one of the distinguished quartette that included Ex-President William H. Taft, Herbert S. Houston, and President Lowell of Harvard. They were in New Haven that week-end to attend a meeting of the Connecticut State Branch of the League at Yale. Mrs. Houston drove me to New Haven Saturday, and that night we dined at the Taft Hotel with "the four troopers" as they called themselves. After dinner we went to their meeting and heard their speeches. It was generally agreed that Dr. Shaw carried off the honors of that evening.

Dr. Shaw introduced me to her friends in New Haven as "Miss Jordan, who wrote my book." Incidentally, she got me off into a corner and persuaded me, much against my inclination, to agree to collaborate with her on a popular history of the Woman Suffrage movement, to be published in book form at one dollar a copy. I was not keen on the idea, and I did not see how I could work it in with my other plans. Her heart was set on it, however, so—to my lasting comfort—I agreed with seeming enthusiasm.

I also promised to pass a week-end with her the following month at her home in Moylan, Pennsylvania, and go over the material she had there. It was only a few weeks later that, motoring back to Massachusetts one day, I heard a news-boy's outcries on the streets of Hartford and saw the screaming head-line in the newspaper he was waving:

Doctor Anna Howard Shaw Dead

She had died very suddenly of pneumonia, after a few days' illness. Perhaps I may be forgiven if I quote here the editorial the New York *Tribune* printed on July 30, 1920, about the book to which Dr. Shaw had always referred, when we talked of it, as "our child":

Whatever memorials her friends may raise, the best preservative of the fame of Anna Howard Shaw will be the autobiography that appeared a few years before her death, *The Story of a Pioneer*. This is sure to be regarded by future generations as one of the most precious source-books of the history of our time. Its genuineness and literary quality will cause it to be read and prized long after the need for suffrage ammunition is over, and to it workers in campaigns as yet unlaunched will look for inspiration.

CHAPTER XXI

ENTER SINCLAIR LEWIS

I WAS now much deeper in the books of other authors than in my own, but some pleasant personal episodes still cheered my way. One of these I mention, to show how briskly a really fine editorial mind can operate.

I was writing my first mystery novel—*Red House*—when John M. Siddall, then editor of the *American Magazine*, wrote to ask if I had anything in the nature of a serial to submit. I replied that I was at work on one and would show it to him when it was finished. I had never met Mr. Siddall, but I liked what I had heard of him; and I greatly liked the man himself when I met him.

A few months after our exchange of letters I finished *Red House* and sent it to Mr. Siddall one Friday afternoon, with the optimistic suggestion that he take it home and read it over the week-end. I had no hope that he would do anything of the kind. He would have dozens of manuscript novels to consider. I would be very fortunate if I heard from him in a fortnight or so. However, he did read *Red House* over that week-end, and he telephoned me Monday morning.

"I like your story," he said without preface. "I think I can use it if we can agree on terms. Can you come to my office this morning and talk about it?"

I could. I was there inside of an hour. Mr. Siddall was a thin, pale, delicate looking man incessantly driven by a consuming energy that eventually burned him up. He told me in his first sentence that his schedule for the present year was full and that he could not publish my novel till the next year. Then he would publish it in six instalments, and he offered me seven thousand, five hundred dollars for the serial rights. It was a fair offer for those days, but I reminded him that he was postponing for eighteen months the novel's publication in book form.

"So I think you ought to pay me ten thousand dollars for the serial rights," I ended.

"All right, ten thousand," Mr. Siddall agreed without an instant's hesitation. "Now I want you to change the title. There's a book just published in England called *Red House.*"

I was slightly dazed by this expedition, but I changed the title to *The Blue Circle* and departed. The entire interview had not taken more than fifteen minutes. I had promised to meet Martha for luncheon uptown at one o'clock. That luncheon was "on me."

I had never met Mr. Siddall before, I never met him again, but up till the time of his death several years later I sold him many short stories. He made his decisions in two or three days, paid one thousand dollars for every short story he accepted, and sent the check in payment within a week. He and George Horace Lorimer of the *Saturday Evening Post* and Mary King of the Chicago *Tribune,* all with the same brisk and businesslike habits of decision and payment, have stood for years at the head of my honor list of editors.

Next to them, but only because these necessarily pay lower rates, are S. A. Baldus, of the *Extension Magazine,* Rev. Francis X. Talbot, S.J., editor of *America,* whose dramatic reviews I have written for fourteen years, and the Reverend Charles J. Mullaly, S.J., editor of the *Messenger of the Sacred Heart.* Not once, in from ten to twenty years of close association, has any one of these editors failed in consideration or courtesy. There are many others, of course, but none with such three-star records. In 1936, Mary King almost equaled Siddall's record. One Saturday I gave her the first reading of my novel, *The Trap*. She accepted it over the telephone the following Wednesday. If I were making a list of the most efficient and best executive women I have ever known I should put Frances E. Willard and Mrs. Ogden Reid at the head of the list, with Mary King as a close second.

I was immensely interested in my efforts to draw new writers of promise into the Harper book family. There was always a thrill in the reading of the first novel of a new writer. Possibly here was another genius! I was fishing in strange waters, and I caught a large fish often enough to keep my enthusiasm alive. I shall always be especially proud of the biggest catch I landed for Harper's.

One day a young man in his late twenties came to the office with a letter of introduction to me from Charles Hanson Towne, the poet. Mr. Towne mentioned in his note, without obvious enthusiasm, that the bearer's name was Sinclair Lewis, and that he had with him the manuscript of his first novel, *Our Mr. Wrenn*. Would I read it?

I would, of course. Reading and judging the merit of novels and other book manuscripts was then my professional job. I looked at Sinclair Lewis. He was a tall, thin, red-haired youth with an effect of exuberant vitality, and with blue-gray eyes that worked overtime. No one could have called him handsome, but he had the widest and most engaging grin I had ever seen. Our first encounter was brief. I promised to read his book and he departed.

I liked *Our Mr. Wrenn*. Later Mr. Towne confided to me that the reserve of his introduction was due to the fact that several publishers had already declined the book. I can't imagine what they were thinking of. Inevitably, it had the beginner's faults; but it held great promise and a strong atmosphere of H. G. Wells, who was young Mr. Lewis' literary idol at the time. Any editor should have recognized its quality, and I deserve no credit at all for doing so. We agreed to publish the book with certain changes, and my long and delightful association with Sinclair Lewis began.

I worked with him on the manuscript, and some of the changes I had to ask him to make were the kind that break an author's heart. He took them all with entire good-humor, and he never lost his grin. When he had done all the reconstruction he thought he could endure at one session, he would sit up suddenly and say, "Now, *praise* me!"

The praise he liked best was my repeated prediction that he would develop into one of the great authors of his day.

"Are you sure of that?" he often asked.

"Absolutely," I always said. Then his grin grew wider. He was sure of it, too. Fortunately we were both right.

As it happened, that summer was especially hot and I had to pass most of it in New York. Our twelve-story apartment building on Gramercy Park had a nicely tiled roof with a safe balustrade running around it. I often invited friends to have a hot-night dinner up there with me—cold chicken, salad, ice-cream and claret cup. Then we reclined luxuriously in steamer chairs and settled the large problems of the day. Only the stars were above us, and New York, flaunting all her jewelry, lay below us. From the East River, a few blocks away, boats moaned up at us as they passed.

I invited young Mr. Lewis to this roof retreat for a conference and meal one hot evening, and he was enchanted. Apparently it was the spot he had been looking for all his life, and he couldn't say enough about it. He left reluctantly and very late, and the next evening he returned uninvited. He said, with his grin, that every one else was out of town, that this was the nicest place he knew of, and that he was sure I wanted him. I did, and he came very often. It is to this roof—now my New York roof for a quarter of a century—that he refers in his inscription in my copy of *Our Mr. Wrenn.*

During this first year he complicated our work by falling in love. He did it violently and tempestuously, as a red-haired youth of his type would be sure to do it, and his courtship was a whirl-wind affair. He told me all about the girl, in great detail, and frequently when I thought we ought to be considering *Our Mr. Wrenn.* She was Miss Grace Hegger. He won her very soon, and immediately brought her to dine with me. She was a charming girl and I liked her from the moment we met. He had asked me not to have any other guests the first evening she came. He said he wanted me to know Grace as well as he did. But immediately after dinner he turned to me imploringly.

"I've never danced with this woman yet," he said. (He always spoke of her as "the woman.") "I'm crazy to dance with her. Won't you play for us and let us get going?"

I sat down at the piano and the young things danced all evening, till the musician at least was worn out.

They were married just before *Our Mr. Wrenn* was published. They were very much in love and both were temperamental, and their first year of married life was an experience of alternate glory and storm. We kept in close touch. I visited them at their first home near Plandome, Long Island, and they frequently came to my New York apartment. When *Our Mr. Wrenn* was published the proud author wrote this inscription on a fly-leaf of my copy:

> To ELIZABETH JORDAN,
> who accepted the Ms. of *Our Mr. Wrenn,* suggested changes that were not just "editorial suggestions" but inspiring and creative finishing touches, and always by her kindliness and good-fellowship and trained knowl-

edge, by hours in the office and on the roof that over-
looks all the city, enabled me to make a book of this.

SINCLAIR LEWIS

And with affectionate greetings from the girl to whom
it is dedicated.

A year later Hal brought me his second novel, *The Trail
of the Hawk*. He had become "Hal" by that time, because
he didn't like his first name and because Hal was a name
Grace liked. We accepted the new novel with three rousing
cheers. It was a beautiful book. No revision was necessary
that time. On every page of it a young genius had laid bare
his heart and soul. Of all the books Sinclair Lewis has
written, I still like that one best. Here's the inscription he
wrote in my copy:

To ELIZABETH JORDAN, friend and boss, discoverer
and maker of *Hawk* as she was of *Our Mr. Wrenn,*
with more gratitude than can be expressed on this one
small page.

SINCLAIR LEWIS

October 20, 1915.

This novel was in a way autobiographical. Hal himself
was at heart a hawk, wild and untamed. Notwithstanding
his devotion to Grace it was hard for him to accept responsibility and the routine of domestic life. But she, too, was
devoted, and wise for her years.

Hal was an appreciative youngster, and in return for what
he was good enough to consider my helpful interest he began
to suggest plots for the short stories I was writing. His
plots were not in my line. Their subjects called for certain
technical knowledge which he had and I had not. I urged him
to write them himself, as a way of increasing his income. At
first the idea did not interest him. He was a novelist, not
a short-story writer, he reminded me; but I finally persuaded

him to work up a dramatic railroad yarn he had outlined to me, and to send it to the *Saturday Evening Post*. Mr. Lorimer accepted it at once.

With his encouragement Hal wrote half a dozen short stories for the *Post* in rapid succession, and was paid five hundred dollars each for them. He always wrote and revised with extraordinary ease. I can still see him standing beside my desk, changing sentences and even whole paragraphs of *Our Mr. Wrenn* without even sitting down to it. He was publicity man for George H. Doran at the time, and was chafing over the need of giving his days to advertising work when every instinct in him was clamoring for freedom to write fiction. His short stories solved his problem. Within a year or two he was able to resign the Doran job and concentrate on his novels. After another short interval he and Grace were lolling on the Florida sands and sending me "valentines" of the bungalow they had rented.

In another light-hearted moment he sent me a post-card photograph of the room in which Martha Washington had died, and labeled it, "View of private suite of the Sinclair Lewises on their yacht, *The Rollicking Banana*, bound south."

This letter, written during one of my vacations in a Maine camp, shows equally well how sympathetic Hal was and how rapidly he was working toward independence:

Saturday

DEAR ELIZABETH,

I've just learned how narrow an escape from drowning you had and I hasten to send you Grace's and my—what is it one extends to a person yanked out of the jaws of death, congratulations or condolences? I fancy you must know how much it would mean to us both in a personal way and as regards my association with Harper's, had you gone. The narrowness of your escape accentuates that.

Hawk is out, and it's a bully looking book. I'll have a signed copy ready for you when you return.

I'm working away on *The Job,* and I've also had two short stories accepted by *Saturday Evening Post* at $500 a piece, which gives promise of the freedom I've yearned for—not yet, but bimeby, mebbe.

Sincerely,
SINCLAIR LEWIS

Sinclair Lewis was often as impish, as mischievous and as unexpected as Mark Twain himself. One of his exhibitions I still remember all too vividly. He and my old friend Bayard Veiller and I were sedately riding downtown one Sunday evening in a street-car. I was sitting between the two young men, and Hal was suddenly moved to impersonate a youth mildly overcome by liquor. We had been dining with dignity and temperance at one of my clubs, and I suspect that Hal had also absorbed all the dignity he could endure at one meal. He was always extremely temperate in those days. On this occasion he put up a really artistic show. There was nothing objectionable about it to any one but me. No effect was overdone; but the whole performance was very funny to every one around us.

Delighted by the art of his companion, Bayard Veiller was moved to prove that he could do the stunt just as well. He could. My obvious annoyance and embarassment added the last touch to the pleasure the delighted spectators took in the little comedy. The young men kept it up till I stopped the car. Then they suddenly and ostentatiously sobered, bowed to the enthusiastic passengers, and escorted me to my destination with the pious and uplifted expressions of young Rollos. It was one of the occasions when my sense of humor was behind a cloud.

The intimacy of some of our later correspondence is illustrated in these two letters:

CARMEL, CALIFORNIA

ANGEL MISS JORDAN,

Tidings of great joy from us to tell you that next December twenty-fifth there will be *three* instead of two little Lewises to wish you Merry Christmas.

I am at once amazed and amused by the situation. Also considerably peeved by the way in which it curtails my activities. But when I don't feel rotten I am tremendously happy. About July or August is the time appointed. The doctor says I am in splendid shape and perfectly normal. I have just returned from San Francisco, where I combined the joys of a daily hot bath (difficult in Carmel) with doctor, visiting, and Christmas gifting.

Of course this changes all our plans. We are returning to New York in the spring by way of Southern California and New Orleans, for I want to be near Mamma and my friends and have the child born in New York. I, who have always looked to London and Paris as the great cities, have apparently not realized the prestige of being born in New York. It was the nearest chance with me (I was almost made in Germany) but the rest of the United States which I have met regards birth in New York as a divine privilege. Therefore....

Have you begun to receive the proofs yet? Hal always returns them within twenty-four hours. When he isn't reading them he is writing short stories, which are being accepted with staggering rapidity.

Your accepting *Mr. Wrenn* and his meeting me seem to have started his joy-ball rolling; and it won't stop, will it?

Such a very happy holiday to you and your mother. I do hope you will like the third Lewis edition as much as you are dear enough to say you like the first two.

Affectionately yours,

December eighteenth   GRACE HEGGER LEWIS

What a party we shall have when we see you! ! !

Sunday

DEAR ELIZABETH,

It's come—a ten-pound, healthy, husky, red-headed boy named Wells, and Grace is feeling fine. She'll be in the hospital

for a couple of weeks—but everything goes fine. Arrival was
on Thursday. . . .

                                           SINCLAIR LEWIS

Hal's third novel was called *The Job,* and was interesting
because it contained his first definite intimation of the literary path he was to follow in later years. All his early books
had good notices. Each, as he wrote it, had an exciting
originality and distinction of style. But he was still far from
Main Street. His books sold well for a beginner's novels.
No one at Franklin Square except myself saw all the possibilities for this engaging new-comer. I once said to him,
    "Hal, do you know what may happen? Here at Harper's
we're doing all the planting, watering, and general developing of this genius of yours. We'll bring out all your first
books. Then, some day, you may suddenly decide that another firm might do more for you, and you may hand it a
book. It would be quite on the cards if that book proved
to be the 'best seller' you and I are waiting for—and if that
new firm got all the cash and credit of it, after we have taken
you through the burden and heat of your first literary years."
    Hal's blue eyes looked hurt. He assured me rather stiffly
that he would never do any such thing, and that I ought to
know him better than to suggest it. He remained with
Harper's during my three years as literary adviser there,
and even for a couple of years after I resigned. Then he
wrote *Main Street* and gave it to another publisher. He was
immediately whirled to fame and fortune—himself rather
incredulous and startled by the experience—on the flaming
tail of that literary comet.
    I never knew why he changed his publishers, for I had
regretfully lost touch with him. But after he and Grace
separated and she returned from Europe she came to see
me, bringing with her their enchanting little son, Wells, then

about ten years old. He was as much like his mother, and as unlike his father, as any small boy could be.

It was pleasant to be associated with younger writers. The youth and immense enthusiasm of Sinclair Lewis and our other recruits were stimulating and rather heady, after years of association with those who had long since "arrived" and were too accustomed to success to get many thrills from it. My heroes had been Mr. Howells, Mr. James, and Mark Twain, all much more than twice my age. My allegiance to them never faltered, but it was fascinating to watch young things coming up and developing. However, my interest in distinguished age continued. I was seeing as much as I could of Julia Ward Howe, then in her eighties, every time she came to New York. It was about this time, also, that I found a new and delightful friend in John Bigelow.

The opportunities of meeting Mrs. Howe were numerous. At most small gatherings where she found herself Mrs. Howe was still being urged to recite her *Battle Hymn of the Republic,* and she seemed to enjoy doing it. Certainly it was a pleasure to listen to her, and to watch the picture of beautiful and benign old age she made as she sat before us. She once confided to me that she was "heading straight for one hundred," and she very nearly reached that goal.

John Bigelow was then ninety, yet he had just finished *Retrospections of An Active Life.* We were close neighbors, as he and his daughter Grace lived on the south side of Gramercy Park, at Number 21. Mr. Bigelow liked to take the short walk that led him to our building, Number 36, and to drop in to tea. He was said to have been the most brilliant and fascinating figure in the diplomatic circles of France when he was America's ambassador there, and great age had not destroyed his charm. His talk was still brilliant, his sense of humor delicious, and his wit amazing. At my teas the younger women were drawn to him irresistibly.

He could always keep a large circle of them interested and amused.

Once, I remember, he and Rachel Crothers foregathered in a corner for an hour, in a concentration that ignored every one else. I had always suspected that Rachel kept her most brilliant lines for her comedies, but it was clear that she was giving Mr. Bigelow some of them that day.

John Bigelow's wife had been one of New York's most distinguished social leaders in her time. She had been dead a great many years, but Mrs. Paran Stevens had often told me amusing stories about her eccentricities. When I met her husband, during the last years of his life, he talked of her by the hour, and his tales of her were always fascinating. One, I remember, had to do with an experience on Lake George. The Bigelows were passing a summer there, and spent much of the time cruising around the lake in their boat. One afternoon they discovered an island new to them. It was only the size of an average country lawn, but Mrs. Bigelow was suddenly moved to explore it.

"It's so peaceful and lovely and lonely that I'd like to rest there a while," she announced. "No, I don't want any one else. Just leave me on it with my book and my sun umbrella. I'll sit on that rug some one has left there. Be sure to come back for me in an hour."

Her family saw her seated under the sun umbrella and the boat departed. An hour later, when the family returned for her, they realized at once that something was wrong. Mrs. Bigelow was perched on the extreme edge of the island with one foot, Mr. Bigelow assured me, extended toward the water. With hands and voice she urged the rescue band to hurry. When the boat reached her she made a flying leap into it, and would have fallen if her son and husband had not caught her.

She was too excited and breathless to explain till she and

the boat were out of sight of the island. Then she confessed that for the past fifty minutes she had been listening to the imploring voices of five young men in the water near her, breathlessly telling her they were quite naked, that their clothes were under the rug that she was sitting on, that they were having chills and cramps, and that they would be very much obliged if she would go away from that island and let them climb up on it and get dressed. Mrs. Bigelow, being severely practical, had suggested that she pile the clothes on the shore behind her and gaze out over the water while the young men retrieved the garments and dressed. The young men, being modest theological students, were taking no chances of that sort.

Another story Mr. Bigelow told about his wife concerned the time she attended the funeral of a dear friend and absently dangled over the end of her pew a large handbag bearing the brilliantly embroidered message, *Bon Voyage*.

Some of my most vivid memories of Mr. Bigelow show him at his own luncheon table, consuming large quantities of sausages and buckwheat cakes while he listened to the verbal ping-pong that went on around him. He ate exactly what he liked and did exactly what he wished to do up till the end of his life. When he was eating something he enjoyed, he confined himself to that function and let others talk.

On one occasion his son Poultney and I disgraced ourselves over Grace Bigelow's story of the attempted suicide of a common friend. The friend had failed to kill himself, and at the time of the recital was in fine health and spirits. The episode had held both tragedy and farce, however, and Miss Bigelow's inability to distinguish between the two was too much for her brother and me. After one fatal exchange of glances we went off into a paroxysm of laughter we couldn't control. Mr. Bigelow stopped eating sausages to gaze at us with severe disapproval. Poultney wiped his eyes.

"If we feel as badly as this over the attempt," he murmured to me, "how *would* we feel if the poor chap had succeeded?"

There is not much of Poultney Bigelow's humor in this serious letter.

> BIGELOW HOMESTEAD,
> MALDEN-ON-HUDSON, N. Y.

DEAR MISS JORDAN,

Yours is a great moral book * with much by play of literary arabesque. Last night I read it from end to end and, of course, fell in love with your splendid social secretary.

Pity 't is that arbitrary censorship hampers the liberty of honest reformers in matters of sex—or marriage. Lawrence did also a great service in *Lady Chatterley's Lover*—but his book has to be bootlegged and it is very expensive—(I refer to the *un*-expurgated.)

How I wish that you had expanded the intimacies of Lucy into realistic happenings. But in that case the *Century* would have declined the book as it did my last one on Doorn and Mussolini and Rome.

If ever you motor hereabouts, pray stop and share a hermit's crust and cat and converse and believe me with best wishes,

> Faithfully yours,
> POULTNEY BIGELOW

P. S. On second thought methinks that Lucy would have captivated me. She has a bit of my weaknesses.

Another writer I saw much of in those days was Mary Austin, who also lived diagonally across the Park from me at the National Arts Club. She had a rare literary gift which, for reasons I never wholly understood, seemed fully appreciated by no one but Mary herself. One reason, I suppose, was that she did not get on very well with editors and other literary associates. She once explained this failure to me by saying, "You must remember that my civilization

* *The Fourflusher.*

is only five years old!" It was, and it wore a bit thin when she saw herself or her work ignored. Before she was twenty she had married a young surveyor, who kept her in the heart of the Great American Desert for a quarter of a century, while he was away most of the time on his various expeditions. Mary's associates were largely Indians. Her human and natural environment gave her an immense amount of fine material, of which she made full use in her work; but it did not fit her for New York social life.

One of the many stories told about her was that at a dinner one evening her host smilingly asked her a question.

"Mrs. Austin," he wanted to know, "how does it feel to be a genius?"

Mary knew the answer to that and let him have it, while her fellow guests listened with awe.

"It makes one very lonely," she sighed.

That story never seemed to me as amusing as it was supposed to be. It was too true. Mary Austin *was* a genius, and she *was* very lonely.

I persuaded her to write a life of Christ for Harper and Brothers, and I did not handicap her with the conditions S. S. McClure was said to have made for Margaret Deland, when he urged her to write one that was "bright and snappy." Mary wrote the book with characteristic scholarship and brilliance. It appeared serially in the *North American Review* under the title Colonel Harvey had suggested, *The Man Jesus*. After all these years it is generally regarded as the best book Mary Austin wrote. She could write good letters, too, which incidentally revealed much of her personality.

Los Angeles

Dear Elizabeth,

I have been motoring all over the States and just stopped for a two weeks' visit with my family; after which, unless I go

back to the Exposition for another spectacle, I shall hit the trail
for New York.

I have spent the time here visiting with my nieces. We have
tried on all my clothes and decided that the best effect is produced by combining my Roman scarf with my bronze slippers
and the best silk petticoat; and now we are reading the Jungle
Book. My new niece is quite the most remarkable specimen
of her kind in captivity and gains her ounce a day in the most
exemplary manner.

I have done no writing whatever, but I have thought out what
I wish to do next winter. If you can make me a reasonable
royalty on the Life, I will no doubt be able to do it. I have
been greatly tempted, though, not to go back at all, and to give
up writing entirely for the more active administrative life which
is offered me here. Talk about the difficulties of dual personality! They are nothing compared to the problem of a dual gift.
I could earn more, live more easily, be happier and no doubt
just as useful to my generation by taking the place held open
for me here by virtue of my gift for producing. Why on earth
I go back to New York for the depressing struggle of a literary
career I don't know. Do you?

Life is so much more human here, so much more Greek in
quality. I suspect that what drives me to the disappointments
and deprivations of literature is the pinch of Puritanism in my
make-up, suggesting the less happy mode as likely to be the
more commendable.

Did you see what my friend Wells had to say of me in his
last book? Do you suppose it is true? Now if he had said that
about anybody else, I would have interviewed her for the purpose of finding out if America really does starve people like
Mary Austin—and why, and how. Isn't it a pity that I can't
use my newspaper sense on myself? I've often thought that
with my instinct for the dramatic I could make such a good
thing out of myself if only I were some one else.

I am tremendously interested just now in the work of the
women police here in Los Angeles. How do you suppose we
stood it all these years, leaving the business of making women
comfortable and safe entirely in the hands of men? And turning girl offenders over to male police who as often as not were
contributors to their delinquency? And having children's play-

grounds in charge of half-educated, politically appointed, often brutal, recently acquired aliens?

How do you suppose we acquired the idea anyway that it is improper for women to go anywhere that children have to go? Do you realize what it means when I tell you that children of nine and ten go about the Exposition unattended and un-offended?

Things like these make California such a livable place, and also contribute to the feeling that to live here is a kind of let-ting down, making fat the soul. . . . Well, I was born into it too soon. Fifty years later I wouldn't have needed to go to New York.

Expect me about the fifteenth.

Sincerely yours,
MARY AUSTIN

October 11

DEAR ELIZABETH,

I arrived yesterday, too tired to call anybody's attention to it, and am still minus my trunks. I shall be glad to see you as soon as I can get on something clean.

In pursuance of our plan of committing all our business to paper, I am replying to your kind offer of a contract for the life of St. Paul, which I found waiting me here. I am unwilling to sign any contract at present for the reason that I am not sure the book will ever be written. I am working on the re-search at odd times, but it will be some time at the present rate before it is ready to write. A book of that kind has to ripen; it must be prayed over as well as studied for.

But the chief reason for delay is that I do not yet know whether I can write it. That you wish me to undertake it is a convincing item, and that I want to do it is another. But it is not a good thing for me to agree to do things very long in advance of being able to do them; for as soon as I have agreed I am immediately seized with a mad desire to do seven or eight totally different things, and I generally do them.

I found a lot of clippings waiting me here, and when I had separated the reviews from the notices which had evidently been inspired by the publishers I was much pleased with them.

What I fear is that many of the papers which ordinarily give me long reviews will simply pass the book over as being too hackneyed in subject to be worth reading. We must talk this over and see what can be done about it.

Suppose you come over to dinner Thursday evening about 6:30.

Sincerely yours,
MARY AUSTIN

March 1, 1917

MY DEAR ELIZABETH,

I have been putting off writing you about Mrs. Burnett's book,* which you so kindly sent me, just because I haven't much to say of it of the sort of thing publishers like to hear. It is charmingly written, as all Mrs. Burnett's books are: but after that I have to add that I took it up with great eagerness and laid it down with disappointment.

Mrs. Burnett gives the impression of having had experiences along this line which would have been interesting and perhaps serviceable to hear. After reading Sir Oliver Lodge's book I had hoped for something of the kind ... but somehow fiction on that subject just now seems out of place. Suppose the dead do hang about in that way trying to get in touch with us and never succeeding except in the case of occasional people who happen to be born in Scotland. What a gruesome place it makes of life. What must all Europe be like now, with the dead plucking helplessly at the sleeves of the living!

Experiences such as she describes in the first part of the book are not unknown among children, and even grown-ups have very acute perceptions of past events in the places where they happened, even if unaccompanied by hallucinations. But there is no good reason for believing that these afford any evidence of "spirits." I had such a one in the cell of Savonarola, and I have had them of persons absent but still living.

I wish that Mrs. Burnett had given us a record of personal experience without attempting to interpret it. Very few people have the requisite knowledge and power of discrimination to be able to say exactly what these very general experiences mean.

* The White People.

On the whole I think our chance of communicating with the dead has been hampered by the disposition to ascribe all sorts of psychic experiences to that agency, when they may have nothing to do with it.

Still I am glad to have read the book. . . .

Sincerely yours,
MARY AUSTIN

Two close friends of Mary Austin's were Mr. and Mrs. Herbert Hoover. One evening during the World War, when Mr. Hoover had returned to America for a few days, to report on his brilliant war work as Food Administrator in Europe, Mrs. Austin invited a dozen friends to her studio to meet and talk to him informally.

I shall always remember that evening. The studio was very small and even the dozen of us crowded it. Some of us sat on the floor, literally at Mr. Hoover's feet. The amazing things about the experience were Mr. Hoover's frankness and his entire trust in us. He talked to us as intimately as if we were his brothers and sisters, and he made the evening one of the most interesting any of us had known. I have often tried, but always in vain, to reconcile that friendly, intimate, fascinating talker with the remote Herbert Hoover of the White House. It cannot be done.

Another friend who wove a charming design into the pattern of my life was Mrs. Custer, widow of the famous General. She was over sixty when we first met, but she lived to be well over eighty, and I saw much of her during those final years of her life. She was a gallant figure, up and doing every day and with only one bug-bear—the fear of being "taken care of." It was a well-grounded apprehension. Everybody loved Mrs. Custer, and most of her friends wanted to make the remainder of her life a restful twilight. She would have none of that. At seventy she light-heartedly started across the world for the Durbar, and I am sure she was one of the most active exhibits of that lively congregation.

"I'm not going to sit still long enough for my knees to stiffen," she once told me, and she never did it. She was very modern, but she loved to talk about the past. She gave me some returns of the school-girl thrills of my early New York experiences when she described her days and nights in the saddle when she went through parts of the Civil War with her husband, "the youngest general in the American Army."

There were tears in her eyes when she described the Custer massacre to me, and the way the news came to her, but her voice was as quietly steady as if she had been talking of the experience of another person. She had met Abraham Lincoln several times, and his young secretary John Hay. She gave me every detail of her visit to the President after her husband's death, and of "Mr. Lincoln's wonderful kindness and sympathy."

"His manner was like that of a tender and understanding father," she ended. Obsessed as she was by her own tragedy she had observed how worn and exhausted the President had looked.

"I have remembered him ever since exactly as he was that day," she ended—"so worn, so tired, so gentle, and so kind."

For many years the survivors of the Custer massacre held an annual dinner and reunion. Their General's widow was always expected to attend this function, and she felt that she ought to do so, great as the strain was for her. Up till a few years before her death she went to every one of those reunions, dreading the experience months in advance and in the end literally driving herself to it by a call on the courage that had never failed her. A few years before her death she told me she had been forced to give them up.

"They were too tragic," she said. "Toward the end there were only seven or eight men left, and at the last dinner I went to there were only five. I had to stay in bed for a week after it. Then I had to tell the five men I could never come again. It hurt me terribly to do that. I did so want to see them through. But they understood, the poor darlings!"

Mrs. Custer was well in her eighties at that time. I think, though I am not sure, that she outlived every one of "the poor darlings."

CHAPTER XXII

Moving Pictures and War Days

I HAD kept in touch with Bayard Veiller, a co-worker of my *World* days, and with his wife—Margaret Wycherly, then and still one of the most cerebral of our leading actresses. Through them I met Helen Tyler, Edgar Selwyn, his wife Margaret Mayo, and many other delightful men and women of the stage. We all unwearyingly talked shop during these encounters, but rarely discussed business. When I read that Edgar and Margaret Selwyn had formed a moving-picture combination with Samuel Goldfish, and that the new organization was to be called the Goldwyn Company, I mentally wished them well and dropped the matter from my mind. I should have been even more amused than incredulous if I had been told that the new company would completely change the current of my life; but that is what it did during the following year.

One day in early October, while the World War was still going on, but before America had entered it, I was called to the telephone to talk to Mrs. Selwyn. I had not seen her for months, and I assumed that the call meant a pleasant luncheon or dinner invitation. But she opened the conversation in a crisp and businesslike way by asking if I would consider an offer to go into moving-picture work.

I laughed and said I wouldn't—that I knew nothing about moving pictures except that I enjoyed seeing good ones. Mrs. Selwyn continued very serious. She said she was overworked and that the Goldwyn Company needed the sort of help I could give it. I have always been sure—probably too

358

sure—of what I do know, but I am no bluffer. Again, and very firmly now, I reminded Mrs. Selwyn of my utter lack of moving-picture experience.

"What of that?" she said almost impatiently. "We've all had to learn the job. We can soon teach you our part of it. What we want is your knowledge of books and authors and the world and life in general. Now, let's talk terms."

This was plausible, but I did not take fire. I had heard too many sad stories of the brisk entrances and exits of authors in the moving-picture world. To end the conversation I spoke as brusquely as Mrs. Selwyn had done.

"I wouldn't consider anything less than twenty-five thousand a year," I said. "And I should have to reserve time for my outside writing and existing contracts."

Mrs. Selwyn's voice came back to me like the joyous chirping of a canary bird.

"All right," she replied. "That will be perfectly satisfactory to us. When can you begin?"

I was dazed by this expedition. I murmured that I must think it over.

"But you said twenty-five thousand," she persisted. "And part time."

"I did," I admitted, "and I expected it to end the discussion."

We talked on. I told her Arthur Brisbane had recently made a contract with me for three editorial columns a week for the Hearst publications. Having added this to a schedule already too crowded, I did not see how I could fit in any more work. In the end I consented to think it over and to meet Mr. Goldfish, President of the Goldwyn Company, for luncheon and further discussion. I did so, and Mr. Goldfish proved as alluring in his fashion as Mrs. Selwyn was. He was suave, optimistic, and as certain as she had been that the Goldwyn studios needed a recruit from the literary world. In the end we came to an agreement. I was to resign from Harper and Brothers and to give Goldwyn, in its Fort Lee studios, the three days a week—Monday, Tuesday, and Wednesday—I had been giving to Harper's. That left me time for my novel and short-story writing and for the three specials a week I was contributing to the Hearst Syndicate. My new title—Editorial Director of the Goldwyn Company—sounded very impressive.

I was sorry to leave Harper's. But Colonel Harvey had already departed to begin his diplomatic career, and Mr. Duneka, though still general manager of the firm, was confined to his New Jersey home by the disease that killed him a year or two later. He was keeping in close touch with Harper's, however, and the following correspondence passed between us:

November 3, 1917

DEAR MR. DUNEKA,

If you listen closely on December first you will hear the sweep of pinions as I take my flight from Franklin Square. In other words, my dear friend, I am handing you my resignation from the staff of Harper and Brothers, to take effect on that day.

Let me add that I am leaving with the utmost good feeling toward every one there. In many ways I am, of course, sorry to go. But with you and Colonel Harvey both away, the place no longer seems the same. . . .

As you and I have always understood each other, I am adding a few personal details in which I feel sure you will be interested. . . .

I enclose a report of my work as literary adviser for the past three years. I also enclose the outline of a letter I plan to send to our list of authors, for any changes you may suggest. Observe how tenderly I write.

Good-bye, dear F. A. D., and God bless you. I shall never forget what a good friend you have always been to me.

Faithfully yours,

ELIZABETH JORDAN

SUMMIT, N. J., Nov. 8

DEAR FRIEND:

I am desolated at the thought of your leaving Harper and Brothers. But, of course, there is nothing else possible, when Fate comes tempting you with large golden apples. What a success is yours!

The firm will miss you, and I shall miss you personally, more than I can say. We have worked together half a lifetime— indeed all *your* adult lifetime—and in those long years I have come to respect your untiring industry, your "manly" virtues, and your fidelity to the work at hand, pleasant or unpleasant.

It is certain that you will make a distinguished success in your new undertaking, but I add the wish that all good luck and happiness may go with you. As they say so beautifully in the Spanish farewell, "Go with God."

I am always,

Sincerely your friend,
F. A. DUNEKA

I also quote here the report I sent Mr. Duneka. It gives the list of the books I arranged for and brought in during my three years as literary adviser, and ends with the additional six books I had recently arranged for and which were published the spring after my departure. It's a pretty good list, if I do say it. The profits on Anna Howard Shaw's Autobiography would almost have paid my salary—not to mention the earnings from Mrs. Burnett's and Kate Douglas Wiggin's books. Also, of course, the list took no account of the endless conferences with authors and would-be authors which had filled so much of my time:

ACCEPTED BOOKS, E. J.

Published

Prayer, by Reverend S. S. McComb, D.D.
Bluebeard, by Kate Douglas Wiggin.
Our Mr. Wrenn, by Sinclair Lewis (his first novel).
Religion and Life, by Reverend Elwood Worcester, D.D.
   (Rector of Emmanuel Church, Boston).

Principles of Correct Dress, by Florence Hull Winterburn.
Good Form For All Occasions, by Florence Howe Hall.
Novel Ways of Entertaining, by Florence Hull Winterburn.
The Prospective Mother, by Marianna Wheeler.
The Young Mother's Hand-book, by Marianna Wheeler.
Modern Dancing, by Mr. and Mrs. Vernon Castle.
The Art of Being Alive, by Ella Wheeler Wilcox.
May Iverson's Career, by Elizabeth Jordan.
California: An Intimate History, by Gertrude Atherton.
The Ladder, by Philip Curtiss (his first novel).
The Story of a Pioneer: An Autobiography, by Anna Howard
    Shaw and Elizabeth Jordan.
The Primrose Ring, by Ruth Sawyer (a novel).
The Life-Builders, by Elizabeth Dejeans (a novel).
The A.B.C. of Housekeeping, by C. T. Herrick.
The A.B.C. of Etiquette, by Anne Seymour.
The A.B.C. of Gardening, by Eben Rexford.
The A.B.C. of Vegetable Gardening, by Eben Rexford.
The Man Jesus, by Mary Austin.
Faith, by Reverend S. S. McComb, D.D.
The Trail of the Hawk, by Sinclair Lewis (his second novel).
Over Paradise Ridge, by Maria Thompson Daviess (a novel).
A. B. C. of Cooking, by C. T. Herrick.
The Art of Conversation, by Florence Howe Hall.
Seven Miles to Arden, by Ruth Sawyer.
A Diplomat's Wife in Mexico, by Edith O'Shaughnessy.
A.B.C. of Home Saving, by Lissie C. Cowlishaw.
The Way to the House of Santa Claus, by Frances Hodgson
    Burnett.
The Incredible Honeymoon, by E. Nesbit.
Lovers' Knots, by Elizabeth Jordan.
Between Two Worlds, by Philip Curtiss (his second novel).
The Story of the Battle Hymn of the Republic, by Florence
    Howe Hall.
Liberty Hall, by Florence Hull Winterburn.
This Way to Christmas, by Ruth Sawyer.
Every Soul Hath Its Song, by Fannie Hurst.
This Is the Life, by Corinne Lowe.
Out of a Clear Sky, by Maria Thompson Daviess.
The White People, by Frances Hodgson Burnett.

The Job, by Sinclair Lewis (his third novel).
Lose Weight and Be Well, Anonymous.
The New Life, by Reverend S. S. McComb.
Diplomatic Days, by Mrs. Nelson O'Shaughnessy.
Herself, Himself, and Myself, by Ruth Sawyer (her third novel).
The Innocents, by Sinclair Lewis (his fourth novel).
The Big Little Person, by Rebecca Hopper Eastman (her first novel).
God: His Meaning in Life, by Reverend S. S. McComb.
A Child's Year Book of Verses, by Ruth Sawyer.

Number of books published since E. J. entered Literary Department—50.

Books Accepted for Publication, Spring 1918

Prayers of Our Times, by Reverend S. S. McComb.
Meditations for Every Day, by Reverend S. S. McComb.
The Reminiscences of Florence Howe Hall.
The Wings of Youth, by Elizabeth Jordan (a novel).
Jim Spurling, Fisherman, by A. W. Tolman (a book for boys).
War Sermons, by Reverend S. S. McComb (autumn 1918).

I needed a month for rest and recreation before I entered the new field, so I did not start the new job till the first of January. That three months' interval between my contract and my arrival at the Fort Lee studios was a mistake. If I had gone in with the Goldwyn Company at once, while the new irons were sizzling so invitingly, the experiment might have turned out differently—even though all precedents pointed to failure from the start. More things can happen in a moving-picture studio in three months than can happen anywhere else in three years. Staggering changes had occurred in the Goldwyn offices.

The results of the Goldfish-Selwyn combination had been disastrous from the start, for reasons which probably no one yet fully understands. On the face of it nothing could have seemed more promising than their venture. Mr. Goldfish, as he has since demonstrated, was a brilliant business man, and both the Selwyns were conspicuously successful playwrights. Naturally, they put on as their first offerings the three plays with which Margaret Mayo had made a large fortune— *Baby Mine, Twin Beds,* and *Polly of the Circus.* As plays, every one of these had been a spectacular success in America and Europe. As pictures, though they were beautifully directed and produced, they simply folded up and caused the Goldwyn combination a big financial loss.

These failures had an effect more disastrous than the money loss, large as that was. It shook the confidence of the new partners in themselves and in one another. If such sure-fire theatrical hits failed, what *could* they safely put on? They were facing these questions and their heavy deficits when I appeared, full of optimism, in January; and they had temporarily reached the point where they were afraid to put on anything at all. Moreover, there was internal warfare among them. The Selwyns, who had seemed one of the most devoted and most congenial couples I ever knew, had already decided on the separation which occurred a few months later. Mrs. Selwyn left the studios almost immediately. Mr. Selwyn lingered a few months longer, obviously heavy-hearted but very dignified and considerate of every one. Then he, too, departed. Mr. Goldfish took over the business, changed his name to Goldwyn, and tried to carry on.

He was a staunch ship in a heavy storm, but he was bewildered by his disasters and temporarily afraid to produce. There was a near panic in the business world. America was on the eve of entering the World War. Add to all these conditions the fact that the winter was the coldest in twenty-five years, that the sides of the studio building on the heights of Fort Lee were of glass, and that the plumbing and heating plants were on strike, and the situation can be imagined.

Mr. Goldwyn had promised me "one hundred per cent of coöperation" as he put it; but it was clear that he was harassed to the point of collapse.

My secretary and I worked in our heavy ulsters. We also wore rubbers, for bursting pipes kept the cement floors wet. I had bought a new automobile and installed in it a new chauffeur. Our daily rides up and down the ice-covered surface of the Fort Lee hill were filled with uncertainties. Serious accidents were constantly occurring. I was also depressed by the discovery that the classic and modern books I earnestly recommended—whose titles were as familiar in my circle as our own names—had never been heard of by most of my new associates. I kept the list. They have all been produced since then, by various companies, and many of them were brilliant successes. At that time they were as alien to the picture world as I was myself.

Nevertheless, there were some high-lights. For the time we were not putting on any pictures at all, but I was meeting a lot of new types, most of them very intriguing. I formed an immediate friendship with George Loane Tucker. He was there as director for a few weeks; but after a little misunderstanding with Mr. Goldwyn he faded away overnight, in the strange fashion picture directors have. My ignorance of the moving-picture game was abysmal, but I knew all about Mr. Tucker's fine work and record. If he had remained he and I could have worked together very harmoniously; but this was not to be.

The Goldwyn Company had three stars at the time—Mae Marsh, Madge Kennedy, and Mabel Normand. Apropos of these Mrs. Selwyn remarked gloomily, during the first weeks of my Goldwyn connection, "Mr. Goldfish is calling for 'drama'—and all we have are three nice little flappers to give it to him!"

I saw little of Miss Marsh or Miss Kennedy, but one day

a young man entered my office, vigorously chewing gum. He was, though I did not know it then, Miss Normand's combined chauffeur, secretary, valet, and business man.

"She wants to see you," he announced at the door, chewing busily.

"She? Who is she?"

"Mabel. She wants to see you."

"All right," I said hospitably. "Tell her to come in."

"She can't. She ain't dressed."

I went to Miss Normand's dressing-room and found her reclining on a wicker divan clad lightly in her panties. She said she wanted a new play and I promised to find one or more for her. The conversation continued:

Mabel: Will you play golf with me in the spring?

I (warmly and sincerely): I'd love to.

Mabel: Will you play tennis with me?

I: I'd like nothing better. But you will have to give me a big handicap.

Mabel: Will you go swimming with me?

I: With pleasure—if you will tow me. I don't swim.

Mabel (stunned): *You don't swim!*

The discovery was plainly a blow to Mabel, who was superb at all outdoor sports. Mr. Goldwyn had advised her to make friends with me, and this was her direct method of attack. She was a big-hearted little creature, delightful in her way, and I found her very entertaining and likable.

I learned to admire the industry, energy and courage of the moving-picture people as much as I admired those same qualities in the actors and actresses in "spoken drama." As workers, they were as plucky, as good-humored, and as indefatigable. When Geraldine Farrar and Pauline Frederick were brought into the Goldwyn Studios to give Mr. Goldwyn the drama for which, quite rightly, he was calling, the situation improved and some pictures were put on. But I was out of my element and I knew it. I was not in the least disconsolate when Mr. Goldwyn moved the studios to California and my experiment ended. It had been deeply interesting and instructive, but it is not a part of my record to which I can "point with pride."

Perhaps Mrs. Selwyn has sometimes felt that she did me an ill turn in luring me from Harper's for a year's mess of pottage. In reality, I am under obligations to her. Without her intervention I might not have found the courage to leave Harper and Brothers even though in my three days a week of work at home I was earning four times my Harper salary. I had the respect of the long-time salaried worker for the check that comes in regularly every week, or month. Mrs. Selwyn's friendly hand had taken that salary plank from me, but I never really missed it. America was beginning her "boom" years. I had all I could do. Through careful investments I already had a good reserve. Before the crash came I had bulwarked myself, as I thought, for life.

By this time America was also in the war. Before she entered I had worked for the allies, as a member of Frank Crowninshield's White Cross Committee of Mercy, and in other ways. Now I gave all the time I could to our own war work, serving on committees, making speeches and selling bonds. Those quiet revelations Mr. Hoover had given us in Mary Austin's studio had made each of his hearers realize the horror of the World War as no published reports could do it. A similar revelation was made by Mr. and Mrs. Frederick C. Penfield when they came over from Vienna and I attended the dinner Mr. and Mrs. James Robert McKee gave for them.

The background of the dinner was the private dining-room of one of New York's big hotels, and there were twenty-four of us at the table. Up till our entrance into the war Mr. Penfield was American Ambassador to Austria and

Mrs. Penfield had been doing remarkably fine war-relief work for the women and children and the sick of Vienna. She had just been conspicuously honored by Emperor Franz Josef and wore on her breast the superb decoration he had given her.

At the end of the dinner, when the coffee and liqueurs had been served and all the waiters had departed leaving the guests alone, Mr. Penfield talked to us as frankly as Mr. Hoover had talked in Mary Austin's studio. Each man paid the friends of his hostess the high compliment of assuming that they were his intimate friends as well, and of telling them inside war news without reservation or even a hint that what he said was confidential. It was, however, on both occasions, and very thrilling. I am quite sure that no word of the inside knowledge we were given those evenings ever leaked out through any one in the two groups.

Other high-lights of memory shine clearly through the years. I was present the night when a certain beautiful Italian countess in charge of a great base hospital in Italy, who had come to America to raise money for her work, began her speech to a huge theater audience with a sentence which made that audience gasp.

"Ladies and gentlemen," said this product of centuries of Italian breeding and culture, "I am here to tell you what a hell of a time we are having on the other side of the ocean."

She had to stop. The vast audience had stiffened, then roared. Of course, it sobered at once. The contrast between the appearance of the distinguished young countess and her language had been startling, but in the next instant her hearers realized that she had not overstated her case.

Maud Skinner had taken me to Charles Frohman's funeral and we had wept together over the tragedy of the *Lusitania*.

"Baby McKee," my little friend of the Cape May cottage,

now a husky young college man, hurried over to France to drive an ambulance for the Allies before America entered the war. From there he wrote his mother:

"The wounded have such incredible courage that one is ready to die trying to help them."

I suddenly became conscious of the passage of the years. Little boys who had sat in my lap in their mothers' homes when they were three or four years old were hustling into training-camps, or coming in their beautiful new uniforms to bid me good-by before they sailed for France. One of them was a submarine commander in constant service until peace came. Margie Shipp's son, whom she and I had so often visited during his days at West Point, was one of the first to go. He had been just a young lieutenant, but he went to the front as Major William Ewen Shipp. Another favorite little pal of mine was now an officer in the Secret Service. At a tea I gave soon after our entrance into the war every young man present wore a uniform, and several of them were god-sons I had held at the baptismal font.

After one of Colonel Harvey's dinners one night at the Metropolitan Club he took his guests to the Cornelius Vanderbilts' home to see some exclusive war pictures and to hear Theodore Roosevelt's famous speech. It was the one in which Mr. Roosevelt said that the two best friends America had in the world were the Atlantic and the Pacific Oceans. But what interested me most that evening was the contrast between the cheerfulness of the guests and the horror of those war pictures.

The Joseph Willards came back for a few weeks from their post in Madrid, where Mr. Willard was American Ambassador. They painted more war horrors. My friend Enid Yandell returned from Paris and described the work of her organization *Appui des Artistes* in feeding the starving artists over there. New York life was a nightmare during those days. One could hardly endure the tension of it.

Martha and I were in our Massachusetts home on Armistice Day. We motored to Boston, a hundred miles away, passing through one celebration parade after another in every town along our route, but seeing very little through the tears in our eyes.

After the war the routine of work quickened with the developing boom. One settled back into a normal groove. Three of my novels were put into Braille for the blind, which pleased me very much. Others were made into moving pictures, and a dozen of them were translated into various languages—French, Spanish, Italian, Norwegian, Swedish, and Danish. I seemed to have a special group of "fans" in Scandinavia.

During this period I had engaged a new Japanese servant who proved to have an interesting history. Incidentally he gave me a new lesson in patriotism. When he came I said to him what I have always said to Japanese who worked for me with a longing eye on my library:

"You may read as many of my books as you care to, Yoshi," I told him, "but as the library is catalogued I must ask you to return every book to its proper place on the shelves after you have read it."

Yoshi smiled.

"Thank you," he said, "but I shall not need your books. I have a library of my own."

I was interested.

"How many books?" I asked.

"Seventy thousand," he told me.

I could hardly believe him then, but it was quite true. He had come to America a lad of twenty for the sole purpose of accumulating a library for his native Japanese town. He

Mrs. William Ewen Shipp   *Mrs. Herbert S. Houston*

The Convent of Notre Dame, Milwaukee

had worked more than twenty-one years, spending every cent
of his earnings on books for that library. The library had
now reached such proportions that its storage over in Brooklyn was costing a big slice of his wages, so Yoshi was planning to take it to Japan in the spring.

Mrs. Willard came to dinner a few nights later and incidentally had a touching reunion with Yoshi, who, it then
appeared, had been her butler in Richmond when Mr. Willard was Lieutenant-Governor of Virginia. She and Mr.
Willard knew all about Yoshi's library. Yoshi now told me
more about it. It was half Chinese, and largely scientific and
biographical. It contained many thousands of German books.
It did *not* contain, Yoshi told me with a superior smile, one
single volume of fiction!

Yoshi, then a man of forty-one, took his library back to
Japan that spring, and presented it to his native town. As
he had cannily foreseen, he was immediately appointed its
librarian and ever since then he has basked happily in the
adulation of his fellow citizens.

Teas and dinners became pleasant commonplaces again.
Mrs. Willard's daughter Belle, whom I had known since she
was a child, married Kermit Roosevelt and went off on hunting expeditions with him. At one of my luncheons she described how she had killed two tigers, one rhinoceros, and
one python that had just swallowed a doe. We all listened
with fascinated interest and awe, till she had to check her
reminiscences to hurry home and nurse the baby....

I had always admired Kermit Roosevelt, since hearing his
arresting comment to his mother:

"Father's a funny man," he told her. "When he's at a
wedding he thinks he's the bride, and when he's at a funeral
he thinks he's the corpse!"

The theaters were having a special boom of their own.

When my friends in the theatrical group put on their new plays charming letters like these from Otis Skinner came my way:

GEO. M. COHAN THEATRE, NEW YORK
SATURDAY

DEAR ELIZABETH:

News of you is always good news, news of your coming on Monday night is even better news. But no, *mon amie,* I cannot sup with you. You are going to sup with me at the Knickerbocker. Do not protest. This is the only way it shall be. Here are the conditions:

You and Mrs. Burnett are going to see my play and you are to save up enough conversation to last you for as brief an interval as I can manage in which to remove my make-up, and you are to apply it to said interval after you reach my dressing-room, which is blessed with a little reception annex. When your souls, properly filled with patience, are in compliant mood, we will all go forth and eat. Until then, my blessing.

Yours always,
OTIS

GEO. M. COHAN THEATRE, NEW YORK CITY
TUESDAY NIGHT

What a wonderful woman you are, Elizabeth! I've known how well you understand the old maxim about the way to a man's heart being through his stomach, because you have fed me with discretion and with a bounteous hand. You know other roads—particularly the road that lies through his *vanity.* If you will sit and hold my hand, I warn you you'll get my ego splashed all over you.

But I thrill and I chortle with your praise, because I know you know. Some people say my play is thin, others say it isn't big enough. I think it *is* big enough—at least *Bellchamber* is big enough because the rascal lets me express the joy of life, and I know no better deed than that. It is work I love and which I can best express. When my audience gets it they climb right over the orchestra into my arms, or at least I feel that they do. Now, could I do that with *King Lear?* No. So I am grateful to my rotten old rascal, *Bellchamber*. He's a really fine chap and he likes me.

Getting the splashes? I warned you. I won't splash any more, because this is written with ink in my dressing-room and this is my last jerk.

God bless you.

Yours,
OTIS SKINNER

The passing years began to take their toll among my women friends. In this letter from Mrs. Arthur Murray Dodge—the last I ever received from her—"the long rest" she so happily writes of proved to be an eternal one. She died in France, and the intimate group that for years had attended her Friday luncheons held a special memorial meeting in her New York apartment, in which we had passed so many happy hours.

SIMSBURY, CONN.

DEAR ELIZABETH,

I have declined to continue as director of the Drama League, as I am going to be abroad all winter. Geoffrey has asked me to stay with him in his new house, which has room for me and my maid. Now that I am free from any direct responsibility, for the first time in my life, I am taking the opportunity to have the long rest I really need, and this has the enthusiastic approval of all the family.

We have taken a house at Cannes for three months, as Geoffrey has two large houses he is doing on the Riviera. He will need to be on hand there most of the time, so it sounds perfect. We shall be getting away from the cold and dampness of Paris at just the right time.

I am offering my apartment for rent. . . . I have had neuritis this summer—six weeks—but am now all right. . . . I shall miss you and my Friday luncheons, but I shall try to get you all together once more before sailing early in November. I shall move to town October fifteenth, staying at 563 for two weeks. . . .

I have a new granddaughter—by Douglas's wife. That makes twenty-six in the family, and more in sight. I begin to feel like a Matriarch. ...

Affectionately yours,
JOSEPHINE D.

The post-war boom was now general. I began to go abroad again every summer. One night in a little vaudeville house in Madrid—not first class but the best Madrid had—a new Spanish dancer came out on the stage. The hour was late, long after midnight, and my friends and I were just about to leave. We had even risen to go when the dancer appeared, but we sat down again. She was not especially young and her costumes were rather shabby, but she had a striking personality and looked as if she could dance. She could. Having begun she danced on and on while we watched her with delight for an hour. I made a prediction.

"She will be a Paris head-liner within two years," I said, "and America will be crazy about her within three years."

The prediction came true. For the dancer with the radiant gift and the shabby costumes was Madame Argentina.

We were all affluent in those days. I remember calling my sister Alice into my study in 1929, before I sailed for Europe, and showing her for the first time a list of my investment holdings. I had made it out that morning, and was feeling uplifted by the discovery that any time I wanted to drop work my dependents and I could live comfortably on the income from my capital. When the crash came we couldn't, of course: but hard work still brought its rewards and I weathered the storm that struck us all. The worst shadows that fell upon me were not those of the long depression.

CHAPTER XXIII

THE LONG, DIM TUNNEL

MY eyes, those faithful allies that had been so sorely tried by night work under arc lights, yet had stood by me so loyally, began to protest against their overstrain. I decided that I needed some new glasses, and I went to my friend and oculist Dr. Colman Cutler, who had prescribed glasses for me for twenty years. I had always been so nearsighted that I often irritated friends and acquaintances, and even members of my family, by not recognizing them when we met face to face; but aside from this myopia there was nothing wrong, and Dr. Cutler had told me the myopia would pass with the years.

"When every one else is putting on glasses you will be taking yours off," was the way he put it.

On the day I chose to visit him New York was again entertaining one of her blizzards. It was a wild and beautiful storm, whose masses of snow were driven onward by a whirling wind. I had been born in the northwest and had passed my school days there. Little blizzards held nothing but exhilaration for me when I was properly dressed to be out in them, and to-day I was prepared. Or was I? The snow was strangely disturbing to my eyes, and I ended by taking a cab to Dr. Cutler's address. I had made an appointment, but I found his offices crowded. Other New Yorkers were having eye trouble. During the following seven years I formed the impression that most human beings are suffering from some form of eye distress. I had never thought much about eyes before.

Notwithstanding my appointment I had to wait almost an hour before I saw the doctor. I filled the interval by studying the other waiting patients. Several of them, sitting in a row as it chanced, seemed almost blind. That tragic vista would have depressed me at any time. To-day, from some deep instinct, it sent a chill down my back. The man in the consulting-room just before me must have been quite blind, for now Dr. Cutler personally led him back into the waiting room and turned him over to his attendant with some friendly and comforting words. Then the doctor greeted me and took me into the consulting-room with him.

It was long past Dr. Cutler's luncheon hour and the distinguished specialist was worn out. He was naturally the kindest and most considerate of men, but he was growing old and he had gone through an unusually taxing morning. He was harassed and tired and hungry, and there were still half a dozen patients waiting. He and I were old friends. My eyes, he was sure, needed nothing but new glasses. Yet to-day the tests did not go normally, and we both became a bit edgy. At last the oculist muttered almost irritably,

"You're not giving me any help at all!"

"I'm nervous," I admitted.

"If you are nervous," the doctor said, "it's something new for you. Suppose we stop now, and you come back to-morrow."

"After waiting an hour?" I jerked out. "No, thanks! Let's have it over. I don't want to waste another morning."

That remark made no hit with Dr. Cutler. He proceeded with the tests, but rather grumpily.

Suddenly before my eyes, fixed to the instrument he was using at the moment, two fiery circles appeared and danced and whirled. My heart stopped as I saw them. There was something sinister and devilish about that elfin waltz. At the same instant Dr. Cutler's manner changed completely.

He became again his normal self—amazingly kind and gentle. He began a new system of experiments, still conducted on my side in silence. At last he laid aside his various instruments, drew a chair forward, and sat down in front of me.

"My dear friend," he began, "you have naturally splendid eyes."

He went on to tell me how good my eyes were, naturally. I was not interested. I knew all about that—and I knew something more was coming. I waited.

"You're in excellent health, too," he went on. "I don't know why these things should have come upon you—especially so many years earlier than they come to most people. But then we don't know much about their cause, really. The one thing we have learned, though, is how to treat them."

"Doctor," I broke in, "what are you trying to tell me? What is it that I have?"

"Cataracts," Dr. Cutler said gently.

"Cataracts?" I echoed faintly. "And—*two* of them? One in each eye?"

"Yes," Dr. Cutler admitted. "But—"

He squared himself to his task. He forgot all about the other patients in the waiting-room and put in fifteen minutes of the kindliest reassurance. He told me how successful cataract operations now were—ninety-three per cent of them, he said, when the patients were in good condition and the operations properly performed.

"And I won't be blind?" I brought out. I knew very little about cataracts.

"Never in your life," the doctor assured me positively. He added that the cataract in my right eye was quite far advanced, and that in the left eye was just beginning. This probably meant that the left eye would stand by till the operation on the right was performed, so that I would never be without some vision. Indeed, the cataracts might not develop further, or might develop so slowly that many years might pass before an operation was required. In any case one could hardly be needed for five years. In the interval I could go right on with my work.

"It won't impair your efficiency," he ended with a beaming smile, "and we will do all we can to retard development. If the operation must come eventually, you will have the best eye surgeon in the world to-day—my friend, Dr. John M. Wheeler."

He was so optimistic by this time that I laughed.

"Doctor," I said, "you're making it seem almost a privilege to have cataracts!" Suddenly I remembered something else. "By the way," I added, "how soon will they show?"

I was having visions of thick white films over the eyes. That was all I knew about cataracts then, and I have carefully avoided reading up on them since. There was nothing to be gained by stimulating my imagination, which had immediately begun to work overtime. Dr. Cutler smiled.

"I don't think they will ever show," he confidently predicted. "They're not that kind."

They never have shown—and I admit that this has been a comfort.

Dr. Cutler went into my family's medical history. Had any of my people had cataracts? They had, I told him. My father had been successfully operated on thirty-five years before by Dr. Nicholas Senn of Milwaukee—a distinguished surgeon of his day. Father had lived fifteen years after that, and had kept his vision to the last. My mother also had a cataract in the left eye. Dr. Cutler himself had discovered this, but I had never allowed Mother to know about it and it had not developed. Reminded of this, Dr. Cutler's face became a rising sun.

"That, I think, explains these in your case," he said.

"Heredity. That's usually the explanation, where there is no other."

He was so pleased by this discovery that he quite forgot my unfortunate end of the situation. My imagination was already hard at work. Was he deceiving me to brace me up? He was so kind he might be. Was I to lose my sight or my usefulness or both? In those moments I felt that I would much rather have received a death verdict. I have never had the fear or horror of death so many have. I could die with decent dignity. But blindness—helplessness, uselessness— being a burden to others. . . . All that was different.

I remembered the patients Dr. Cutler was so kindly for- getting, and rose to go. As I did so, the cumulative burden of the coming seven years fell on me like a tangible weight. . . . There were to be tests—all sorts of tests, to make sure my general condition was as good as it seemed. I agreed to have them made at once, and departed. Out in the storm and away from Dr. Cutler's warmly comforting presence panic gripped me. I got into a taxicab and rode home in a nightmare.

When I got back to my apartment I found it empty. The day was Thursday, and Young, the faithful butler who has been with me for thirteen years, was off duty. Martha was in her down-town studio, and Harriet at her desk in the Columbia University Library. I stood before a window in my study, facing Gramercy Park, and looked out at the storm. It was a beautiful storm. How long would I see beauty? How long would I see *anything?*

I must have stood there an hour. It was a strange hour, in which I faced the complete readjustment of life that I was convinced lay before me. Not blindness. I remembered my father's successful results at a period when eye opera- tions were not as skilfully performed as they are now. He had not lost his sight. But my wings were clipped. Much of my liberty and independence were gone, and I knew it. I could never again fly as far as in the past. That took some thinking about. . . .

Behind me, on my desk, the telephone bell rang. When I took up the receiver the voice of Miss Blanche Nichols, Dr. Cutler's secretary, came over the wire. She had been the doctor's office-head for many years, and in my opinion was one of the world's best examples of the right person in the right place. I had met her in my yearly visits to the oculist, and had admired her fine efficiency and her perfect office manner. That manner was now full of friendly sympathy and understanding. Her first words told me how long I had been standing at that study window.

"Miss Jordan," she began, "I couldn't help overhearing Dr. Cutler's talk with you, and I've been wanting to call you up ever since. I had to wait over an hour till the office cleared and Dr. Cutler went to luncheon. I know what a blow you have had, and I'm so afraid you're feeling terribly depressed. May I tell you a few things I'm sure will help you?"

I murmured that she was very kind.

"The situation isn't nearly as bad as you think it is," she went on. "You see, I know hundreds of men and women who have had cataract operations and are going about after them with splendid sight. Why, even women of eighty do knitting and fine embroidery work after such operations— and old men read their newspapers in peace and comfort. . . ."

There never was a kinder impulse than the one which prompted Miss Nichols' telephone message that day. I shall be grateful to her up till my last hour. Her charming voice went on, telling me of public men and women, still in the ring, who had undergone cataract operations years ago and had forgotten all about them.

"It doesn't seem possible to you now," she ended, "but

after a few weeks, when you've got over the first shock of this, you will go on as if nothing had happened. You may never need the operations. But if you do, they will simply mean a fine new eye equipment." She ended impressively, "One thing is certain. You are *not* going into darkness!"

That talk *did* buoy me up. I remember, too, my final reaction: "If octogenarians are taking this in their stride, I certainly can do it."

After dinner that night I told Harriet and Martha of my situation. They were stunned and incredulous. Martha cried out passionately, "I won't *have* it so! I *won't!*" It was her first and last loss of poise as we went together along a new and darkening highway. I repeated Dr. Cutler's and Miss Nichols' comforting assurances, and my friends cheered up as I had done.

For five years after that hour I never again mentioned the subject to them, or to any one else except Dr. Cutler, Miss Nichols, and my family physician, Dr. Howard Gillespie Myers. There was no reason why any one else should know, and no reason why Harriet and Martha and I should further discuss the condition. The most important of all precautions was the need of keeping the truth from my mother, now over eighty. Since I left the Goldwyn Company we had passed six months of every year, from June to November, in our country home in Massachusetts. This winter, for the first time, Mother had remained there. The twice-a-year move, though she had no part in the strain of it, disturbed her, and she liked the country. She would try one winter in it, she announced. If she enjoyed it she would remain with my sister and our young ward, Clothilde, who were also there the year around. My sister, too, would be deeply disturbed by my eye condition. Neither she nor any one else outside the little group I have mentioned had any knowledge of it till the first operation was imminent five years later.

"We'll have Dr. John M. Wheeler perform it when the time comes," Dr. Myers told me, when the successful tests were made.

I was glad he and Dr. Cutler had reached the same conclusion about the surgeon, even before they consulted. I was also impressed by the fact that both doctors had assumed the operations would be necessary.

I had a bad month or so over the readjustment the new situation demanded. Tests. Daily eye-drops. Frequent visits to the oculist. The reassuring verdict that the tests and various analyses proved my general condition fine. Then Harriet and Martha and I went abroad for three months of rest and beauty in Spain, Italy, France, and Switzerland. After I came home, as Miss Nichols had predicted, I got into my new stride and went on—very comfortably the first year or two, so far as the eyes were concerned.

But other new and harassing troubles were coming at me from every side. As the financial depression increased and the financial screws tightened all along the line, men and women stopped reading books and magazines, or borrowed them from the libraries. Magazine editors ceased to buy new stories and special articles and filled their periodicals with material that had piled up on their manuscript shelves during their care-free years. The situation of authors became very serious. One literary magazine illustrated it by a frontispiece in its Christmas number showing an author swooning over his typewriter while Santa Claus, standing helpless behind him, sadly shook his head. The value of my gilt-edged securities had dropped to one-fifth of what they had been. My earned income dropped correspondingly. Even so, I still had a good reserve and was not yet sharing the panic of most of my literary friends.

My corroding anxiety now was my mother's physical condition. After more than eighty years of almost perfect health, she had entered upon her last illness. I had always prayed that when this came the end would be mercifully swift for her. Instead, she lay for five months in a strange stupor, attended day and night by two watchful nurses who could do little but watch, and with doctors almost equally helpless, coming and going. There seemed no disease. There seemed nothing to be done. The superb human machine that encased her was simply and very slowly running down.

At first she was conscious a few hours every day, and we sat beside her and talked or read aloud to her. Daily, by her wish, I played the piano for at least an hour, in my study just across the upper hall from her room. In these intervals her brain was amazingly alert, as it had always been. She was interested in the news of the world, in books, in music. Among the books I read to her was *The Good Earth*. She was not disturbed about her illness. I had told her she was "taking a rest cure." She was convinced that nothing could happen to her when my sister and I were with her. It was necessary, of course, for her nurses to move and massage her every two hours, and she resented this. She had no knowledge of her long intervals of stupor. Every time she was aroused she was convinced that she had been awakened from a refreshing nap.

"I should be quite all right," she put it, "if those nurses would stop trying to make me comfortable!"

She lay thus during one of the longest and hottest summers Massachusetts has ever known. The windows of her big room opened on the garden, and cross-currents from scientifically arranged electric fans cooled the atmosphere.

"She may lie like this a year or more," the doctors said, "or she may go any moment."

My sister and I were afraid to leave the house, almost

afraid to leave her room, even with two nurses guarding her.

The "nerves" of which most writers talk so much and which had troubled me so little, began to whisper their sinister suggestions. One of them reiterated that I must watch my helpless mother at night—that the nurse on duty might fall asleep. Night after night, for months, I was in and out of the sick-room at all hours from midnight on. I never found both nurses off-duty. One of them was always there, sitting within easy reach of her patient, reading or sewing under a shaded lamp. Sometimes, too restless to go back to bed, I sat down and shared the vigil. At such hours I had a strong feeling that my father was with us. He would be, of course, if he could. He had adored my mother to the last hour of his life and had died holding her hand. . . .

As the months passed Mother's intervals of consciousness grew shorter daily, till at last there was no interval at all. She lay there, already lost to us, it seemed, motionless though with no other sign of paralysis, eyes closed, ears deaf to our voices.

One day when this final condition had continued for many weeks I thought I observed a slight change in her when I bent over her.

"It's I, Mother," I said clearly and cheerfully, though my heart had stopped beating. "I'm just kissing you good morning."

This time there was no doubt about the response. Her fingers tightened on my hand. Her cheek moved, almost imperceptibly, to be kissed again. For just an instant her soul had returned from the far space to which it had retreated during those tragic weeks. It was the last time. She lived a fortnight longer; but she never came back again.

The following year my old convent, now Mount Mary College and University of Milwaukee, gave me the honorary degree of Doctor of Letters. It had offered the degree twice before, but my absence in Europe the first time, and my mother's illness the second time, had made it impossible for me to go West. This time I went, and my home town and old classmates gave me a welcome that warmed my heart. I was in need of cheering. My sight was steadily failing, and the depression still lay over us like a dark blanket. . . .

I was still going to the theaters, when I could get front seats. One night when the attraction was Escudero and his Spanish dancers, I found myself directly behind Mrs. Charles Lindbergh, who was watching him with a party of friends. As it happens I have never met either of the Lindberghs. I looked at Mrs. Lindbergh with special interest, and was struck by charms I had not found in her photographs. Her complexion was lovely, her face brilliantly animated, and her smile wholly charming. It was clear that she was having a delightful evening and that her companions were amusing her very much. Her photographs always look serious, so I was especially impressed by her gaiety.

Colonel Lindbergh, as usual, was up in the gallery, away from his wife and friends, with his hair smoothed tightly to his head and his coat collar high around his chin to help him to escape the recognition and affectionate mobbing of admirers. This, I was told, was his usual procedure. He always went to the gallery of a theater, joining Mrs. Lindbergh in their car when the performance was over.

I have often thought of Mrs. Lindbergh's high spirits that night and recalled her happy face. No premonition of tragedy had touched her, but her baby was kidnapped just three nights later.

The following year I went to a Northampton business college and took a course in typewriting by the touch system. This was "preparedness"—and time proved its wisdom.

I am perhaps devoting too much time to the matter of eyes—so much more important to me than to any one else. I do it because the experience had such a happy ending, and because it offers such encouragement to thousands upon thousands of other victims of cataracts. I must make it clear that all the optimistic predictions of Dr. Cutler were borne out. I still worked steadily. I still wrote a novel a year. I still acted as president of the Gramercy Park Club, and as a member of the Executive Committee of the Gramercy Park Association. I still planned and directed the Christmas lighting of Gramercy Park, though I could no longer look at the lights from my windows. I even carried on my dramatic reviewing, sitting in the front rows of the orchestra and using powerful opera glasses. The year before the first operation, I admit, was not as cheery as it might have been. The vision of the right eye was practically gone and that of the left was rapidly going.

"Stand it as long as you can," Dr. Cutler cheerfully advised.

I lived that year in a heavy London fog, in which even the faces of my intimate friends were lost and their figures moved dimly around me. I could no longer look down from my windows on Gramercy Park. There was no park there— merely a spectral gray mist. I managed to keep on with my work, using the touch system on the typewriter and having my copy read aloud to me. I kept two secretaries busy. I found the touch system very helpful that year. Indeed, I could not have worked on without it.

Inevitably, I gave up most of my social life, to the puzzlement of my friends. There was too much danger of accidents. I had lived in my Gramercy Park apartment for twenty years. I knew every inch of every room and could move about safely. In the homes of my friends, however well I thought I knew those homes, dangers lurked. I was finical in my precautions. I changed my care-free stride to a cautious creep. It was no time for me to break a leg or an arm— though at the period it would not have depressed me greatly to know that I was to break my neck. Notwithstanding my extreme caution I once almost fell down an entire flight of stairs in the old Stuyvesant house on Gramercy Park. Another time I "fell upstairs" in the side entrance of an uptown shop, and narrowly escaped breaking a wrist. The end of my social activities came when I went to the opera with a party of friends one Saturday afternoon. I still had to have music. But five of the women in our box tried to help me downstairs when we were leaving. *That* was a revelation. I had fondly imagined I was still concealing the fact of my dimming vision. Evidently I was not.

Martha dropped most of her own activities that year and was my shadow, guarding me everywhere I went, but the strain on her was great. After the opera experience I remained at home most of the time, putting in the days at my desk and being entertained in the evenings by intimate friends who came to dinner, or by Martha and Harriet, who read aloud to me till their tongues must have ached. Nowhere on this earth could there be more devoted friends than those two, whose friendship bore so long and severe a test. I was in an increasing fog. Even most of my piano music had to go. Reading new music had been among my greatest pleasures. Now, of course, I could not see the notes. There was little satisfaction in playing day after day, month after month, the music I already knew and which held such poignant memories of my mother.

I took a certain satisfaction in meeting my problems as they came. I learned to dial the telephone by the touch system, as well as to operate the typewriter that way—working out the former method myself. I had a place for everything and everything was meticulously in its place. I learned to hold an investigating finger under every faucet I turned on, to make sure that I had also turned it off.

It was at this period, when such mind as I had was almost exclusively on my eyes, and I was in a mental condition to chew the paper on the apartment walls, that Dr. Cutler warningly shook his venerable head at me.

"You must not get eye-conscious!" he said.

Several months before this my sense of humor had tucked its tail between its legs and crept away from me like an unwelcome puppy. That remark brought it rollicking back for an instant, looking up at me, ready to play.

When spring came I felt that I had reached my limit, and I went to see Dr. John M. Wheeler at his hospital in the Medical Center. There the atmosphere was strictly scientific and the work done by the staff impressively skilful. I put in a day going through all the required tests known to eye surgery. Drops, tests, and an interval. More drops, more tests, another interval.... The waiting-rooms were lined with humans going through similar tests or waiting for consultations. I felt like a log in a lumber mill, passing with increasing acceleration from one skilled worker to another. When I finally reached Dr. Wheeler he was all I had expected to find him—very quiet, more than a bit remote in manner, but emanating kindness and a confidence that one leaned on as on a rock.

"Why are you so anxious for the operation now?" he asked after his examination.

I murmured that I wanted to put in the summer getting over it, before next winter's work.

"Why not use the summer to get ready for it?" he smiled. "Why not have it in October?"

"You advise that?"

"I think so," he said thoughtfully.

It was a blow, but I accepted it and went to Massachusetts to wait.

My friends had to know now, or all sorts of wild rumors would circulate among them. They took the revelation in various ways. Some of them, like Martha, would not "have it so." Others, the most trying, wept on my breast. A few bore the news with great cheerfulness. Josephine Daskam Bacon, an intimate friend for thirty years, was so optimistic about it that I coldly rebuked her.

"You seem to think this experience is a trifle," I said.

"So it is," Josephine explained. "It's a trifle compared to what it might be, and your various experts tell you it's only temporary. Why worry about it?"

That is a Spartan philosophy, but a correct one—though easier to recommend than to follow. The next four months were the hardest. I suddenly discovered that I was seeing double the little that I saw at all, and this was something of a nightmare. I sent a startled letter to Dr. Cutler in New York and was assured by return mail that the experience was a common one and nothing to worry about. But I felt that I was washed up on the beach of life. Martha and my sister and I passed most of the time motoring over the mountains behind a chauffeur who was the peerless driver he considered himself but who was also rather hard to look at.

"It's bad enough to see one Richard in the driver's seat," I grumbled. "To have to look at *two* of him for hours every day is the turn of the screw."

I kept my eyes closed most of the time; a good plan any way one looked at it.

The operation repaid me for those difficult months and years. In itself, of course, it was an ordeal. One is entirely conscious, and one is expected to remain absolutely motionless and to help the surgeon, while a blazing light pours from overhead on an eye that instinctively rejects light. The operable eye had been given a local anesthetic. For just an instant, when the operation began, my heart seemed to stop. In the next instant I had called my nerves to heel and they responded like obedient dogs.

I suppose I shall be as motionless in my grave as I was during the thirty-two minutes I lay on that operating table. Certainly I shall never be as motionless anywhere else. There was a shrouded group around me—doctors and nurses in their gowns and masks—but absolutely no sound except Dr. Wheeler's quiet, assured voice.

"Move the eye a little to the right. . . . That's good. . . . Now a little to the left. . . . Look up. . . . Look down. . . ."

No pain whatever. . . . A sense of instruments being used, and of what they were doing. . . . The awful fear at first, that one might unconsciously move or twitch. . . . Time passing—or was it standing still? . . . At last the surgeon's voice on a new note.

"It's all over—and everything is fine!"

He himself adjusting the bandages and the black mask. . . . The stretcher-ride back to my room where Martha was waiting—with a cheerful book to read aloud. After that a week of blackness and utter immobility, during which one gets very nervous and restless inside and remains like a log to outward seeming. Nothing but fruit juices and water the first five days, but who wants food? Two nurses to raise one's head if a pillow must be shifted a few inches. . . .

What I wanted, and got, was Martha's reading—which went on steadily and beautifully most of the hours of every day, with the radio relieving her at intervals and Harriet taking up the reading in the evenings. I have never been able to keep still and twiddle my thumbs, and those days I was not even allowed to twiddle the thumbs. But I am always full of love and virtue when read aloud to, if the book is interesting, and we had brought a cart-load of new books to the hospital to make sure these books would be. At night, when I couldn't sleep, I chatted with my night nurse. She watched me like a hawk every second, to see that I did not stir. Once, during the fifth night, I thoughtlessly thrust a toe from under the bed covers. The shock to her was great. She discoursed on it . . .

I had expected quite a thrilling moment when the black mask and bandages were removed and I cried triumphantly, "I can see!" There was no excitement whatever, except in me. Dr. Wheeler and his entourage always move like an army with banners. They were there, but they had known perfectly well that I would see. To them the only excitement comes on those rare occasions when the patients do *not* see. Even those, I am sure, they take with a great professional calm and a grim resolution that the patient *shall* see before they are through with him.

My biggest thrill came five weeks later, the first time I put on my new distance glasses. Notified that they were ready I had gone up to the optician's to get them and have them adjusted. Alice, my sister, who had come on from Massachusetts to help me through the tedious weeks following the operation, was with me. The shop was dim, as most opticians' shops seem to be. I wore my new glasses out to the sidewalk and stopped there transfixed.

It was a perfect day and a new and singularly perfect world faced me. The fog was gone! Dizzy with excitement I stumbled into my waiting cab and we started uptown. Fifth Avenue lay before me, alive and beautiful beyond words. The men and women on the sidewalks had ceased to be dim shadows or black moving masses. They had heads and faces and arms and legs. I could see their eyes and the color of their neck-ties and the details of their clothing. I could see the shops and the exhibits in the windows.

It was all so thrilling and so incredible that I kept up a fire of exclamation. I pointed out these phenomena to my sister. I was so stirred that for a time I did not realize her lack of response. Then I turned and looked at her, seeing her face for the first time in more than a year. She was speechless, with tears pouring from her eyes. I could even see the big drops on her cheeks. . . .

Life became more normal, offered new and lofty encounters. One of these was the development of a briefer one begun twenty years before. I was then writing something for which I needed special knowledge of Japanese customs. I said to my friend Agnes Houston, "I wish I could meet a high-bred Japanese woman. I'd like to ask her some questions."

To Agnes Houston any expressed wish of a friend was a wish to be gratified immediately if that was possible. Forty-eight hours later she had me seated at a luncheon table beside the Baroness Shidzue Ishimoto. The Baroness, now referred to in American newspapers as "the great lady of Japan," was then a bride visiting America soon after her honeymoon. She was eighteen or so, very pretty, and rather hard to distinguish from a cherry blossom. We talked all through luncheon and then segregated ourselves in a corner and finished the conversation. Eighteen years later she came to America again to lecture here. She had blossomed into the leading woman of her country. Again I met her under Mrs. Houston's wing, but this time at a crowded tea. I said, "We met years ago, Baroness, but you will not remember that."

"Indeed, but I do remember it," she told me. "I remember every word of our talk that day."

I credited this to Japanese courtesy. Two years later, in

January, 1937, the Baroness returned for another lecture tour. Our common and most uncommon friend Agnes Houston had just died, and the hearts of her friends were heavy. The Japanese Baroness and I had both loved her, and our grief for her drew us together. I wished to do for this charming Eastern visitor some of the things Agnes would have done. She dined with me several times, and we went to the theater. It was at my table that she leaned toward me one night and said smilingly but with a serious undercurrent in her voice, "I think I should tell you that you are responsible for many of the things I have tried to do. It was what you said to me twenty years ago that strengthened my resolve to help my people."

I had been deep in suffrage and war work during the Baroness's first visit to America. The tributes I offered to Dr. Anna Howard Shaw, Mrs. Ogden Reid, Mrs. Norman Whitehouse and other leaders, during my first talk with her, must have been among the seed that led to the Baroness Ishimoto's superb harvest.

Later I proudly quoted her remark to our ward Clothilde, now a college junior.

"I have been talking to you steadily since you were two years old," I ended. "Can you remember one single remark of mine?"

"I can," said Clothilde, with a seraphic smile. "One. You told me to work like the devil while I work and play like the devil while I play."

She would remember just that!

In 1934 Mrs. Alice Hargreaves, the original of *Alice In Wonderland,* made her first visit to America, in her eighties, to receive the honorary degree of Doctor of Letters from Columbia University. She deserved it, for it was she who, standing at Lewis Carroll's knee, persuaded him to put into a book the marvelous tales he had made up for her.

She was interested in America and its people, but she was not wholly happy here. She was guarded on every occasion by her son and her daughter, and this voyage to the new world must have been inspired by the last flicker of that childish spirit of adventure which had made her appreciate *Alice*. To me there was always about her, in this new environment, a definite suggestion of strain and anxiety. She was Alice, but she was no longer at home in *Wonderland*.

I had the second big eye operation a year after the first, and following that the same year the two smaller ones that are usually necessary to complete the good work of restoring vision. But, meantime, I had my good eye to stand by, and it did so gloriously. The smaller affairs were merely matters of ten or twelve minutes on the operating table, and a week or less in the hospital. Four eye operations in two years— each performed by Dr. Wheeler—is something of a record. But they have all been supremely worth while.

Vision again! No one can imagine what that is who has not seen vision going. Years of depression? Yes. Years with a stiff professional handicap? Yes. Operations? Yes. But where would one have been without those operations?

I began these memories in the shadows, looking back at the sunshine of long ago, filtering down into dim woods. It is not to be wondered at that, with the fourth operation just behind me and a new and brighter life before me after seven years of near-retirement, I should end them even as I began, with

"Three rousing cheers!"

INDEX

Abbey, Edwin, 214, 215
Abbey, Mrs. Edwin, 214
Aftenposten (Christiania), 293
Alden, Ada Foster Murray (Mrs.
Henry Mills Alden), 174, 175,
176, 251
Alden, Anne Field, 175-176
Alden, Henry Mills, viii, ix, 179, 265,
267; a great god in the American
literary machine, 173; belated
honeymoon, 174, 175; *Lady
Rose's Daughter*, 177; life-long
friend of Mr. Howells, 180; home
in Metuchen, 186; a prediction,
195; fiftieth anniversary as editor
of *Harper's Magazine*, 251
Aldrich, Thomas Bailey, 199
Alexandra, Queen, 214, 215
Alice in Wonderland, 393
Allen, James Lane, 180
America, 338
American Magazine, 337
"Amy Leslie," 244
Anderson, William E., 14, 15, 19,
23
Andrews, Harry E., letter, 245
Andrews, Mary Raymond Ship-
man, 262, 264, 277; letter, 278
Anthony, Susan B., 333
Argentina, Madame, 374
Atherton, Gertrude, 121, 178, 186,
199; arrival in New York, 86-88;
letter, 110; in Munich, 281, 293
Atlantic Monthly, 148, 149, 238
Austin, Mary, 350, 367, 368; let-
ters, 351-355
Awakening of Helena Ritchie, The,
198, 258

Ayer, Harriet Hubbard, 95-97, 155-
158

"Baby McKee." *See* McKee, Ben-
jamin Harrison.
Bacon, Deborah, 152-154
Bacon, Josephine Daskam (Mrs.
Selden Bacon), 139, 152ff, 196,
251, 389
Baldus, S. A., 338
Bangs, John Kendrick, 260, 262
Barbour, William D., 222
Barbour, Mrs. William D., 142, 222,
223
"Bart Kennedy, Genius," 140
"Battle Hymn of the Republic,"
199, 347
Bavarian Alps, 281-283
Becket, John à, x, 139, 144, 145-
148; death of, 152-154
Bennett, James Gordon, 25
Bermuda, Bailey's Bay, 281, 284-
286, 319, 320
Besant, Annie, 74-77
Beveridge, Kuhne, 87
Beyer, Mrs. Edward. *See* Jordan,
Alice.
Bigelow, Grace, 347, 349
Bigelow, John, 347, 348, 349
Bigelow, Mrs. John, 348, 349
Bigelow, Poultney, 139, 349; let-
ter, 350
Big Stone Gap, 40-46
Binner, Paul, 24
Blavatsky, Helene, 74-77
Blue Circle, The, 338
Bly, Nelly, 23, 38

(1)